TWENTIETH-CENTURY ENGLISH HISTORY PLAYS

Twentieth-Century English History Plays

From Shaw to Bond

Niloufer Harben
Lecturer in English
University of Malaya

BARNES & NOBLE BOOKS
TOTOWA, NEW JERSEY

First published in the USA 1988 by
BARNES & NOBLE BOOKS
81 ADAMS DRIVE
TOTOWA, NEW JERSEY, 07512

ISBN: 0–389–20734–9

Printed in Hong Kong

Library of Congress Cataloging-in-Publication Data
Twentieth-century English history plays.
  Bibliography: p.
  Includes index.
  Contents: Saint Joan/George Bernard Shaw—The
lady with the lamp/Reginald Berkeley—The rose without
a thorn/Clifford Bax—[etc.]
  1. Historical drama, English—History and criticism.
2. English drama—20th century—History and criticism.
I. Harben, Niloufer.
PR739.H5T8   1988   822'.91'080358   87–1024
ISBN 0–389–20734–9

For My Mother

Contents

Acknowledgements

I would like to express my deep appreciation to Professor Katharine Worth, Head of the Department of Drama and Theatre Studies, Royal Holloway and Bedford New College, University of London, for her guidance and inspiration while supervising the research undertaken for my Ph.D. thesis which forms the basis of this book. My grateful thanks also to those who have taken an interest in it, especially Miss M. J. Moore and my family for their support and encouragement.

The author and publishers wish to thank the following who have given permission for the use of copyright material: Faber & Faber, for the extracts from John Osborne, *Luther*; and Calde & Boyars, for the extracts from Edward Bond, *Early Morning*; and Faber & Faber and Harcourt Brace Jovanovich, Inc., for the extracts from T. S. Eliot, *Murder in the Cathedral*, Copyright 1935 by Harcourt Brace Jovanovich, Inc., renewed 1963 by T. S. Eliot.

1

Introduction: The English History Play in the Twentieth Century

Although the history play is a most popular genre among English playwrights of this century very little research has been done in the field. In particular, because it is a large and difficult subject, critics have generally tended to shirk any attempt to define the scope and the limits of the genre. Such attempts at definition as have been made are mainly based on Elizabethan playwrights and practice, and very little work has been done along these lines in relation to the twentieth century. The term 'history play' has often been used rather loosely and in the twentieth century the existence of such a genre has not been clearly defined or sufficiently elucidated. Various preconceptions surround the term so that our understanding of its meaning is, at best, hazy. It therefore must be critically rewarding to examine it afresh, seeking to define more precisely the scope and limits of the genre.

There is the need for a comprehensive definition of the term which covers plays of different approaches. But it is easy to lapse into too catholic a sympathy for all treatments of history; this ultimately is an abdication of judgement because it does not add clarity to our understanding of the form and can only leave us in a morass of ambiguity and indecision. Thus a statement such as: history plays are plays which are 'based on history or having a historical theme' raises more questions than it allays doubts as to what constitutes the genre. Tucker Brooke, writing of Tudor drama in 1912, recognized the need for a definition of the history play but could arrive at none inclusive enough to embrace all he chose to consider histories. Yet he admits that 'any ambitious discussion of the genre, unless based on sane definitions, is in danger of losing itself hopelessly in the attempt to follow such quasi-historical will-o'-the-wisps as *George a Greene* and *James IV*'.[1] A real duty is neglected when no criteria are set. Sympathy for a variety of concerns and approaches does not preclude the need for some severe discrimination in judgement. While it is clearly inadmissible to fall into the error of only including forms which are readily acceptable or comprehensible to oneself, some framework is required for discussion to become meaningful.

The history play often carries with it the implication that the writer's intention is to fulfil the function of the historian, showing a strict regard for historicity in the presentation of the facts and their interpretation. Scholarly insistence on historicity as the ultimate concern of the artist writing in this genre would reduce the full scope, power and flexibility of the form. A definition which required this would exclude works with a serious historical concern whose treatment leans towards the more purely imaginative. If we recognize that the genre need not be so defined as to demand strict historical accuracy, might we be led to the conclusion that the classification of a play as history need not be more than a broad indication of its subject or theme?

That, however, would mean that the playwright has the licence to make of history anything at all, resulting in sheer travesty of the term. Undoubtedly a line has to be drawn somewhere, for a total disregard for historical truth would be a distortion of truth itself. By this we mean that there has to be a valid basis for the point of departure of the artist, however subjective his vision. He has to come to terms with his subject and show a deep and serious interest in the past, free as he is to think critically and independently about it. The writer's power of intuition enables him to penetrate beneath the surface of documented fact to explore the possibilities of human character and situation within the context of actual experience. Undeniably the artist's invaluable contribution is his unique imaginative insight, yet there has to be some basis for historical truth, or what he presents would not be history or truth at all.

But this brings us to the rather overwhelming question of whether there is such a thing as historical truth. This has been a much debated question among philosophers.[2] The reaction to the positivist view which stressed the primacy and autonomy of facts in history and claimed the possibility of 'ultimate history'[3] led to an extreme scepticism and the purely relativist doctrine that 'since all historical judgements involve persons and points of view, one is as good as another and there is no "objective" historical truth'.[4] The interaction between the historian and his source material and the interdependence of these two factors in the writing of history caused many to doubt the meaningfulness of the term 'fact' in history.

What however do historians say on this matter? E. H. Carr, in his interesting discussion of the problem, foresees the danger of total relativism which pressed to its logical conclusion 'amounts to total scepticism, like Froude's remark that history is a "child's box of letters with which we can spell any word we please"'.[5] But Carr himself claims that not all the facts about the past are historical facts; they become so only after the historian has elected them to a special place of importance.[6] He is countered by G. R. Elton who argues convincingly for the independent reality of historical facts. That an event can be known, he says, is all that is required to make it a 'fact of history'. If the historian asserts his sovereignty over the facts he is a traitor to his calling, for history becomes whatever the historian likes to make of it.[7]

Though one places a greater emphasis on the historian and his subjective perception of the facts, and the other on the pre-eminence of the data and an objective critical approach to them, both project the more or less accepted view that history essentially involves the interaction of two elements – the past or rather what is left of it in traceable form and the historian's skill in its reconstruction and interpretation. The first duty of the historian is to respect his facts after he has ascertained them through a scholarly, critical assessment of all sources. After this it is a matter of relating fact to interpretation and interpretation to fact. Elton claims that the professional historian's method may not be infallible but it creates a foundation of generally assured knowledge beneath the disputes which will never cease: 'No historian would suppose his knowledge can be either total or infinite. But this does not alter the fact that it is knowledge of a reality, of what did occur, and not something that the student or observer has put together for study.' 'Inability to know all the truth about the past, is not the same thing as total inability to know the truth.'[8] This seems sound reasoning. Thus we can conclude that there is such a thing as historical truth and though it is unattainable in an absolute form, it exists and is the historian's only proper ambition.

But what significance does this hold for the historical playwright? Do the roles of the historian and the historical playwright diversify or is it the dramatist's intention to fulfil the purposes of the historian? Irving Ribner in his book, *The English History Play in the Age of Shakespeare*, published in 1957, states that, though the dramatist's first objective is to entertain a group of people in a theatre, 'when he goes to history for his subject matter, however, he assumes the functions of the historian as well'.[9] But the function of the historian is to contribute to the build-up of both fact and interpretation, the product of systematic, controlled research. Historical fact is difficult to ascertain and the dramatist can hardly be expected to bring to the subject the professional study necessary for a disciplined, scholarly assessment of the facts. The establishing of facts, the provenance of documents, the criticism of sources are strictly the jurisdiction of the specialist, areas, in fact, where the historian addresses himself to other historians. Even on the side of pure interpretation, the historian is bound to subdue his imagination to the controls of scholarship and accept the primacy of his sources, whereas the artist goes to history for his inspiration, but is free to explore the universal truths embodied in his subject. What then are the limits of the historical playwright? There have to be some controls within which he is free to exercise his imagination.

As far as the facts and sources are concerned, the limit of the historian is the limit of the playwright. But where interpretation is concerned the playwright should be free to approach his subject imaginatively and sympathetically while it may be incumbent on the historian to be critical and sceptical. However, since this is an area where conjecture plays a large part in the writing of history, the playwright should be able to bring to his understanding of the facts an artist's perception and sensitivity which allow him to place himself in each character's position and look upon the situation from different points of view. Here he can bring into play his unique insight into the springs of human character and motivation, provided it is controlled by an overriding respect for what is actually there in evidence.

But, since evidence is in many cases not clear cut, there is often a problem not of interpreting fact but of establishing it which gives rise to historians seeing differences in the facts themselves. What then are the bounds of the playwright? Well, as G. R. Elton points out, though there may be numerous theories about a particular event or issue there is 'a very large body of agreed knowledge on which no dispute is possible, and though this body of knowledge may not by itself provide a very sophisticated interpretation of the past it is entirely indispensable to any study of it'.[10] It is this area of generally accepted fact that a playwright should respect and not wantonly abuse. Obviously by this we do not mean minor alterations such as transpositions of time and place, the telescoping of events and imposing of artistic form and movement which are legitimate dramatic devices. Shaw dramatizes confrontations that never happened in *Saint Joan*, but his dialogues are based on relevant historical facts. But major distortions which violently affect the nature of character and events portrayed can hardly be justified. There is, however, a category of play which can be excepted given sufficiently imaginative treatment. Major exceptions to the general rule are crucial to my purpose and an important exception of this kind is dealt with in my discussion of Edward Bond's *Early Morning* which takes flagrant liberties with external facts in order to project a deeper historical truth.

A characteristic feature of nineteenth century historical drama, however, is that playwrights tended to look to history for possibilities of romance and spectacle and showed little regard for historical truth. Schiller's treatment of the Joan of Arc story is a case in point. He causes her to fall in love with her enemy, an English knight called Lionel, and mercifully saves her from the horror of the burning episode. She is made to die heroically on the battlefield instead. The Church does not figure at all in his play and the question of heresy never arises. He thus shirks the aspects of historical fact he found disagreeable or incompatible with his purpose. More recently there has been much controversy over Howard Brenton's play about the Churchills in which he takes considerable liberty with character and motive. Therefore it is important to determine how free a playwright can be with historical material if his play is to be considered a history. A definition should allow considerable room for imaginative insight and expression, but not for indiscriminate fabrication where a disservice is done to history and an injustice to those concerned.

The writer does not have to serve as a spokesman for any particular version of history. Rather, he can bring to his exploration of the past a personal awareness and his own artistic integrity. He does not have to be slavishly dependent on his sources. If he accepts without question the judgement of his sources he will be merely presenting a certain account of an event in history. And it is necessary to remember that historical knowledge is by no means a static thing, for new facts are constantly being discovered which

lead to a revision of supposedly established facts and a discrediting
of earlier theories. As H. Lindenberger notes, Shakespeare's portrayal of Richard III, deriving as it does from Thomas More and the
Tudor historians, bears little resemblance to a modern portrait of
the king and 'if the reality of a historical figure or context is defined
according to the standards of contemporary academic historical
writing, all but a few plays would seem scandalously inaccurate'.[11]
Historians themselves have to contend with new material continually coming to light. G. Clark, writing in 1957, observes, 'No
historian hitherto has had at his command all the sources which
might be relevant to his subject; none has ever completed his work
so that no newly emerging source could invalidate it.'[12] Thus, since
history itself changes according to increasing knowledge and
shifting historical perspectives, playwright and historian alike can
only be true to the facts as he knows them in his time and place.

What cannot be denied as truth is the significance which past
events and figures embody for man. The artist in his vision includes their impact on posterity, what they have come to mean
through the passage of time, projecting yet another truth reflective
of the human condition. This then is another aspect of the history
play. It takes into account not merely the thoughts and ideas of a
specific day and age, but also what another day and age has made
of these as reflected in the mind and imagination of the playwright. A pronounced feature of the twentieth-century English
history play is the overt treatment of the past in terms of the
present. This approach can be seen to stem from Shaw. He au-
daciously challenged the conventions of nineteenth-century historical drama which attempted to create a semblance of historical
reality in the form of the 'right' historical atmosphere through
elaborate costumes and sets, artificial speech and sentiments.
Hence the shock of Londoners when Shaw's Julius Caesar came on
stage speaking plain English![13]

Shaw succeeded in bringing about a radical change in taste and
outlook on the part of audiences as well as playwrights. Since
Shaw, most historical playwrights can be found blatantly reflecting
their own time. This can be seen in major playwrights such as
Edward Bond whose use of startling anachronisms is an important
feature of his work, and even in minor playwrights such as Gordon
Daviot. The pacifist angle in her play, *Richard of Bordeaux* had
immense appeal in her time, according to Sir John Gielgud who
played the lead role and directed the first production. He was

continually mobbed by crowds in the street as he left the theatre and looks back to it as the greatest 'fan' success of his whole career.[14]

One way of distinguishing the major playwright from the minor is the former's ability to draw connections between past and present which are not obvious and to establish an image not only for his own generation but for successive generations as well. A really powerful playwright can create new myths in dealing with history. Thus we find not only a lesser playwright like Daviot but major playwrights like Shaw and Bond impelled to challenge the tremendous impact Shakespeare has had on our notion of the past. Some of their plays such as Daviot's *Richard of Bordeaux* and *Dickon*, Shaw's *Caesar and Cleopatra*, and Bond's *Lear* are attempts to redress the balance and offer a corrective to Shakespeare's view or a fresh perspective. Shaw and Bond are playwrights powerful enough to impress images of their own on the modern consciousness.

Historical plays of modern playwrights often refer more directly to the legend than the fact. This brings us to another important consideration – the place of the romantic and legendary associations that spring up around every great historical figure and event. The inevitable question that arises is when does history become myth? If a great part of the impact of the history play lies in the artist's perception of history through another age's eyes with all the ramifications and reverberations of time gone by, is the writer prevented from bringing into his conception the mythic dimension that is so much a part of our sense of the past? What these historical figures and events have come to mean to us often surpasses mere historical fact. The fascination of mythical elements, even for those historians who would disavow them, is immense and they are consistently perpetuated to become an irresistible part of the legend surrounding a historical personality or event.

As to the question of truth, historians themselves are not always agreed. Edward Renan's opinion is that the whole truth about a historical figure is not to be found in documents: 'To what would the life of Alexander be reduced if it were confined to that which is materially certain? Even partly erroneous traditions contain a portion of truth which history cannot neglect.' He points out that those who rely entirely on documents will find themselves in a quandary when they have to contend with documents which are 'in flagrant contradiction with one another.'[15] It was a 'true instinct' that led Herodotus, 'the Father of history', to include in his narrative stories which might or might not have evidential value, according to F. J. Weaver. In his book, *The Material of English History*, published in 1938, he explains:

> Stories that are obviously mythical, and probably invented to explain some tradition, often contain suggestions of the real origin of the tradition. So to the modern study of history in its various branches a seeming medley of material is freely admitted, solely on its merits – not only charters, deeds, and other such documents; laws, treaties, and proclamations; annals and chronicles; but also diaries, memoirs, and private correspondence; genealogies and wills; commercial papers and house-hold accounts; ballads, songs, myths and folk tales, anecdotes and oral traditions; place-names, idioms, and the development of language. Different techniques are required for testing different classes of material and for estimating the value of their contribution to history, but each class has its own contribution to make.[16]

So historians themselves find they cannot afford to neglect any sources, documentary or non-documentary, capable of adding dimensions to their understanding, which the conventional sources of history do not provide.

The boundary between history and legend is impossible to demarcate exactly even by historical experts. Therefore a modern psychologist. E. H. Erikson, in his approach to history asserts that 'the making of legend is as much part of the scholarly rewriting of history as it is part of the original facts used in the work of scholars. We are thus obliged to accept half-legend as half-history, provided that a reported episode does not contradict other well-established facts; persists in having a ring of truth; and yields a meaning consistent with psychological theory'.[17] The way in which an historical event is seen and felt is extremely significant, and can have far-reaching effects on the future, creating history in its image. Legends have a different reality from historical fact, but they have a vital reality nevertheless and can be deeply revealing of the nature of humanity and the historical process. Thus, as has been observed, we are gradually finding our way back to the old wisdom, in the words of Kathleen Raine, that 'fact is not the truth of myth, myth is the truth of fact'.[18]

If the historian and the psychologist cannot afford to totally ignore the mythological dimension in their study of the past, neither can the dramatist. It is his duty to be properly instructed with regard to the facts, but not to keep narrowly within its bounds. He must be free to render the truth of the situation as he sees it. He might explore its mythological aspects and bring to it a particular focus or concern, but that is all part of the historical interest and reality. History is the observer and the observed, and this holds true whether it is approached by historian, psychologist or playwright. Each throws his light and none can bring all-round illumination, but each has a unique and valuable perspective to bring to bear. The subjective element makes of history something of an art just as the objective element makes it something of a science. A certain balance has to be achieved, but neither aspect can be denied.

Historical perspectives are continually changing in accordance with the bias of the writer and the age. Each generation rewrites history in its own image. Thus, the historian, Charles Wayland Lightbody states that 'there are no final value-judgements of time and history, but always new judgements, reflecting new conditions surrounding those who do the judging'.[19]

Historical works therefore comment as much on the writers and their own time as on the periods about which they are written. Critics often deny or minimize the value of Shaw's plays as history because he treats the past overtly in terms of the present and projects a distinctly modern perspective. But not only was Shaw primarily concerned with the present and interested in the past only as it relates to the present, he also had grasped that one cannot escape from the limitations of one's own temperament and environment. As early as 1907, he writes in the preface to his essay, 'The Sanity of Art':

> I deal with all periods; but I never study any period but the present, which I have not yet mastered and never shall; and as a dramatist I have no clue to any historical or other personage save that part of him which is also myself, and which may be nine tenths of him or ninety-nine hundredths, as the case may be (if indeed, I do not transcend the creature) but which any-how is all that can ever come within my knowledge of his soul. The man who writes about himself and his own time is the only man who writes about all people and about all time.[20]

There is a fundamental truth in this which relates to any writer's approach to the past and applies as much to the historian as to the dramatist. It has now long been accepted by historians that historical judgements give to all history 'the character of "contemporary history" because, however remote in time events there recounted may seem to be, the history in reality refers to present needs and present situations wherein those events vibrate'.[21] Shaw anticipates this important truth, enunciated in 1938 by Benedetto Croce, the Italian historian cum philosopher whose influence, as an English historian, C Webster, explains, 'came from his insistence that past history only existed when relived in the minds of historians in the light of their own experience, that all history is for this reason contemporary history, something that they apprehend because they have become part of it'. Webster goes on to comment:

> There are some who think that this is one of the great pitfalls of the present day and that it tends to make historians interpret the actions of men of previous ages as though they had the same environment as themselves. My own view is that it is just the analysis of our own experience which enables us to understand more completely that which is so different from it. The process will in any case take place in some form or other and it is far better that it should be done consciously.[22]

This surely justifies the modern historical playwright's often radical reading of the present into the past, since it is an inescapable part of the writing of history. A writer sometimes mirrors intensely personal experiences. In *Murder in the Cathedral*, T. S. Eliot's own personal sense of fragmentation may be seen reflected in the dilemma of his protagonist. While working on *Emperor and Galilean* Ibsen stated in a letter that what he was putting into the play was a part of his 'own inner life', what he described were things he had himself experienced in different forms and the historical theme he had chosen had a closer connection with the currents of his own age than one might at first think. This he regarded as an 'essential demand to be made of every modern treatment of material so remote, if it is, as a work of literature, to be able to arouse any interest'.[23] A man cannot escape from himself or from the political, social and cultural environment to which he belongs. Though it is undeniable that our apprehension of the present is indelibly affected by the conditioning of the past, it is no less true that our understanding of the past is inextricably bound up with our experience of the present.

Another factor of crucial relevance in arriving at a definition of the history play is the question of the nature of the subject matter. There has been a tendency among critics in dealing with past playwrights to stress political themes and issues as a playwright's distinct concern in the writing of historical drama.[24] But today history is no longer thought of merely in terms of politics. One of the limitations of historical science in the nineteenth century, Herbert Butterfield states, was that it 'studied the events of a nation and the changes in the world too much from the point of view of government'. Our whole notion of general history has been affected by the enormous amount of work done in the cultural field and the remarkable development of economic history.[25] The present-day concept of history has broadened immensely to encompass practically every sphere of human interest and activity in the past. It follows that though most history plays revolve around political figures and events, we should not exclude works which have a different focus. For example, Edward Bond's play on Shakespeare, *Bingo*, should not be discounted as a history on the grounds that he is a literary rather than a political figure. Shakespeare's significance as a universal literary monument can hardly be denied to have had a world-wide influence on the lives of men and as such he is a historical phenomenon to be reckoned with. Whether Bond's portrait of Shakespeare is adequately based in history would be the question to explore in considering the play as a history.

Another point of historical debate is the choice of period. Elton traces the issue back to Thucydides who questioned the possibility of any history except contemporary history on the basis that only personal experience and observation could guarantee knowledge and accuracy:

2,500 years later, that argument is still sufficiently alive for an American historian to ask the ironical question whether the past should concern the historian at all. In giving a warning against an excessive preoccupation with the contemporary, he adopted a position probably more common today than that of Thucydides, if only because developing techniques have given us a better control over the evidence for more distant ages and left us aware of the exceptional difficulties involved in discovering and assimilating the evidence for our own times.[26]

The main arguments in this position are that the full range of sources does not become available until later and that objectivity and perspective are hard to achieve in dealing with contemporary history.

David Thomson, editor of the twelfth volume of *The New Cambridge Modern History*, agrees that the writing of contemporary history involves the scholar in problems that in some ways are less acute for the historian of ages more remote. However he argues cogently that the contemporary historian enjoys some compensating advantages·

> His sources, if not complete, are superabundant. He has the feel of the events, the sense of atmosphere, the appropriate presuppositions for sympathetic understanding. The very immediacy of his interpretation may endow it with value for his successors. In any case it is important that professional historians should not shirk the duty of making available to those who must try to shape the immediate future the best understanding of the age that their techniques and skills can achieve: for to abdicate this duty would be to abandon the field to propagandists and soothsayers.[27]

The matter of choice of period ultimately rests on the individual historian's preference and belief. Obviously then the historical playwright should be left free to deal with remote eras, as T. S. Eliot does in *Murder in the Cathedral*, as well as those less distant, as Edward Bond does in *Early Morning*. But there are plays which look to even more recent times such as Trevor Griffith's play, *The Party*, which treats events in the late 1960s. If it can be admitted, Edward Bond's *Saved*, would also be a candidate. But that would open up the term too far and I prefer to draw the lines more strictly. I suspect it is better to reserve the term 'history' for plays where there is some little interval of time between the author and his subject because of the gain in perspective, for otherwise a play can so easily be built on assumptions that may be shattered soon after.

Early twentieth-century historical dramas, as can be seen from the plays of Shaw, reveal a tendency to concentrate on the impact of the exceptional individual on his environment. More recently the situation has been reversed and dominant figures are presented as embodiments of social, economic and political forces, as can be seen from the plays of Bond. Stemming mainly from the widespread influence of Marxian ideas on modern thought, there is a tendency to set, in place of heroic figures, material and economic factors as the motor power of historical development. This is reflected in the current mode of historical thinking. C. H. Wilson, in his professorial inaugural lecture at the University of Cambridge in 1964, relates how a reviewer trained in an older school of history, Sir Harold Nicolson, remarked of a volume on the late nineteenth century, that it represented this new trend:

In the old days, he wrote, a little nostalgically, we should have been provided with a narrative of facts concentrated on the personalities of Napoleon III or Alexander II. But now Marx and Darwin claim as much attention as Bismarck or Mr Gladstone. Personalities are less important than social and economic trends. "Thus (he concluded bravely) we are given here many bright pages about pig-iron."

Wilson points out that:

the need to place individuals in their social context (which is one half of the permanent historical equation) is probably more readily accepted amongst practising historians today than the need to measure the mark of individuals upon their surroundings (which in true orthodoxy is the other half of the equation).[28]

It does not matter which half of the historical equation the dramatist concerns himself with. It should be entirely his prerogative whether to focus on the individual's influence on his time, or to project him as representative of the social, political and economic forces of his age, or to explore the relationship between the two, as John Osborne does in his play, *Luther*.

But here another question arises. Need there be historical figures and events in a play to make it eligible as a history? There is what Lindenberger calls the 'unhistorical history play', citing Hufmansthal's *The Tower* as an example of a play essentially concerned with historical issues, but not based on any 'real' history.[29]

Then there are the vast number of mythological plays constructed around rather dubious historical sources where legend soon takes over. Some of the plays of John Arden and Edward Bond are so inspired and many of these, like Bond's play, *The Woman*, get to the essential concerns of history more truly than many overtly historical dramas. A play can be centred around historical issues rather than actual characters or occurrences and surely this is a kind of history play which a definition should be flexible enough to include.

It becomes clear from the preceding discussion that the crucial question is how free can a playwright be with history. What has to be determined is just where and how a playwright is at liberty to be inventive with history and where and how he is not. To arrive at this it is necessary to explore the area of divergence between history and drama. History and the history play are two distinct, disparate forms of writing with markedly different aims and have to abide by their own rules and conventions. A play is a play and to that effect, of necessity, creates its own internal frame of reference. What cannot be denied is that any attempt to reconstruct the past involves some degree of fantasizing with facts known or discovered adding to the mystery of what is irrecoverable in any total sense. Drama perforce involves this to a much greater extent than the writing of history. As Lindenberger aptly points out, the very term 'historical drama' suggests something of its nature, 'the first word qualifying the fictiveness of the second, the second questioning the reality of the first'.[30] What I feel we should not do is to make the mistake of stressing the historical element to the detriment of the dramatic or the dramatic element to the detriment of the historical. What has to be achieved is a fine balance and it is precisely the nature and scope of this balance that I intend to explore.

History is governed by the very necessary discipline of having to limit its focus to what is actually there in evidence. It would, therefore, sometimes have to be dry and insufficient. Drama cannot afford to be so strictly limited by the facts. It certainly cannot afford to be dry! The dramatist has to engage with past experience in a far more committed way if his play is to come through with any conviction. The dramatist has to read into history in order to convey the totality of an experience and he gains something by this greater imaginative appropriation of the past. The history play, therefore, has to be, in a sense, more historical than history.

A historian is more directly interested in historical knowledge for its own sake, concerned to add to that build-up of learning about the past. A playwright's interest in history would be more from the perspective of what it can possibly bring to our awareness of what life is and can be. The true difference between the poet and the historian, according to Aristotle, is that 'one relates what has happened, the other what may happen'. Poetry therefore 'is a more philosophical and higher thing than history: for poetry tends to express the universal, history the particular'. By the universal, he means, how a person of a certain type will on occasion speak or act, according to the law of probability or necessity. And even if the poet:

> chances to take an historical subject, he is none the less a poet; for there is no·reason why some events that have actually happened should not conform to the law of the probable and possible, and in virtue of that quality in them he is their poet or maker.[31]

A salient point emerges from this. A playwright's truth is imaginative truth. He writes with a poet's unique insight into human character and intuitive grasp of life. His sense of the probable, of inner consistency between character and situation, is a dominating element in the creative process even when he goes to history.

Sir Philip Sidney, in his defence of poetry, supports Aristotle. History is tied 'to the particular truth of things and not the general reason of things'. He argues effectively that the historian is often forced to assume the role of poet and that 'the best of the *Historian* is subject to the *Poet*'. The historian is bound to tell things as they are, cannot be liberal, without being 'Poeticall of a perfect patterne'. 'Manie times he must tell events, whereof he can yeeld no cause, and if he do, it must be poetically.' Neither 'Philosopher nor Historiographer could at the first have entered into the gates of popular judgements, if they had not taken a great passport of Poetrie.'[32]

It is undeniable that the imagination has an essential place in the writing of history because history is both scientific investigation and analysis, and imaginative reconstruction and insight. David Knowles affirms that 'a historian may well, in his assessment of character, show the same genius of sympathy that we recognize in a poet'.[33] Herbert Butterfield indicates that there are striking

affinities between historical and dramatic thinking. It demands
something of the imagination of the literary man, he says:

> to turn a bundle of documents into a resurrected personality and
> to see how a heap of dry facts, when properly put together, may
> present us with a dramatic human situation.
>
> . . . In the last resort historical students must be like actors, who
> must not merely masquerade as Hamlet on one night and King
> Lear on another night, but must feel so and think so, and really
> get under their skins – the defective historian being like the
> defective actor who does not really dramatise anything because
> in whatever role he is cast, he is always the same – he can only
> be himself.[34]

Here we find history and drama being brought together in a
startling theatrical image which reveals the historical and dramatic
imaginations to be closely interlinked.

The historian's main method of communication is through
words and he has to rely predominantly on the efficacy of words to
record or interpret the stream of events and the behaviour of men.
Drama is action, enactment. The dramatist's medium is not just
words, but actual people placed on a stage and required to move
and be. Even if the play is a play of ideas, exploring abstruse
philosophical concepts, these have to be translated into concrete
human terms because the playwright has to deal with people on a
stage, not bloodless abstractions. These people can break or make
a dramatic situation because they bring their own truth and understanding to bear. Visual and aural elements play an essential part
in the communication of meaning in the theatre. Words can be
crucial or trivial, for at times what is happening is more important
than what is being said. Words can be contradicted by action
which is a comment in itself. We retain the ritual when we distrust
the words or the efficacy of words.

Drama, thus, operates on different levels. Its purpose is to
communicate, to engage or involve an audience. Though the
historian would, generally, wish others to read the history he
writes, his readers' response is not a direct concern. Drama includes the immediacy of an audience's response as an integral part
of the theatrical process. For drama is a collective experience – an
interaction between playwright, director, actor and spectator. It
does not allow for a fixedness of interpretation, a view or meaning

which is single and apparent. Drama, by its very nature, is dialectical so there has to be a dialogue and tension of opposites if it is not to destroy the mechanics by which it works. Then it passes through the subjective consciousness of innumerable other people as the producer approaches the play; the actor, his part; the audience, the production. Thus its final effect is often unpredictable as there are so many variables involved and the meaning that emerges cannot be ensured. This, however, is its strength and its truth for reality ultimately can only be perceived through subjective minds and impressions.

So drama parallels the way we are confronted by issues in life. Truth is finally inscrutable and can only be apprehended through a filter of subjective impressions. Drama provides this multiple perspective, refracted as it is through the minds of playwright, director, actor and audience. This is how we meet any truth in life, the onus of interpretation finally resting with each individual as he makes sense of it in his own terms. Drama presents this deep reality inherent in its very form. The history play when acted is as subject as any other play to the dictates of drama intrinsic to its nature. Ultimately the effect of the play as drama will depend not so much on the manifest intention of the playwright as on whether it registers with the audience as true to the complexity of the human situation.

A central part of the theatrical experience is the inner drama that takes place in each member of the audience as he relates to what is taking place. At its highest level drama creates a heightened state of consciousness in its audience which renders it more alert and receptive. It raises and intensifies so that an audience feels it has been in touch with reality in a compelling way and been given a profound insight into the human condition. Through this sense of communion at a deep level an audience can find itself released and renewed; and somehow strengthened and increased to face life anew. When drama achieves this it is close to a spiritual experience as demonstrated by T. S. Eliot's *Murder in the Cathedral* or Charles Williams's *Thomas Cranmer of Canterbury*. Like all drama the history play should go as far as it can in this direction. Indeed our sense of the past often contributes to this feeling of deep involvement.

It therefore becomes apparent that the history play as a play generates its own controls just as history imposes its own limits for the historian. The playwright is bound to his chosen discipline just as the historian is to his. But this leads us to consider whether the history play possesses a distinguishing quality which renders it unique in any way in drama. And it is undeniable that the history play does wield a distinctive power arising from the fact that, while other plays make no pretence to be more than a simulation of reality, the history play tacitly claims to be engaging with reality, for its effect is often based on the audience's belief that it is dealing with a past actuality. When emotionally stretched, the audience cannot seek relief from anxiety by dismissing what is presented as unreal, purely a figment of the writer's imagination. The audience *feels* that it is being faced with certain ineluctable facts of existence because what is happening on the stage is reinforced by the sense of history.

This can be turned to potent effect by the dramatist. Often the inescapable identification with the past leads to an intensity of response and involvement because we see the action on the stage brimming over into a continuum of events of which we are a part. At such moments certain projected 'truths' about human existence are brought home with frightening urgency, as in Shaw's *Saint Joan* and Edward Bond's *Early Morning*. We get the sense of an inevitable chain of consequences which draws us in as part of the drama since the world portrayed has an undeniable relationship with our own world of present thought and action. The historical playwright, thus, owes it, not only to his subject, but also to his audiences, to be regardful of historical truth since the idea of factuality is never entirely absent from their minds. Any definition of the history play, therefore, should include this obligation on the part of the playwright.

In seeking to arrive at a definition in the field of drama, one recognizes the wisdom of M. C. Bradbrook's concern that since 'the history of drama is the history of interaction between the author's imagination, the actor's skill and the spectator's expectation', the definition of a work should cover the play in being, the dramatist's idea of it and the response of the audience as part of the play.[35] And if the history play is to be justified in its possession of this formidable power inherent in our idea of and reaction to the play, there must be a basis for it in the approach of the playwright and therefore in the definition of the genre.

It is my contention, therefore, that a history play is a play which evinces a serious concern for historical truth or historical issues though the expression of that concern and the treatment of those issues may take protean forms. This would exclude plays whose concern with history is sketchy and peripheral, plays which are romantic and sentimental in their approach to history, which reveal an ignorance of or indifference to the facts. It excludes plays with only faint pretensions to historical or political concerns, where history is exploited merely for its sensational and theatrical possibilities. A play is not a history when historical truth is a matter of relatively small importance and character is based on fabricated evidence, or when generally accepted facts of history are altered to serve a central theme or purpose. As an illustration we might look at three varying approaches to the history of Thomas Becket by Tennyson, T. S. Eliot and Anouilh. Tennyson's *Becket* is a classic example of the kind of play which looks to history for possibilities of romance and sensation. What takes precedence over the conflict between Thomas and Henry, between the institutions of Church and Crown, are the romantic entanglements and intrigues woven around the facts of history. As has been observed, 'Quite unhistorically, the rivalry between Queen Eleanor and Fair Rosamund is used to provoke the catastrophe.'[36]

Anouilh's *Becket* is another play that would not qualify as a history. It is founded on a long outdated account of the subject – *The Conquest of England by the Normans* by Augustin Thierry – which Anouilh chanced to come across and from which he derives some of the main premises of his play. E. Martin Browne has indicated that Anouilh's picture of Becket, is based on the idea, now exploded:

> that he was a Saxon, a member of the conquered race in an 'occupied' country. The Normans would never let him be one of them: even when he wielded almost absolute power for Henry he felt this inferiority . . . and indeed it is true that 'for this drama it was a thousand times better that Becket remained a Saxon.'

Anouilh knew the facts but chose to disregard them. He says, 'no one except my historian friend [who had told him of the errors] was aware of the progress of history'. The theme of a man suffering from the neurosis of the subjugated in an occupied country had an obvious interest and relevance for Anouilh.[37] But his lack of interest in history is plain. He makes no pretence at historical veracity. Thus his play cannot be termed a history since it is deliberately based on a false premise and he has imposed motivation on his character and altered the known facts of history to justify it.

In contrast, T. S. Eliot's approach to the subject reveals a serious concern for historical truth. His play is based on a sound knowledge of the facts. While it treats the external conflict between Church and State, it is also an immensely inward play, probing the deep spiritual conflict within Becket himself. Eliot might have projected some of the agony he was experiencing at the time in his own personal life into his dramatisation of Becket's inner turmoil, but there is ample basis for his portrayal in the records themselves. Eliot goes back to the original sources which he treats with scrupulous respect, but he also reads widely and is aware of the complexity of historical views on the subject. Thus *Murder in the Cathedral* emerges as the play I would consider a history play.

Considerable space has been given to discussing the kinds of approach and treatment of history the definition would include, so it is not necessary to go into this again here. But, to summarise, whether playwrights deal with historical subjects of varied nature and in diverse manner, whether these subjects have a basis in fact or in myth, the distinguishing feature of the history play must be a concern for historical truth or historical issues. It must be re-emphasized, however, that historical truth is *more* than history which, as one historian defines it, 'is all the remains that have come down to us from the past, studied with all the critical and interpretative power that the present can bring to the task'.[38] Historians would be the first to agree that we cannot pronounce on the past 'with a frightful degree of certainty'.[39] We cannot be sure we have the whole truth no matter how ingeniously the evidence is built up. Only a fraction of the whole can ever be known and in the attempt to recover it – the certain, the probable and the speculative will co-exist.

Historical truth is, thus, disengaged from any single person's view of it, but each has his light to bring. The historian's torch is systematic controlled inquiry and scholarship. The dramatist's is imaginative sympathy and insight. Thus his imagination must be allowed full play over his material. He is not bound rigidly to his sources or to the views of approved prophets. He must be free to show us events from unexpected angles. But there are limits to this freedom, if he is not to lose hold of the concern for historical truth itself. A playwright is free to read into history as long as no violence is done to history and he has reasonable grounds for his portrayal. There must be a basis for his vision in history, no matter how inward into psychological states or outward into social and political debate he takes it.

In order to ascertain whether this concern for historical truth or historical issues, established as the basis of my definition, is present in a given play, each play requires close individual examination on its own terms. Thus in subsequent chapters, the ideas raised in somewhat abstract terms in this introduction are pursued through a detailed study of certain plays. The history play is a very popular form among English playwrights of this century and obviously there are a great many plays that could have been chosen. The plays considered have been selected for their varying approaches to history and because they provide telling illustrations of many of the ideas discussed. Major works by writers of the first rank have been included, such as Shaw's *Saint Joan*, T. S. Eliot's *Murder in the Cathedral* and Edward Bond's *Early Morning* because writers of this quality are creative and dynamic in their approach to history. They strike out in fresh directions, stimulating new trends of thought and experiment. Popular works by minor playwrights have also been considered, such as Gordon Daviot's *Richard of Bordeaux*, Robert Bolt's *A Man for All Seasons* and Peter Shaffer's *The Royal Hunt of the Sun* because they were immensely successful in their own time and reflect the response of popular taste.

I have considered not only the historical aspects of these plays, but also their particular value and effectiveness as drama. For, as history is concerned to separate what is essential from what is trivial, what is enduring from what is transient; in the final analysis the real significance of a history play, as with any play, is its capacity to explore the universal implications of a human situation and penetrate to the truth of the human condition. The ultimate criterion by which it should be judged is the nature of our response. We experience the flash of recognition or the shock of the unexpected and are convinced only by the compelling truth of the artist's portrayal of life.

2
George Bernard Shaw:
Saint Joan

In a study of twentieth-century English history plays George Bernard Shaw is a good playwright to start with, not merely from the point of view of chronology. The modern approach to historical drama can be seen to start with him. The immense influence he exerted in his own time and continues to exert among English playwrights of this century is reflected in the fact that nearly all the playwrights dealt with in this book mirror some measure of his impact. He is evident in the background of the works of minor playwrights such as Reginald Berkeley, Gordon Daviot and Clifford Bax; as well as major playwrights like T. S. Eliot, John Osborne and Edward Bond. Much of what we have grown accustomed to expect from a modern history play was brought about by Shaw's originality and daring in challenging the hidebound practices and conventions of nineteenth-century historical drama.

Saint Joan has been selected for close individual attention in this chapter because it is a major historical work of the twentieth century and illustrates the new tradition of history play stimulated by Shaw, with his emphasis on discursive rational elements, an anti-heroic tone and diction, an overtly modern perspective and a consciousness of different possible views of an event. But as Shaw is seminal in the field, before coming to *Saint Joan* in particular, some attention has been devoted to establishing the precise nature of his originality in the mode.

Nineteenth-century English playwrights were mostly drawn to history because of opportunities it afforded for theatrical display. As Martin Meisel observes, 'the history play of the nineteenth century was characterized by three qualities: elaborate spectacle, romantic intrigue and flamboyant histrionics'.[1] History provided a splendid backdrop against which to weave intricate webs of exotic romance and intrigue. Events were sensationalized, characters sentimentalized and historical issues subordinated to the petty round of personal disputes and passions. Thus in plays like Tennyson's *Becket* (1893) the 'love' interest is the focus of dramatic sympathy and the real issues involved in the clash between Henry and Becket recede into oblivion. The extremely successful plays of Stephen Phillips and Bulwer-Lytton were in this romantic, melodramatic tradition which catered to the popular taste of the time.

There was no serious attempt at historical authenticity though playwrights went out of their way to create the 'correct' historical atmosphere through superficial externals of historical period or personage. Vast sums were lavished upon elaborate sets, costumes and accessories. But these were merely factitious aids to produce the impression of historical reality. '"Correctness of costume" was a phrase invented to excuse pageantry, as was "accuracy of locale" for spectacle.'[2] It was regarded as important for the past to be portrayed as profoundly different from the present, and writers took pains to create the semblance of a period removed in time through the psychology of their characters whom they invested with highly impassioned artificial language and sentiments. Londoners were therefore startled when Shaw's rational, mild-mannered Julius Caesar came on stage speaking 'plain, even slangy English'[3] and the historical illusion was rudely shattered by startling anachronisms such as 'Egypt for the Egyptians', 'Art for Art's sake', and Beaconsfield's 'Peace with Honour'.

Shaw reacted strongly against playwrights who were shallow and opportunistic in their approach to history. His genuine concern for historical truth caused him to dismiss their products as 'historical romance, mostly fiction with historical names attached to the stock characters of the stage'.[4] Asked by Roy Nash of the *Manchester Evening News* in 1938 whether a dramatist writing a historical play should be allowed to clothe his characters in 'garbs of romance', Shaw replied:

> If the characters are clothed in romance, as you so romantically put it, they are not historical. No historical character is worth dramatizing at all unless the truth about him or her is far more interesting than any romancing. A good play about Rip Van Winkle is not spoiled by calling it Rip Parnell; but it does not thereby become an historical play. Shakespeare always stuck close to the chronicles in his histories. And they survive, whilst hundreds of pseudo-historical plays have perished.[5]

Clearly, Shaw himself regarded a historical play to be one which respected its sources and showed a concern for historical truth. This does not mean that he believed in a slavish adherence to historical facts and records. He was only too well aware of the demands imposed on the historian or dramatist by literary or dramatic form. In an interview in *Today* he states:

> Historical facts are not a bit more sacred than any other class of facts. In making a play out of them you must adapt them to the stage, and that alters them at once, more or less . . . things do not happen in the form of stories or dramas; and since they must be told in some such form, all stories, all dramatic representations, are only attempts to arrange the facts in a thinkable, intelligible, interesting form – that is, when they are not more or less intentional efforts to hide the truth, as they very often are.[6]

In Shaw's history plays historical facts do indeed take diverse, interesting forms because Shaw is extremely inventive in his treatment of history. He can be found continually seeking out new approaches but by no means is he guilty of 'intentional efforts to hide the truth.'

Shaw's first history play, *The Man of Destiny* (1897), paradoxically subtitled a 'fictitious paragraph of history' was written in reaction to Sardou's play about Napoleon, *Madame Sans-Gêne*, in which Shaw complains, Napoleon is 'nothing but the jealous husband of a thousand fashionable dramas, talking Buonapartiana'.[7] In a caustic review of a London production of the play in 1895, Shaw exclaims at the expense involved in the production of this:

> huge, mock historic melodrama which never for a moment produces the faintest conviction, and which involves the exhibition of elaborate Empire interiors, requiring half an hour between the acts to set and not worth looking at when they are set'.[8]

Shaw's play is built around a fictitious encounter between Napoleon and a strange lady, and though it has all the classic ingredients of romantic intrigue, it depends for its effect on the deliberate frustration of the audience's expectations. Despite the imaginary situation Shaw's characterization of Napoleon is based in history. He humanizes the figure of Napoleon, presenting him as an ironic blend of the admirable and the ignoble, yet focusing on qualities of mind and will which account for his genius. As R. N. Roy points out, Shaw's portrait outraged many, for 'Napoleon had become a romantic hero whom even sober historians depicted in the grand manner'.[9]

A modern historian, however, would have no trouble crediting Shaw's picture of the positive and negative aspects of Napoleon's character. David Knowles talks of 'Napoleon's supreme lucidity of mind as an organiser and administrator, his admirable energy, his clairvoyance in campaign or on the field of battle, his daring in conception of great schemes.' 'Yet', he says, 'the character behind this, as seen in his personal relations, in his diplomacy, and in his spoken and written words, seems to lack a corresponding generosity and nobility, as it also lacks warmth and grace and sincerity.'[10] Though *The Man of Destiny* is constructed around a fictitious episode, it cannot be discredited as history on this ground, because Shaw presents us with a view of Napoleon that can be endorsed by historical facts.

In Good King Charles's Golden Days (1939), paradoxically subtitled 'a true history that never happened', is another play where the external situation is an artistic contrivance through which Shaw highlights essential historical truths. It is a lively conversational piece which brings together notable historical figures of a period – Isaac Newton, Charles II, George Fox and Godfrey Kneller – who embody in themselves dominant social, religious and political forces of the time. To foreshadow the supercedence of Newton's mathematical theories by those of Einstein a century or two later, Shaw gives Hogarth's famous dictum, 'the line of beauty is a curve' to the painter Godfrey Kneller. In all other essential respects, Shaw is faithful to history.

R. N. Roy accuses Shaw of taking 'outrageous liberties with the facts of Newton's life'[11] when these liberties amount to little more than minor matters of locale, the telescoping or transposition of events. Lord Keynes talks alarmingly of Shaw's 'wild departure from the known facts' in describing Newton 'as he certainly was not in the year 1680'. But, as Keynes himself observes, Shaw 'with prophetic insight' into the possibilities of Newton's nature, gives us 'a picture which would not have been very unplausible thirty years later'.[12] Shaw is not unscrupulous or indiscriminate in the changes he makes to the external facts of history for these changes are motivated by a concern with a deeper historical truth, and enable him to attain considerable breadth of vision.

John Bull's Other Island (1904) illustrates the kind of history play, referred to in the introduction, which does not contain actual historical figures, but is nevertheless centred around historical issues. The play's fictitious characters and events present us with a sort of paradigm of Anglo-Irish history. The Englishman, Tom Broadbent, taking over Larry Doyle's old love, Nora Reilly, and entrenching himself in Ireland politically and economically, symbolises the acquisition and exploitation of Ireland by the English, romantically, politically and economically. The play deals with various historical questions – the conflict of racial types, the dispossession and displacement of the Irish peasantry, the religious and political identity of Ireland. It provides us with an acute insight into English and Irish national character as revealed by their relations in history.

Caesar and Cleopatra (1898) with its anti-romantic, comic–ironic view of the hero stimulated a whole new trend in the approach to history, not merely for dramatists but novelists, historians and biographers as well. As Archibald Henderson observes, 'The contemporary school of ironical biography began, not with Lytton Strachey's Queen Victoria, but with Bernard Shaw's Caesar'.[13] Shaw humanized the heroic figure, portraying him as a mixture of the unique and the prosaic. In an article in *The Play Pictorial* in 1907, he writes:

> . . . we want credible heroes. The old demand for the incredible, the impossible, the superhuman, which was supplied by bombast, inflation, and the piling up of crimes on catastrophes and factitious raptures on artificial agonies, has fallen off; and the demand now is for heroes in whom we can recognise our own humanity . . .[14]

Shaw's impact was widespread. Thus we find an immensely influential twentieth-century playwright like Brecht applauding Shaw's 'refreshing conviction – that heroes are not exemplary scholars and that heroism is a very inscrutable, but very real conglomeration of contradictory traits'. Shaw, he says:

> knows that we have the terrible habit of forcing all the attributes of a certain kind of people into one preconceived stereotyped concept. In our imagination the usurer is cowardly, sneaky and brutal. We would not think of permitting him to be even a little courageous, sentimental or soft-hearted. Shaw does.[15]

Shaw's influence on Brechtian protagonists must surely be felt in plays like *Galileo* and *Mother Courage*. The powerful nature of Shaw's impact on modern drama is revealed in the fact that the penchant throughout this century is for a debunking of the heroic. The hero is most often viewed as an ironic, equivocal compound of body and spirit, instinct and intellect, blindness and imagination.

Shaw's iconoclasm, his delight in upsetting rigid, conventional notions is an inescapable part of his approach to history. *Caesar and Cleopatra* challenges not only popular romantic illusions, but also Shakespeare's characterizations of Caesar and Cleopatra which have moulded the general conception of these historical figures. Shaw's play provides balance of perspective by presenting a contrasting view. There has been much critical controversy over the play's value as history. Much to Shaw's annoyance the play in his time was dismissed as 'historic extravaganza' or 'comic opera'.[16] Throughout his life, Shaw insisted on its historicity. Critics generally have denied the claim. H. Ludeke maintains that 'Shaw's portrait of Caesar will not stand up under close historical scrutiny.'[17] Stanley Weintraub asserts that 'G. B. S.'s Caesar is no more than Shakespeare's Caesar the Caesar of history.'[18]

Yet despite their contrary views of Caesar, these two writers present us with invaluable insights into the possibilities of his nature, basing their visions on historical fact. The historical records themselves are imperfect and there are considerable discrepancies in what survives. Thus as G. B. Harrison points out,

> There is often wide difference between writers of all ages; yet all of them base their findings on the same source. Certainly Caesar was ruthless in his drive to power but once power was assured his intentions appear to have been both statesmanlike and benevolent. Nor is it surprising that the pompous aristocrat portrayed by Shakespeare should be so different from Shaw's tolerant, rational, worldly-wise and avuncular statesman of *Caesar and Cleopatra*.[19]

The early accounts of Caesar's Alexandrian expedition are slight and I suspect that Shaw chose the period because it allowed him considerable freedom over his sources. His concern with the play's viability as history is evident from the trouble he took to check its historical aspects with Gilbert Murray, the noted classicist, modifying his account in the light of Murray's comments. Murray accepts Shaw's portrait of Caesar as quite plausible. In a letter to Shaw, he writes, 'You make a good defence of all points of my attack, especially about Caesar. I own I don't understand him; and your reading may be the right one.'[20]

Shaw, as usual, has indulged in his penchant for making extravagant, even contradictory claims. At an early stage in the writing of the play when it was suggested to him that he had read Mommsen and other historians, he flatly denied it:

> Not a bit of it. History is only a dramatization of events. And if I start telling lies about Caesar it's a hundred to one that they will be just the same lies that other people have told about him . . . You see I know human nature. Given Caesar and a certain set of circumstances, I knew what would happen, and when I have finished the play you will find I have written history.[21]

Behind the deliberate exaggeration Shaw is making a valid point. He was only too well aware of the sophistication required in dealing with historical material and the complexity of historical views. Historical perspectives shift according to the bias of the writer and his age and Shaw was conscious that he was presenting history in the light of his own time. The playwright brings to history his acute insight into human nature, and his sense of internal logic linking character and circumstance is an important part of the contribution he has to make.

Shaw later repeatedly asserted that he took the chronicle without alteration from Mommsen after reading extensively from Plutarch to Warde-Fowler. He found that Mommsen had conceived Caesar as he wished to present him.[22] Shaw's conception of Caesar as a great statesman and practical realist undoubtedly owes much to Mommsen. But he by no means presents Caesar purely in the Mommsen light as some have claimed. Mommsen is unqualified in his adulation of Caesar and his summing up of Caesar's character is extreme indeed. 'The secret of Caesar's character lies in its perfection, he says. 'Caesar was the entire and perfect man. . . . As the artist can paint everything save only consumate beauty, so the historian, when once in a thousand years he encounters the perfect, can only be silent regarding it . . . '.[23] It is precisely this kind of absurd idolatry that Shaw flatly condemns. His own portrait of Caesar is much more mixed and ambivalent and shot through with comic irony.

The purpose behind Shaw's frequent references to Mommsen was probably to place himself in the pro-Caesar tradition of Mommsen and other nineteenth-century historians. Referring to the hero restorations of Mommsen and Carlyle he says:

> allow me to set forth Caesar in the same modern light, taking the platform from Shakespeare as he from Homer, and with no thought of pretending to express the Mommsenite view of Caesar any better than Shakespeare expressed a view which was not even Plutarchian'.[24]

Shaw's concept of historical progress involved the pivotal role played by heroes which was in keeping with the outlook of nineteenth-century historians and philosophers such as Carlyle, Nietzche and Hegel who saw the individual as the motor force of historical development. The history of the world, according to Carlyle, is the biography of great men. 'In all epochs of the world's history we shall find the Great Man to have been the indispensable saviour of his epoch: – the lightning without which the fuel never would have burnt.'[25] For Shaw too the great man is the agent of civilisation's advance; he prefigures the superhumanity of the future. In holding to this view Shaw was very much a Victorian.

The contention that *Caesar and Cleopatra* is unreliable as history rests on two main grounds. One is Shaw's attributing responsibility for the death of Pothinus to Cleopatra when, though various possible causes might have led to his assassination, most historians agree that it was done at Caesar's command. Shaw in switching blame has been accused of a gross violation of history. Gale Larson argues forcibly that this is not a horrendous distortion of history', since Caesar was celebrated for his clemency and both adverse and sympathetic historians, ancient and modern, have praised him for this quality. 'Edwyn Bevan, a twentieth-century historian, writes that "Pothinus, convicted of being in correspondence with the enemy, was put to death by Caesar – ostensibly by order of Cleopatra."' Bevan, like J. P. Mahaffy (a nineteenth-century historian whom Shaw seems to have drawn on for his characterization of Cleopatra), 'accepts the ferocious side of Cleopatra and can conceive of her ordering Pothinus' death. Thus, Shaw, attributing this murderous act to Cleopatra in no way violates her historically known character'. He has therefore in effect transcended a fact of history so that a larger truth of historical biography would remain inviolable'.[26] I agree with this view. A violence would have been done to history if Cleopatra had had a reputation for clemency and Caesar for vengefulness, but Shaw distorts a fact of history to preserve an essential truth embodied in his image of Caesar.

The other main ground for contention involves what has been described as the 'entirely pedagogic nature' of the relationship between Caesar and Cleopatra that is represented in the play.[27] This, it is generally surmised, is largely due to the falsification of Cleopatra's age at the time. Shaw makes her sixteen when she is supposed to have been twenty. Critics have suggested that Shaw might have been misled by the deceptive nature of a reference in Mommsen. But numerous historians have given contradictory information about Cleopatra's age and Shaw had sufficient grounds for portraying her as a young immature girl, merely from Plutarch's comment that Caesar had known Cleopatra when she was 'a girl ignorant of the world' whereas when she met Antony she was in the time of life when women's beauty is most splendid, and their intellects are in full maturity'.[28] That is basis enough for a playwright for, as argued in the introduction, a playwright is not a historian and is not required to weigh the evidence.

Besides, though Shaw deliberately plays down the romantic side of the relationship as a foil to Shakespeare's portrayal, he by no means denies it. There are numerous pointers in the text itself. Right from the start we are told that 'this Caesar is a great lover of women'[29] and Caesar meeting Cleopatra incognito informs her that Caesar 'is easily deceived by women. Their eyes dazzle him; and he sees them not as they are, but as he wishes them to appear to him'. He predicts that she 'will be the most dangerous of all Caesar's conquests.' (Act 1, pp. 187,191) When Pothinus asks Cleopatra how she is so sure that Caesar does not love her as men love women she replies, 'Because I cannot make him jealous. I have tried.' This really is no answer and Pothinus leaves unconvinced: 'The curse of all the gods of Egypt be upon her! She has sold her country to the Roman, that she may buy it back from him with her kisses' (Act 4, p.259).

Furthermore actresses who have played the part of Cleopatra such as Mrs Patrick Campbell, Gertrude Elliot and Vivien Leigh have brought out the flirtatious nature of the relationship. The legend is well known and Shaw hardly needed to labour the point.

Besides the play is intended as a direct contrast to Shakespeare's *Antony and Cleopatra*. Hence the hilarious scene at the end where Caesar in his departure from Egypt almost forgets to say goodbye to Cleopatra. When she appears looking cold and tragic in striking black, he exclaims, 'Ah, I knew there was something. How could you let me forget her, Rufio?' (Act 5, p. 288). *Caesar and Cleopatra* has a reasonable enough basis in historical fact to warrant the term history'. It offers us a counter vision to Shakespeare's in a very different key. One mark of a great playwright like Shaw is the ability to challenge Shakespeare and abide the comparison. Later I shall be considering a lesser playwright, Gordon Daviot, who attempts it but fails.

Of all Shaw's history plays it was *Saint Joan* which marked a turning point in modern historical drama because of its universal impact. Shaw based his play upon original documents, the contemporary reports of Joan's trial and the subsequent rehabilitation proceedings, scrupulously avoiding historians' accounts and the extensive literature on Joan until he had completed the play. The official Latin texts of both trials had been edited by Jules Quicherat in the 1840s and published in five volumes of documented history. Quicherat's scholarly work was translated into English for the first time in an abridged edition by T. Douglas Murray, *Jeanne d'Arc*, published in 1902. In 1920 Joan was canonized by the Roman Catholic Church and Shaw must have been struck by this ironic reversal of judgement in history. Early in 1923 Sydney Cockerell, the curator of the Fitzwilliam Museum at Cambridge, having recognized the dramatic possibilities of the historical material, handed Shaw a copy of Murray's book. Shaw had always felt drawn by the figure of Joan and now his imagination was fired by contemporary reports of one of the most enthralling trials in history. He wrote the play within six months.

Saint Joan was first produced in New York on 28 December 1923 with Winifred Lenihan in the title role, and in London on 26 March 1924 with Sybil Thorndike as Joan. It was published in 1924. The play was heralded as a triumph both in New York and London, and subsequently produced throughout Europe where it met with equal acclaim. In France a production of *Saint Joan* by Georges and Ludmilla Pitoëff opened on 28 April 1925. A tremendous success, it ran for over a hundred performances in 1925 and was revived year after year for the next ten years. It revolutionized the nature of French historical drama. As Daniel C. Gerould comments:

The humour, fantasy, and anachronisms that the critics had found in *Saint Joan* became accepted characteristics of the new genre of historical drama which was best represented in the works of Giraudoux. . . . Ultimately the real originality of Shaw's *Saint Joan* and the source of its influence in France lay in Shaw's application of comic irony and modern psychology to a historical subject which had previously been considered entirely serious.[30]

Shaw's break with the romantic melodramatic tradition of his time constitutes his innovation, but this was not achieved without a struggle. In the *New York Times* of 13 April 1924, some time after the first New York production of the play, James Graham reports a fierce controversy raging in Paris about *Saint Joan*. This was sparked off by a dispatch in the Paris theatrical publication, *Comoedia* from its New York correspondent, M. Thomas, alleging that the author had insulted Joan. Shaw is accused of being sacrilegious as well as boorish and ungallant. Shaw hit back in defence in a letter to the London correspondent of *Comoedia*:

> I love the real Joan, but the conventional Joan of the stage makes me sick. The protagonists of my play, although they appear on the stage as soldiers and feudal noblemen, are in reality the Church, the Inquisition and the Holy Roman Empire. All united irresistibly to destroy a warrior saint. I have not belittled Joan, as would have been the case if I had turned her story into a melodrama about a wicked Bishop and a virtuous virgin. I have carried the tragedy beyond the taste of lovers of such melodrama and probably beyond their comprehension.[31]

The figure of Joan had been grossly sensationalized and senti-mentalized in the theatre so that it had become something of a cliché. She was depicted as either the diabolical witch of the business as in *Henry VI* or as a romantic love-lorn maiden as in Schiller's *Die Jungfrau von Orleans*. Shaw found the pseudo-Shakespearean Joan ending in 'mere jingo scurrility'. He called Schiller's play, 'romantic flapdoodle' and dismissed all modern attempts known to him as 'second-rate opera books'.[32]

Shaw's assertion that Schiller's play 'has not a single point of contact with the real Joan'[33] is hardly an exaggeration. Schiller takes flagrant liberties with history. The Church does not figure in his play at all and the question of heresy never arises. La Hire and Dunois are shown vying for Joan's hand in marriage. A supernatural element is introduced in the form of a knight in shining black armour who warns Joan against entering Rheims. She pays no heed and before the gates of Rheims disarms an English officer with whom she instantly falls in love. Joan is torn between this love for her country's hated foe and her great mission to save France. The play ends with Joan dying heroically on the battle field. Historical truth is abandoned altogether in the interest of wild romanticism.

Plays about Joan in Shaw's time went in equally for romance and sensation. Such realism as there was in Tom Taylor's *Joan of Arc*, produced at the Queen's Theatre in 1871, was for the sake of spectacle as evident from the following review printed in *The Times* (21 April 1871):

> Seldom or never has a more imposing picture been placed upon the stage than the Cathedral at Rheims. The taking of the Tourelles is a spirited battle scene and when the mystic maid, fully armed and carrying her standard, rode upon the stage, the enthusiasm of the spectators knew no bounds. The scene in the torture chamber elicited great interest of somewhat an appalling nature. The drama follows Joan in her adventurous fortunes to her ultimate imprisonment for witchcraft and death at the funeral pile. Certainly we have arrived at the age of realism, when an actress is seen standing upon a mass of apparently burning faggots. The highest praise must be bestowed upon the manner in which the drama has been placed upon the stage. It is an enormous success.
>
> (*Standard*)

The heroine of *Jeanne d'Arc* (1906), the play by American playwright Percy Mackaye, is a pale, ethereal figure, and an inevitable love interest is the focus of dramatic sympathy. D'Alençon is shown in wild transports over Joan, exclaiming lines of sickly sentiment:

> "Always you are with me." Did she say these
> words

> Or am I dizzy with this incense of her? . . .
> "Always you are with me!" Always, always!
>   Here –
> On the air, this moonlight, everywhere – her
>   face
> Encounters mine in glory.[34]

(Act 4, p. 128)

But when he attempts to kiss her as she lies sleeping he is prevented by the dazzling winged form of St. Michael keeping vigil over the virgin maid. The immediacy and vitality of Shaw's modern colloquial idiom in *Saint Joan* was in bold defiance of the convention of employing artificially impassioned, highly stilted verse in historical drama to suggest a time and place removed from the present.

Shaw saw a successful London production of Mackaye's play and when he was asked what he thought of the part of Joan, he replied:

> Yes, I saw Miss Marlowe play it. She was very soft and sweet: that is, about as little like Joan as Joan's charger. Nobody could possibly have burned Miss Marlowe. Job himself would have burned the real Joan. Mind, I am not blaming Miss Marlowe: she did the job she was given and did it very well. She was called on to make Joan pitiable, sentimental and in the technical melodramatic sense 'sympathetic.' And whoever does that makes Joan's fate unintelligible, and in my opinion, makes Joan herself vapid and uninteresting.[35]

Shaw abhorred these melodramatic stereotypes where the real Joan is idealized and romanticized out of existence. His concern was to make Joan credible in actual human terms and project the distinctive qualities that made her a force to be reckoned with in history. But the tremendous pressure exerted by popular taste and theatrical tradition can be seen from the fact that even in early productions of *Saint Joan* the drag towards the conventional often asserted itself and Shaw had to take pains to counteract it. In a letter to the Theatre Guild about the first American production, he writes, 'Simenon must not make the scenery fantastic. It may be very simple; but it must suggest perfectly natural scenery. Joan was an extremely real person, the scenery should be keyed to her reality.' They were also asked to avoid leading to 'that upstage effect with a very feminine operatic-looking Joan in the centre'.[36]

Shaw once criticized Wendy Hiller's interpretation of the role of Joan:

> Joan wasn't a cataleptic – she was forcible and sure from beginning to end, and never played pianissimo . . . when you come on in the Trial scene, kick the chain from step to step instead of dragging it. Let the kicks be heard before you come on: and when they take the chain off do not rub your ankle pathetically, but bend your legs at the knees and stretch them as if you were going to take on the whole court at all-in-wrestling – And call the man a noodle heartily, not peevishly. Get a big laugh with it. And now go your way in the strength of the Lord; but do not despise the instruction of the old bird – G. B. S.[37]

Referring to a certain continental actress's playing of the role, Shaw complained:

> She made the audience weep, but for all the wrong reasons. She played St Joan like a servant girl who has to go to jail for three months for stealing milk for her illegitimate child. Now that is a tragic situation, I admit, but it is definitely *not* Saint Joan![38]

But gradually the Shavian point sank home, stimulating a radical change in public taste and outlook. At the 1938 Malvern Festival Elizabeth Bergner played Joan and the following comment on her performance would surely have met with Shaw's approval:

> Miss Bergner displayed beauty, pathos and charm, but there was nothing of the soldier, nothing of the peasant, and nothing of the obstinate saint. Only the martyr. Nor did Miss Bergner capture the rude common sense which made Miss Thorndike's presentation acceptable as history.[39]

The play's historical reliability has come in for vigorous discussion. When *Saint Joan* was first produced it aroused considerable reaction. J. M. Robertson devoted a whole book to refuting the historicity of the play, but his book is full of illiberal diatribes and narrow-minded pedantry. Strict historical verisimilitude is his concern and the play is picked apart for its variation from history in all kinds of minutiae. Shaw, he asserts, has shown little respect for 'historiographical rectitude' and invented a 'doctrinaire figure which has no historical actuality'. Again we find the desire for an idealized stained-glass window image of Joan. Who can fail to see, he says, that:

> when the noble figure of the tranced visionary, with her sheer burning medieval faith in God and the Saints, inspiring disheartened soldiers and populace to a kindred faith in her Mission, is transmuted to that of a kind of early Feminist Reformer – a Superwoman with a genius for artillery and tactics, reforming a demoralised army – we have lost a real historic figure and gained a mere whimsical contraption.[40]

T. S. Eliot commends Robertson's book and calls Shaw's Saint Joan 'one of the most superstitious of the effigies which have been erected to that remarkable woman'.[41] She:

> is perhaps the greatest sacrilege of all Joans: for instead of the saint or the strumpet of the legends to which he objects, he has turned her into a great middle-class reformer and her place is a little higher than Mrs Pankhurst. If Mr Shaw is an artist, he may contemplate his work with ecstasy.[42]

The shock to the sensibility of a major artist like Eliot is a measure of the originality of Shaw's treatment of history, especially since Eliot was in fact deeply influenced by *Saint Joan* as can be seen from his play *Murder in the Cathedral* where he adopts the same anti-heroic tone and modernity of spirit.

Historians themselves were at that time committed to a reverential approach to heroic figures like Joan. Writing in 1925, a Belgian historian with a special interest in the medieval period, J. Van Kan, commends *Saint Joan* as the 'first serious attempt to give a dramatic rendering of the figure of France's sublime heroine based upon a truly historical foundation'. But he draws attention to 'certain historical inaccuracies which are the cause of small, but nevertheless unnecessary, blemishes in the character of the Heroine Maid, and which distort the surroundings over which she spread her angelic light'. For example he finds it wrong 'to lay in the mouth of Joan words which have a tang of boastfulness' for 'anything with the least hint of boastfulness was worlds removed from the Maid'.[43] The distinguished Dutch Medieval scholar, Johan Huizinga, writing in 1925, laments the absence in *Saint Joan* of a 'high dramatic style'. Shaw's play is 'too much lacking in the qualities of tragic poetry to be commensurate with the sublimity of his subject'.[44] Huizinga refers to a book he had written on fifteenth-century France and the Nationalists in which he hardly mentions Joan. This had been considered an error by some historians, but what had kept him from including Joan was a sense of harmony and a 'vast and reverent humility'.[45] It is hard to imagine any scholar now being able to justify a serious omission on those grounds! But even sober historians of the time treated Joan as a removed exalted figure to be held in pious awe and veneration.

It was precisely this kind of Johannolatry that Shaw was revolting against. He by no means lessens Joan's stature – she is a very splendid figure indeed, but immensely real as well. He did not want audiences to see Joan as a sublime spirit safely remote from themselves, so that they would fail to recognize the relevance of her predicament to contemporary situations. Shaw's primary concern was with the present, not the past; thus he was bent on driving home the play in contemporary terms, pointing to modern equivalents. Sybil Thorndike was told that Joan was like a suffragette.[46] In his preface, Shaw compares Joan's situation to that of Sylvia Pankhurst and Edith Cavell. The question raised by Joan's burning, he says, is a burning question still. That is why he is probing it. If it were only an historical curiosity he would not waste his readers' time or his own on it for five minutes.[47]

Both early and contemporary critics can be found faulting the play as history because of its overtly modern perspective. 'The atmosphere is not that of the Middle Ages'.[48] While admitting that the Shavian history play is the source of one of the most powerful conventions of modern drama, Margery Morgan thinks it reveals a total lack of historical perspective. She describes 'such "historical" drama' as 'merely a special area of fantasy'. The consciousness of Shaw's characters is modern; they speak anachronistically with a foreknowledge of subsequent events.[49] David Daiches asserts that:

> Shaw, like the great XVIII moralists, believed that the generalizations about the society you knew best, your own contemporary society, are valid for men at all times, and thus he cheerfully assumed that he understood Caesar or Saint Joan on the basis of

modern analogies. But he did not understand them, for he lacked historical imagination; and these characters became in his hand modern Shavian heroes rather than convincing historical characters.[50]

Shaw is accused of imposing on the past the psychology of the present. 'He makes no attempt to escape from the limitations of his own temperament.'[51]

But Shaw recognized that one cannot escape from the limitations of one's own temperament and environment. As argued in the introduction, a dramatist can hardly be faulted for interpreting the past in terms of the present since it is an inevitable part of the writing of history. Historians themselves have come to accept its occurrence in some form or other and many feel that it is far better that it should be done consciously. Thus modern historians tend to interpret the behaviour of men of the past as though they had the same environment as themselves. Since Shaw, modern historical drama has taken on this distinctive feature of registering the past overtly in terms of contemporary concerns and conditions. All the playwrights in this study adopt this approach to history and a dynamic modern playwright like Edward Bond employs with riveting effect the Shavian technique of making an audience sit up through the force of startling anachronisms which bring past and present together, driving home the contemporary relevance of what is being portrayed.

The other main reason for which Shaw is accused of a serious distortion of history relates to his portrayal of the trial. It is claimed (erroneously I think) that Shaw projects the trial as non-partisan when it was politically biased. Most critics, even those who generally acknowledge the play's fidelity to history, share this opinion. Louis Crompton asserts that 'only at one point does Shaw seriously misinterpret Joan's career' for he sees Joan's trial as pre-eminently a confrontation between a new prophet and the representative of the status quo. But the Hundred Years War was a French civil war as well as an Anglo-French conflict. Joan's party was opposed by a group of Frenchmen who were pro-English and pro-Burgundian. 'To the extent that he belonged to this party, it is impossible to regard Cauchon as an unbiased spokesman for medieval Catholicism.'[52] Eric Bentley too writes that 'Shaw departs from the facts in at least one essential point, namely in representing the trial as scrupulously fair.' 'To this end Shaw gave an inquisitor arguments such as no inquisitor would have ever approved, let alone employed, and made Bishop Cauchon amiable and rational.'[53]

Yet one has only to examine the records of the trial to see how close Shaw keeps to the arguments used, and how amiable and rational Bishop Cauchon and the Inquisitor went out of their way to be or to appear. Historians themselves are not agreed on this question of the trial's partiality. Huizinga finds Shaw doing 'violence to history in presenting the judges as limited but respectable persons', but he talks of Shaw's 'relative rehabilitation of Joan's judges' as one of the 'most exciting and most original' aspects of his work. He concedes that the proceedings of the 1431 trial of condemnation were in many respects more reliable than those of the rehabilitation trial of 1456 and that, as far as the Archbishop of Beauvais was concerned, Shaw could appeal to the sources on more than one point to support his picture of a well-intentioned Cauchon. And he admits that though Joan 'was asked cunning questions that she could not answer, though the reasoning was formalistic and one-sided, the crucial issue – whether Joan had been able to develop her amazing power owing to divine help or demonic – was a very serious one'. But even if the whole trial need not be seen as sheer wickedness and conscious bias, he nonetheless finds it hard to maintain the historicity of a well-meaning Cauchon, since many of the judges were his creatures and a few of them did raise their voice against him.[54]

Another respected historian, Charles Lightbody, writing more recently in the 1960s, does not agree with this view. He finds it 'difficult, despite the almost universal execration to which Joan's judges have been subjected in modern times, to read the Trial Record without feeling the deep sincerity of the ecclesiastics' in their quarrel with Joan. Of Pierre Cauchon he says:

> It is one of the ironies of history that this man should have gone down alike in popular and literary tradition as one of the blackest villains of all recorded time, worthy of comparison only with Pontius Pilate, because of his leading part in the trial of the peasant maid from Lorraine, whom, we must believe, he regarded sincerely as a heretic and a witch, a poisoned sheep which it was a matter of Christian duty to remove before it tainted the whole flock.[55]

It is this popular image which theatrical tradition had helped to perpetuate that Shaw is concerned to shatter:

> The old Jeanne d'Arc melodramas, reducing everything to a conflict of villain and hero, or in Joan's case villain and heroine, not only miss the point entirely but falsify the characters, making Cauchon a scoundrel, Joan a prima donna, and Dunois a lover. But the writer of high tragedy and comedy, aiming at the innermost attainable truth, must needs flatter Cauchon nearly as much as the melodramatist vilifies him.[56]

If Shaw tones down the personal bias in the part of Cauchon it is to highlight the greater historical truth. His aim is to reveal the vast political and religious forces that moved into action against Joan, and prevent us from making Cauchon, the Inquisitor and the other judges, scapegoats for the institutions which they represented.

Shaw has solid historical grounds for this view. The trial received tremendous official backing. According to W. P. Barret, 'the distinguishing feature of the trial is the immense weight of authority behind it'. Pierre Cauchon was 'assisted by the collaboration of the Inquisition in the person of Jean le Maître, who, with an ill and reluctant humour, agreed to participate only after an especial commission from the Grand Inquisitor of France instructed him to do so. But more important still, Cauchon had the support of the University of Paris, especially in its eminent representatives Beaupère, Midi and Courcelles, who were among the assessors.'[57] At this time the University of Paris was at the height of its medieval fame. It possessed supreme authority in law and theology and was, moreover, under English domination.

If Shaw whitewashes certain historical figures it is because he does not want the audience evading responsibility by merely shifting blame. It is too simple to draw an easy moral by reversing the judgement, making Cauchon the villain of the piece, as was done twenty-five years after Joan's death when his body was dug up and thrown into the common sewer. Shaw shows that the responsibility for Joan's death lies equally with the institutions involved and with every member of society who actively or passively supports such decisions. The driving force behind Shaw's works is a passionate moral concern. *Saint Joan* was written in the period after the first World War when a second could be seen impending. One of Shaw's motives in writing the play was to shock people into an awareness of the consequences of the way they think, in the face of a 'world situation in which we see whole peoples perishing and dragging us towards the abyss which has swallowed them, all for want of any grasp of the political forces that move civilization'.[58] The audience is made to recognize that as unthinking members of a system they might have been part of the social machinery that burned Joan and might be burning her still in a different form today.

It is also a measure of Shaw's achievement that he is able to distribute dramatic sympathy by giving weight to different points of view. But though Shaw provides Joan's adversaries with arguments of substance he by no means exonerates them or presents the trial as free from political bias. It is certainly not his view as has been claimed that the 'execution of Joan was a regrettable but thoroughly understandable measure taken by upright men in full confidence of their judgement' who had they shared her visual acuity 'would have followed her joyfully instead of bringing about her death'.[59] Discussing the Inquisitor with Henderson, Shaw once said that he thought Lemaître 'a most infernal scoundrel'. This has been dismissed as yet another example of Shaw's 'impish conversational manner'.[60] But the truth as to Shaw's own view might well be contained in just such light exchanges where Shaw, the eternal masquerader, might have felt free to let slip his mask. In four postcards he sent to Mrs Patrick Campbell in 1913, long before embarking on the play, Shaw talks of doing a Joan play some day, referring to 'a poor cowardly riffraff of barons and bishops who were too futile to resist the devil'.[61] And he reproaches the actor, Clarence H. Norman, for misinterpreting his role in *The Apple Cart* stating:

> I am disgusted at the ease with which nice clothes and a pleasant address, with rank, impose on everybody. My infernal old scoundrel of an Inquisitor in St Joan got away with it like a cathedral canon; and now here you are swallowing my gentlemanly Magnus as a god! I'm surprised at you'.[62]

Though Shaw is concerned to highlight the political and religious forces at work behind the figures of Warwick and Cauchon, he does not disguise the fact that personal factors play a significant role. Joan symbolizes a threat to the system and therefore a threat to those who are so closely identified with it. Warwick expresses his fear of what Joan stands for when he remarks to the English chaplain, Stogumber, that if this cant of serving their country takes hold of men, it is 'good-bye to the authority of their feudal lords, and good-bye to you and me'. He suggests that the Bishop of Beauvais too is not exempt from personal considerations, having been 'turned out of his diocese by [Joan's] faction'. Warwick himself blatantly reveals that his desire for Joan's removal stems from political and self interest. He crudely goes about the arrangement of it as if it were a commercial transaction. He is prepared to 'buy' the maid at any price and is willing to pay 'little commissions' to middlemen as long as they 'deliver the goods' (Sc. 4, pp. 126–7).

The urbane Cauchon is more subtle and sophisticated in his determination to vindicate himself and the Church under the plea of dire spiritual need. The Church cannot be seen to be 'subject to political necessity'. To justify its position Joan is viewed as an arch heretic, a monstrous threat to the stability of the world. 'The Pope himself at his proudest dare not presume as this woman presumes.' She is of a cancerous breed which if not 'cut out, stamped out, burnt out' will bring 'the whole body of human society into sin and corruption, into waste and ruin', and result in 'a world of blood, of fury, of devastation, of each man striving for his own hand: in the end a world wrecked back into barbarism'. Yet irony lies in the fact that he seeks to prevent this by an act that is utterly barbaric in itself. The vehemence of Cauchon's outcry appears to stem from a passionate concern for Christendom: 'I shudder to the very marrow in my bones when I think of it. I have fought it all my life; and I will fight it to the end' (Sc. 4, p. 135). But the excessive nature of his outpourings lends a false note to his response. In him we see the front man presents to the world, but through constant flashes of wit, Shaw exposes the reality beneath the façade. Cauchon fiercely opposes Warwick's notion that Joan is a witch. 'She is a heretic.' A witch aligns herself with diabolical forces. A heretic goes against the established doctrine of the Church. The Church's scale of priorities is clear. Warwick is happy to concede the point as long as the result he desires is assured – 'My Lord: I wipe the slate as far as witchcraft goes. None the less we must burn the woman.' Cauchon is outraged that the Church should be treated as a 'mere political convenience'. He is no 'political bishop'. He is so righteously impassioned as to be almost convincing. But the words that follow are revealing. 'My faith is to me what your honor is to you', he tells Warwick (Sc. 4, pp. 131–2). This is ironic since Warwick has no sense of honour, and has made no secret of the fact.

The hollowness of Cauchon's lofty professions becomes increasingly apparent. If we give careful ear to the tone of the prose we recognize the performance within the performance. Cauchon may not deliberately be playing false with the world. What is infinitely worse is that he may be playing false with himself. Shaw conveys the intensity with which men will play a role in order to evade a personal sense of guilt.

Throughout this scene Cauchon and Warwick are shown quite unable to appreciate the other's professional viewpoint. Warwick thinks Cauchon exaggerates for he cannot see Joan 'superceding the Church by a great heresy'. Cauchon expresses equal disbelief at Warwick's notion that Joan is a 'cunning device to supercede the aristocracy'. Her belief that 'kings should give their realms to God and then reign as God's bailiffs,' he sees as 'quite sound theologically' (Sc. 4, pp. 136–9). By locking them one against the other, Shaw reveals how prone people are to construe matters in a form that is conducive to their own interests. The dubious moral basis for this alliance is satirized. There is farce in the way Shaw makes them express their different grounds for contention. Cauchon's concern arises from the fact that Joan 'has never mentioned the Church and thinks only of the king and herself,' Warwick's because 'she has never mentioned the peerage and thinks only of the king and herself.' Both amount to heresy, spiritual or secular. Shaw humorously has Warwick label her spiritual heresy 'Protestantism' and Cauchon label her political heresy 'Nationalism'. They unite over the body of Joan in mutual agreement that if Cauchon will 'burn the Protestant,' Warwick will 'burn the Nationalist' (Sc. 4, pp. 138–40).

Shaw juxtaposes their two heavily rationalized positions against the irrational stance of Stogumber. Their coldminded reasonableness contrasts sharply with the naked savagery of the English chaplain who from the start exclaims: 'By God, if this goes on any longer I will fling my cassock to the devil, and take arms myself, and strangle the accursed witch with my own hands' (Sc. 4, p. 125). Yet to all intents and purposes this is the unpalliated truth of their combined attitudes. It brings home the barbarism of what is being proposed underneath all attempts to justify and civilize it. 'Progress,' Shaw has said, 'depends on our refusal to use brutal

means even when they are efficacious.'[63] Stogumber is a caricature
of the blind patriot. His hysteria for blood reveals a poverty of
intellect and imagination. Critics have aptly suggested that Shaw
must have perceived the parallel between English feeling against
Joan in 1429–31 and the anti-German jingoism which so deeply
disturbed him during the First World War.[64] Through Stogumber
Shaw highlights what Cauchon and Warwick conceal beneath a
civilized social exterior. This is reinforced at the close of the scene
when each makes a final pronouncement as to his intention:

> Cauchon: I will not imperil my soul. I will
> uphold the justice of the Church. I
> will strive to the utmost for this
> woman's salvation.
> Warwick: I am sorry for the poor girl. I hate
> these severities. I will spare her if
> I can.
> Chaplain: I would burn her with my own hands.

> (Sc. 4, p. 140)

The sugar-coated falsity is seen against the stark truth. In view of
the threat Joan poses to the establishment, at the heart of the two
carefully built-up positions is the same sort of blind zeal that
Stogumber epitomizes. But society cannot afford to admit to the
naked reality. It requires the veneer of civilization to maintain its
authority. To preserve its code of existence, it has to justify its
actions and thus often legalizes its crimes.

Joan's judges are naturally concerned to assure themselves and
all the world that there 'has never been a fairer examination' and
that Joan is being tried 'by her most faithful friends, all ardently
desirous to save her soul from perdition' (Sc. 6, p. 159). The
historical judges proclaimed as much. Through subtle forms of
evasion and rationalization a man can succeed in convincing himself that he is acting according to his conscience under the inexorable pressure of circumstance. The Inquisitor's magnificent address to the court on the evils of heresy is supremely compelling
and has been seen by one critic as 'an impromptu speech, spoken
by a man of wide experience and great wisdom'.[65] It gives the
impression of being all that and more. One could easily be taken in
by his arguments as many have been because of the combination in

his manner of pleasant urbanity and imposing official authority.

Yet a closer examination of his speech reveals it to be a masterful piece of oratory artfully designed to exert tremendous psychological pressure. Mark Antony's speech to the Roman mob in Shakespeare's *Julius Caesar* is not more subtly manipulating. It anticipates every effect Joan is likely to have on the court and one by one strips her of every safeguard. They are not to judge Joan by the natural gentleness of her appearance and disposition, the austerity of her life, the sincerity of her faith, the charity of her actions. Yet he gives them nothing by which they *are* to judge her. He continually drives home his greater experience in dealing with these matters in such phrases as 'if you had seen what I have seen', and 'I have seen this again and again.' If they had his knowledge the most tender-hearted among them 'would clamor against the mercy of the Church in dealing with it'. This would make them hesitant about coming to any conclusion contrary to his, and inclined to defer to his judgement as a specialist in the field. He puts them on guard against their natural compassion while yet convincing them that they are all 'merciful men'. He himself is 'compassionate by nature' as well as by profession and would go to the stake himself sooner than do the work he did if he did not know 'its righteousness, its necessity, its essential mercy'. This brings to mind Mark Anthony's speech where through the power of suggestion the mob is convinced that they are 'all honourable men' about to do the only honourable thing. In like vein the Inquisitor assures the members of court that they are 'all merciful men'. He warns them on forfeit of divine mercy against hardening their hearts, but then goes on to say with cold deliberation:

> But if you hate cruelty – and if any man here does not hate it I command him on his soul's salvation to quit this holy court – I say, if you hate cruelty, remember that nothing is so cruel in its consequences as the toleration of heresy.
>
> (Sc. 6, p. 166)

Inexorably the point is driven home. Their emotions have been so artfully worked upon that they are unconscious of the paradox in what is being said – be cruel if you hate cruelty. By the end of this long speech they are effectively indoctrinated. Except for Brother Martin, the rest are quite pliant, reacting precisely as intended, convinced that they are doing the righteous thing, the necessary thing, the merciful thing. Louis Crompton interestingly points out that the arguments Shaw gives to the Inquisitor are 'exactly those used by the nineteenth-century Quaker historian H. C. Lea in his monumental *History of the Inquisition* to justify the extermination of the Albigensians, whose ultra-asceticism and contempt for marriage could only, in Lea's view, 'have probably resulted in lawless concubinage and the destruction of the institution of the family'. The Church's official defence of the Inquisition to be found in an article in the *Catholic Encyclopedia* quotes Lea extensively and Shaw apparently studied the essay most carefully in preparing his play.[66]

Wrongs are often justified as a means to an end which is always represented as the right end. Shaw is a master of polemical dialogue and he gives weight to opposing points of view because he is well aware that truth is many-stranded. He presents each individual within his own frame of reference so that the rationale by which he works is seen. The play thus provides different perspectives of an event and the audience is challenged to come to terms with these. But though the judges appear perfectly justified in their own eyes, Shaw also shows us cracks in the surface which reveal hidden motives and vested interests which make the impartiality of the judges and the trial suspect.

Despite controversial discussion the play's historical treatment has aroused, *Saint Joan* has been highly acclaimed by modern historians. Charles Lightbody considers it a 'great play' and the 'only notable historical work which modern Leftist thought' has contributed to the subject of Joan of Arc.[67] Henri Gullemin asserts that it 'contains the best that the superabundant literature of Joan has to offer us; it is a fine play, grave, sensible, intelligent and profound'.[68] G. G. Coulton describes it as a 'fine dramatic success', affirming Shaw's portrait of Joan as 'practically true to the records'. But he dismisses Shaw's preface as 'childish'. 'The itching for cheap paradox has overmastered him and he flounders blindfold among the documents.'[69] Non-historians too have faulted the play as history on the basis of the preface. Robertson finds the final impression left by the preface 'simply one of chronic intellectual incoherence'. Shaw puts 'with equal emphasis incompatible views on every main aspect of the case he raises'.[70] But this is probably precisely Shaw's intention. One must be careful not to confuse the debater of the preface with the dramatist of the play.

A tension can always be detected between Shaw's prefaces and his plays for he revelled too much in argumentative comedy to explain away his plays. They exist in their own right, apart from their prefaces which were often written some time after the plays were completed. *Saint Joan* for instance was first produced in 1923 and the preface was not written till May 1924.[71] It is worth noting too that Shaw often warned actors and actresses against reading his prefaces.[72] He criticized Wendy Hiller's interpretation of Joan, attributing it partly to her having done too much homework including the reading of his preface.[73] In the preface Shaw deliberately overstates his case to shock the reader out of his complacency and get him grappling with the issues for himself. This would not help an actor since it might obscure his understanding of his part. It would be folly to fault a play as history on the basis of its preface. The preface to *Saint Joan* is a lively demonstration of Shaw's brilliant gift for wit and ratiocination. As he has said, 'the way to get to the merits of a case is not to listen to the fool who imagines himself impartial; but to get it argued with reckless bias for and against. To understand a saint you must hear the devil's advocate . . . ' .[74]

An examination of Shaw's historical source for *Saint Joan*, T. D. Murray's *Jeanne D'Arc*, reveals how remarkably close Shaw has kept to it. The play brings out with extraordinary effect the salient qualities of Joan's unique character as revealed in the records. She is a person of great force of will. Her amazing faith and vision are only too evident, but she is immensely practical as well and in no way introspective or morbidly religious. In 1890, after seeing Sarah Bernhardt as Joan of Arc, Shaw complained, 'she intones her lines and poses as a saint'.[75] The records reveal that though she was venerated as a saint by many, Joan never posed as one. One witness during the rehabilitation trial of 1456 recalls how when women came to visit Joan, bringing pater nosters and other objects for her to touch, Joan laughed and said, 'Touch them yourselves. Your touch will do them as much good as mine'.[76]

Shaw brings out the magnificence of her bearing during the trial – the courage, the good humour, the trenchant commonsense and ready wit, the sanity that never left her. The mental superiority that Shaw credits her with is another pronounced feature that emerges from the records. She refused to be intimidated by the official gravity and sheer weight of ecclesiastical authority confronting her. Despite the strain of long exhausting interrogations during which she was assailed with questions from every side,

Joan showed amazing clarity of mind and a memory power which astonished those present. On one occasion when questioned with regard a point she had answered before, Joan said, 'I asked about this eight days ago, and thus replied.' One of the notaries insisted that she had not, but when the proceedings of that day were read out Joan was proved right. At this she turned round good-naturedly and warned him that 'if he made mistakes again, she would pull his ears!'[77]

In the play, Joan displays the same acuity of mind and quality of good humour. She calls Courcelles a 'rare noodle' when he insists she should be tortured since it was customary procedure (Sc. VI, p. 172). In the records, as in the play, the judges can be found making a grave issue of Joan's wearing of male attire and being met with her sane insistence that it was a trifling matter. She often saw them making needless difficulties out of nothing and, with her downright commonsense, cut straight through to the heart of the matter. Despite her extreme youth and inexperience, her handling of profound theological issues unsettled her judges. Her answers to subtle, loaded questions seemed inspired. They confounded her judges and once the sitting broke up in consternation. She was asked, 'Do you know if you are in the grace of God?' and she replied, 'If I am not, may God place me there; if I am, may God so keep me.'[78] Shaw includes this almost word for word in his dramatization of the trial:

> Cauchon: Dare you pretend, after what you have
> said, that you are in a state of
> grace?
> Joan: If I am not, may God bring me to it:
>   if I am, may God keep me in it!

> (Sc. 6, p. 175)

Joan's utterances are full of her personality and Shaw captures her spirit by weaving into the play many of her actual statements with hardly any alteration. The following are just two instances:

> There is a saying among children, that 'Sometimes one is hanged
> for speaking the truth.'

> (*Jeanne D'Arc*, p. 18)

It is an old saying that he who tells too much truth is sure to be
hanged.

(*Saint Joan*, Sc. 6, p. 171)

In what likeness did Saint Michael appear to you? . . . Was he
naked?
Do you think God has not wherewithal to clothe him?

(*Jeanne D'Arc*, p. 42)

How do you know that the spirit who appears to you is an
archangel? Does he not appear to you as a naked man?
Do you think God cannot afford clothes for him?

(*Saint Joan*, Sc. 6, p. 176)

Shaw reinforces Joan's assertive nature by contrasting her
against such negative spirits as Charles and Baudricourt. The
outwardly belligerent, superficially energetic, self-opiniated Captain Baudricourt is seen to collapse before Joan's inner strength of
will. He is a caricature of the petty official with an inflated sense of
his own importance. Joan is not one bit intimidated by his pose of
the commanding officer. She hails him unceremoniously – 'Be you
Captain?' – and immediately brings him down to size. As she
cheerfully forewarns him, he finds it 'all coming out quite different' from what he intends. Charles, though no fool, cuts an equally
ludicrous figure at points. In marked contrast to Joan, he is clearly
one who is not up to his calling. He 'never asked to be king' and
would rather be 'left alone'. But Joan will not have it. 'It's no use,
Charlie,' she says, 'Thou must face what God puts on thee. If thou
fail to make thyself a king, thoult be a beggar: what else art fit for?'
To emphasize the situation, Shaw farcically has Joan almost physically supporting the Dauphin as with a grotesque effort he musters
the courage to snap his fingers defiantly in his Chamberlain's face
(Sc. 2. pp. 112–16).

Joan epitomizes the active principle in life in her determination
to 'dare, dare, and dare again, in God's name' (Sc. 2. p. 115). She
unites faith with action. Her philosophy is not to sit back in
expectation but to attempt in faith. Dunois before Orleans cautions
Joan, 'The rafts are ready; and the men are embarked. But they
must wait for God.' She flashes back, 'What do you mean? God is
waiting for them.' His warning that not a man will follow her is
met with the reply: 'I will not look back to see whether anyone is
following me' (Sc. 3, pp. 120–2). The records are full of examples of

this kind of verve. 'Act and God will act!' she declared.[79] When told by a member of the committee of theologians which the King's council appointed to examine her, that if God willed to deliver the people of France from the calamity they were in then it was not necessary to have soldiers, she exclaimed, 'In God's Name! the soldiers will fight, and God will give the victory.'[80] Asked for a sign before they sent an army with her to Orleans, Joan replied, 'In God's Name! I am not come to Poitiers to shew signs: but send me to Orleans, where I shall shew you the signs by which I am sent.'[81] Shaw has beautifully captured the irresistible force of energy and inspiration that Joan embodied in his play.

Joan's military genius, especially her skill in the use of artillery, is testified to by numerous witnesses in the rehabilitation trial. Shaw emphasizes this extraordinary ability of Joan's. She is shown impatient with Dunois and the rest of the French court at their slowness to act: 'You don't know how to begin a battle; you don't know how to use your cannons. And I do.' This draws the dry comment: 'Not content with being Pope Joan, you must be Caesar and Alexander as well' (Sc. 5, pp. 148–50). Here Shaw has clearly been influenced by Murray's introduction where he talks of the mystery of 'an untutored and unlettered girl of eighteen years old', displaying a skill and judgement worthy of Napoleon himself and 'in two short months accomplishing more than Caesar and Alexander accomplished in so much time, and at an age when even Alexander had as yet achieved nothing'.[82]

Murray also provides the germ for a central conflict in the play – the conflict between imperialism and catholicism on the one hand, and nationalism and protestantism on the other:

> Jeanne's special merit was that she saw the possibility of a great French nation, self-centered, self-sufficient, and she so stamped this message on the French heart that its characters have never faded. Ecclesiastics, on the other hand, with their conception of a Universal Empire and a Universal Church, thought little of National aspirations or claims.[83]

Shaw builds on this, presenting Joan as a forerunner not only of nationalism but of protestantism as well. He was not the first to project her in this light because, as Lightbody notes, German writers had been foremost in expressing this view, but Shaw's play 'rendered familiar to the modern world the concept of Joan as a nationalist heretic, a champion of the right of private judgement'.[84]

Critics have taken Shaw to task for portraying Joan, in all respects a good Catholic, as a martyr to the Protestant cause of the primacy of the private conscience. 'It is, of course, in the portrayal of Protestantism as ultimately the decisive factor in Joan's fate,' writes M. A. Cohen, 'and in particular, in the motives ascribed to Cauchon and other members of the Burgundian Church, that Shaw took his biggest liberties with history.'[85] But Shaw has strong historical backing for presenting Joan's refusal to defer to the judgement of the Church as the key issue upon which the case against her is built. The judges in their examination of Joan can be found returning to this question again and again:

Will you refer yourself to the judgement of the Church on earth for all you have said and done, be it good or bad? Especially will you refer to the Church the cases, crimes and offences which are imputed to you and everything which touches on this Trial?
On all that I am asked I will refer to the Church Militant, provided they do not command anything impossible. And I hold as a thing impossible to declare that my actions and my words and all that I have answered on the subject of my visions and revelations I have not done and said by the order of God; this I will not declare for anything in the world. And that which God hath made me do, hath commanded or shall command, I will not fail to do for any man alive. It would be impossible for me to revoke it. And in case the Church should wish me to do anything contrary to the command which has been given me of God, I will not consent to it, whatever it may be.
If the Church Militant tells you that your revelations are illusions, or diabolical things, will you defer to the Church?
I will defer to God, Whose Commandment I always do. I know well that that which is contained in my Case has come to me by the Commandment of God; what I affirm in the Case is that I have acted by the order of God: it is impossible for me to say otherwise. In case the Church should prescribe the contrary, I should not refer to any one in the world, but to God alone Whose Commandment I always follow.[86]

Shaw keeps very close to the original dialogue in his dramatization of this issue, interpolating comments from the assessors which highlight the significance of what Joan is claiming and

reveal her to be totally unconscious of the enormity of her pretensions (Sc. 6, pp. 173–4). Joan is viewed by her judges as a threat to
the unity and stability of the Church. She is seen to prefigure the
birth of Protestantism and the judges warn of the consequences
that will follow from it. Shaw endows them with a foreknowledge
of the future, extending the historical scope of his play. As Katharine Worth points out, the case for the opposition presented by
Cauchon:

> is bound to be credited with real force by a modern audience
> who are in a position to check the accuracy of the prophetic
> observation Shaw has allowed him. Had this been otherwise,
> not only would the truthfulness of the action have been cast in
> doubt, but the extraordinary nature of Joan's insight would have
> been obscured.[87]

Shaw registers a sense of the multiple layers of meaning that
accrue to an occurrence in history in the light of subsequent
events, and by so doing includes a larger dimension of time which
the audience is a part of. The wider perspective he brings to bear
serves to increase rather than reduce the play's historical value.

Shaw in *Saint Joan* demonstrates that the individual in his pursuit of truth will always be alone in society, the extraordinary
individual, most often destroyed because of the threat he poses to
the establishment. The individual committed to truth by nature is
open to revelation, alive to the infinite possibilities of life. He
therefore figures in stark contrast to society with its inherent
tendency to overstructure and codify, so that bent on preservation
rather than growth it tends to turn in on itself, leading to stagna-
tion and decay, rather than movement and life. In *Saint Joan* we
experience the private will against the public as Joan strives to live
true to the voices within while the political forces at work in society
marshall against her. No possibility of compromise is held out and
Joan dies unreconciled – 'His ways are not your ways' (Sc. 6, p.
184).[88]

As a character Joan comes through as extremely real and compelling. Her irrepressible will and bouyancy of spirit explode all
vanity of social form and pretension. Against the hypocrisy and
guile of aristocrats at the court of Charles or judges at her trial, she

appears a 'poor innocent child of God' (Sc. 5, p. 142). She experiences the essential isolation of the individual in her pursuit of truth because for them truth is a matter of social and political expediency. Their narrow self-interest and self-seeking are set against her absolute commitment and self-sacrifice.

Eric Bentley sees the conflict between vitality and system as a central feature of Shaw's plays. Shaw, he says, 'often places a model "vital" character in the midst of a group of reprehensible mechanized ones'.[89] Joan's predicament can be seen in these terms. What she stands for – inspiration – and what society represents – institution – are fundamentally opposed in character. Joan is a creature of divine impulse – free and dynamic. Shaw depicts almost all the other characters as servants of the system - artificial, dehumanized, imprisoned in conformity. Right through the play the social concern with form and ritual is contrasted with Joan's natural vigour and spontaneity. Shaw deromanticizes her, departing radically from the traditional image of a lofty, ethereal figure, shrouded in a haze of sanctity. Surrounded by the formal, hierarchical figures of the court, she stands out as a vital country girl, obviously sprung from the soil but infused with a sense of vision.

Shaw juxtaposes this creature of ideas and impulses against the professional man of ideology and tradition. The individual who is divinely inspired is generally beyond human comprehension because he is often seen to fly in the face of social norms and expectations. In society even the extraordinary is expected to fit into a conventional pattern. Thus we find the Archbishop of Rouen declaring, 'The creature is not a saint. She is not even a respectable woman. She does not wear women's clothes. She is dressed like a soldier, and rides around the country with soldiers.' To some she is mad, a 'cracked country lass' (Sc. 2, p. 102). The English, smarting from the humiliation of defeat in battle, naturally enough see her as an 'accursed witch'. To the Church she is a heretic. To the French army she leads she is 'an angel dressed as a soldier' (Sc. 2, p. 99). And to others she is 'a bit of a miracle' in herself. (Sc. 2, p. 90). But no one denies that 'there is something about the girl,' a 'dangerous power' that makes her a phenomenon to be reckoned with (Sc. 5, p. 155). She is spirit-driven, spirit-inspired, and against this force nothing can prevail. She heeds not the vast opposition raised against her, but only the irresistible voice of God within.

Shaw draws freely on the available symbol and legend in Joan's story: her voices, the predicted death of the blasphemer, the identifying of the Dauphin, the changing of the wind at Orleans, the cross of sticks held up to her at the stake and the heart left unconsumed by the flames. Some of these are provided with rational explanations, others are not. But Joan is consistently depicted as irradiated with the force of inspiration. Shaw illustrates that it does not take away from her stature if she is seen as genius or saint. Her inspiration, however interpreted, is no less a reflection of the sublime. Joan herself has a fuller, freer sense of the rational and she is quite happy to accept a natural explanation for the supernatural. When Baudricourt suggests that her voices come from her imagination she finds no reason for contention – 'Of course. That is how the messages of God come to us' (Sc. 1, p. 92). Shaw makes much of Joan's quality of common sense and attributes this and many of her gifts to the fact that she is a woman. Joan is the only significant woman character in the play and in contrast to the male figures around her, she appears refreshingly free from cant, pose and rigidity of outlook. She has a woman's intuitive power which enables her to assess a situation very quickly, dispensing with needless complexities and cutting through to the crux of a matter. She is shown continually running up against men who are extremely legalistic and bound by convention. The attitude of narrowly sticking by the book dominates their speech and actions. Some form of legality is obviously needed in a complex society, but it can get out of hand for it is the cold inhuman following of rules that can lead to terrible lunacy like Nazism. It is lunacy of this sort that led to the judicial murder of Joan. The letter of the law was strictly adhered to but a gross injustice was perpetrated. Pierre Champion, considered by many historians the leading twentieth-century Joan of Arc scholar, describes the trial as 'a masterpiece of partiality under the most regular of procedures'.[90] In the play Joan's judges are shown similarly concerned to make the trial as unimpeachable as possible by a punctillious observance of procedure and Shaw has the Inquisitor in the Epilogue rising to speak for all judges 'in the blindness and bondage of the law' (Epilogue, p. 206).

Throughout the trial scene Shaw maintains a fine balance between the serious and the comic. The humour does not take away from the sober reality, but serves as an effective check on the emotions. Shaw controls the response of the audience, preventing them from being overwhelmed by the awareness of impending catastrophe. The humour keeps them sufficiently detached, able to function critically. The serio-comic tone is handled with much power and sensitivity for the tragic sense is never vulgarized and the scene builds to an extremely moving climax.

From the start Joan does not have a chance. Her judges are out to incriminate her as a heretic despite the fact that 'many saints have said as much as Joan' (Sc. 6, p. 164). Shaw deliberately pushes matters to the point of absurdity to show how almost anything can be seen as heresy if one is determined to interpret it as such. They accuse her of trying to escape and when she logically points out that 'If you leave the door of the cage open the bird will fly out,' D' Estivet pounces on her reply – 'That is a confession of heresy. I call the attention of the court to it.' Joan is suitably deflating in her plain-seeing of this as 'a great nonsense'. She herself is the epitome of clarity and good sense, quite justified when she protests, 'But you will not talk sense to me. I am reasonable if you will be reasonable' (Sc. 6, p. 170). Her answer to their threat of torture is sane and to the point. There are no heroic pretensions. She cannot bear to be hurt and, if hurt, will say anything to stop the pain, but it will be a pointless exercise since she 'will take it all back afterwards' (Sc. 6, p. 171). Asked for one good reason why an angel of God should command her to dress as a soldier, she cannot see what could be 'plainer commonsense'. She is a prisoner guarded by soldiers. If she 'were to dress as a woman they would think of [her] as a woman; and then what would become of [her]?' Their persistent sense of horror provokes the caustic demand, 'Do you want me to live with them in petticoats?' (Sc. 6, p. 177).

Joan is disarming in her openness and candour and vitality of response to life. She brings her own reason and experience to bear. This is what is finally threatened. Unable to prove her voices false, the court insists they are diabolical and demands that she accept the inspired judgement of the Church. For Joan this is to ask the impossible as it would mean repudiating her awareness of inner truth, the credibility of her own mind and spirit which in the final analysis is all the individual has to measure reality with. As she protests in genuine distress, 'What other judgement can I judge but by my own?' (Sc. 6, p. 175). Joan possesses an inner freedom of being which is ultimately the only real freedom an individual has. It allows her the courage to exercise her own rational judgement in coming to terms with life. It is significant that it is only when she cannot reconcile her faith and her reason that she plunges into despair and self-doubt:

> Oh, it is true: it is true: my voices have deceived me. I have been mocked by devils: my faith is broken. I have dared and dared; but only a fool will walk into a fire: God who gave me my common-sense, cannot will me to do that.
>
> (Sc. 6, p. 179)

She is driven to recant. But when she sees that they intend to imprison her for life, keeping her away from all beauty and light, everything that brings her back to the love of God, and by their 'wickedness and foolishness' tempting her to hate Him, she recognizes that their counsel 'is of the devil' and hers 'is of God'. It is now she who reverses the situation, pronouncing judgement on them as not fit for her to 'live among' (Sc. 6, pp. 183–4). Sainthood is a phenomenon not easy for men to accept since it often results in a remorseless exposure of human frailty. Light judges as well as illuminates, and the nature of its revelation can be deeply discomfiting.

In contrast to Joan's passionate outcry, the formal recitation of the grim sentence is cold and stark indeed. Shaw's version of the recantation, the absolution and the final sentence of damnation and excommunication derives closely from the official account. The speeches are merely compressed and the lines broken up for dramatic weight and thrust. For example, part of the final sentence in the original records reads:

> . . . for these causes, declaring thee fallen again into thine errors, and under the sentence of excommunication which thou hast formerly incurred, WE DECLARE THAT THOU ART A RELAPSED HERETIC, by our present sentence which, seated in tribunal, we utter and pronounce in this writing; we denounce thee as a rotten member and that thou mayst not vitiate others, as cast out from the unity of the Church, separate from her Body, abandoned to the secular power, as indeed by these presents, we do cast thee off, separate and abandon thee . . . [91]

Shaw uses almost the same terrible words of abandonment, but invests the sentence with dramatic edge and resonance by giving it a ritualistic character which drives home the sense of awful finality. Cauchon and the Inquisitor rise and solemnly intone the sentence antiphonally:

Cauchon: We decree that thou art a relapsed heretic.
The Inquisitor: Cast out from the unity of the Church.
Cauchon: Sundered from her body.
The Inquisitor: Infected with the leprosy of heresy.
Cauchon: A member of Satan.
The Inquisitor: We declare that thou must be excommunicate.
Cauchon: And now we do cast thee out, segregate thee,
                 and abandon thee to the secular power.

(Sc.6, pp. 184-5)

It is a chilling moment and the scene ends with Joan being rushed out to the flames. The Epilogue which follows this sensational climax is crucial to the play's meaning and purpose. It deliberately frustrates any wish on the audience's part to be left on an exalted tragic note. As has been said, dramatists, influenced by the general iconography of Joan, had tended to depict her as a sublime heroic figure. Audiences of early productions of *Saint Joan*, with this theatrical tradition behind them, expected the play to end with a glowing vision of heroism. Shaw's originality and daring can be seen in his shattering these expectations in order to make people sit up.

Ever since the play's first reception, the Epilogue has aroused spirited controversy and it continues to be regarded by a large body of critics as a crude excrescence. When the play was first produced, the Epilogue was greeted with heated objections even by avid Shavian enthusiasts who felt it was a shocking anti-climax. It destroyed the historical illusion and tragic mood, detracting from the play's impressiveness. Audiences were disconcerted by Shaw's audacious blend of the farcical and the sublime. James Agate in *The Sunday Times* (30 March 1924) refers to 'a faintly jovial, quasi-satirical and wholly unnecessary epilogue conceived in a vein of lesser exaltation'.[92] J. Kooistra's comment in 1925 is representative of early critical opinion:

If her tale is one with a glorious ending, the epilogue, with its mixture of satire, buffoonery and grandeur fails to convey that message . . . its incongruous elements disturb the noble impression left by the preceding action. It is a signal instance of miscalculated effects, perverse destruction by the artist of his own creation, and lamentable want of good taste.[93]

Modern critics can be found echoing the same sentiments. When the play was revived in London in 1960, there were similar cries for the omission of the Epilogue by noted literary figures.[94] John Fielden agrees with critics who have argued that 'the epilogue, loquacious and tinged with humor as it is, destroys the mood achieved by Scene 6'.[95] Eldon C. Hill asserts that 'the controversial epilogue which brings Joan back to earth for her 1920 canonization, detracts from the tragic effect'.[96]

It is however precisely this tragic mood or effect which Shaw wishes to avoid. The Epilogue, he insists, is indispensable. 'Without it the play would only be a sensational tale of a girl who was burnt, leaving the spectators plunged in horror, despairing of humanity.'[97] The audience must not leave the theatre on a fatalistic note, overcome by the tragic nature of Joan's end. It is not the individual awareness and inner change that tragedy effects that Shaw is concerned to bring about, but social consciousness and social change. He does not want the audience to condemn the political and religious institutions that destroyed Joan while unquestioningly accepting their modern counterparts. The epilogue drives home the point of the play. It unsettles any comfortable notion that the audience might be tempted to entertain about a savage past and a civilized present. The audience is forced to look at themselves and made to realize that as unthinking members of a system, they too may be contributing to such disasters as have ravaged human history.

In the Epilogue Shaw shows us that a spirit like Joan is her own salvation and ultimately cannot be destroyed. She is 'up and alive everywhere'. Her sword 'shall conquer yet'. The greater human tragedy lies in the nature of the world reflected. Truth never seems to be accepted without violence. The world still has no place for its saints and can only extol them at a safe distance in time. The glorious litany of praise raised to Joan is merely a matter of form and pretence and Joan's response recalls Christ: 'Woe unto me when all men praise me! I bid you remember that I am a saint, and that saints can work miracles. And now tell me: shall I rise from the dead and come back to you a living woman?' (Epilogue, pp. 202–6). One by one each person shuns the idea of her return.

Shaw includes the audience in this rejection of Joan by bringing in a representative of their own time. The twentieth century government official who first comes in to announce Joan's canonization is a caricature of petty officialdom. He appears very much standing on his dignity. Yet for all his starchy formality and impressive official jargon, he is typically ineffectual when it comes to making a decision. A mindless puppet of the system, he bows himself out of an awkward situation by deferring judgement:

> The possibility of your resurrection was not contemplated in the recent proceedings for your canonization. I must return to Rome for fresh instructions.
>
> (Epilogue, p. 207)

True to the dehumanizing nature of all bureaucracies, he is unable to function beyond his immediate role of glorified messenger-boy. Inevitably each individual's personal interests become inextricably tied up with his position. Thus we find even the executioner stiffly rejecting the idea of Joan's return, voicing a familiar sentiment, 'As a master in my profession, I have to consider its interests, And after all, my first duty is to my wife and children' (Epilogue, p. 207). Shaw demonstrates that every member of society, however small his function, can contribute to the hostility and rigidity of the establishment by his attitude of subservience and self-preferment. He highlights the sterility and destruction caused when a man allows his personal will and identity to be submerged in the system so that he becomes a mere cog in the social machine.

The audience is shocked out of complacency through this startling and profoundly ironic reversal. Joan is still a mere pawn on a complex political chessboard. It is still a world of false fronts and sham graces and the public veneration of Joan is yet another role being played. Joan is the only one who never plays a part. She is always herself. Even in the Epilogue we see the 'role' of saint as something quite apart from her. She *is* a saint and does not have to act the part society now assigns to her. The twentieth-century government official formally announces that 'on every thirtieth day of May, being the anniversary of the death of the said most blessed daughter of God . . . it shall be lawful and laudable for the faithful to kneel and address their prayers through her to the Mercy Seat'. But Joan, a totally free and unconventional spirit, exclaims, 'Oh no. It is for the saint to kneel!' She chuckles at the idea of herself a saint: 'But fancy me a saint! What would St Catherine and St Margaret say if the farm girl was cocked up beside them!' (Epilogue, pp. 203–4). Shaw presents her no remote ethereal figure but as delightfully real and familiar as ever.

All the others too are little changed. Brother Martin is still seeing and yet not seeing. He condemns the second trial as a travesty of justice but fails to see that almost everything he accuses it of, though more subtly disguised, can be seen to apply to the first trial in some measure. And for all his 'fine words' celebrating the fact that 'the white robe of innocence has been cleansed from the smirch of the flame', he is still the man who has good intentions, but lacks the courage to act on his inner convictions. As Charles bluntly informs him, 'If you could bring her back to life, they would burn her again within six months, for all their present adoration of her. And you would hold up the cross, too, just the same' (Epilogue, p. 193). He is the kind of man who can only lament an injustice after the event.

Charles, shrewd and pragmatic as ever, takes the 'world as it is' and keeps his nose 'pretty close to the ground'. It is patently clear that political considerations brought about the rehabilitation trial. In response to Ladvenu's distress at the injustice of the proceedings, he replies, 'My friend: provided they can no longer say that I was crowned by a witch and a heretic, I shall not fuss about how the trick was done.' Cauchon is still stubbornly self-deluded, intent on asserting, 'I was just, I was merciful, I was faithful to my light' (Epilogue, pp. 192–7). He is still blind to the gross contradiction between his words and his actions. When Stogumber admits he did a very cruel thing once because he had not seen what cruelty was like, Cauchon is quick to rebuke him: 'Were not the sufferings of our Lord Christ enough for you?' 'Must then a Christ perish in every age to save those who have no imagination?' Like Cauchon, Stogumber has remained purblind. Opposing the resurrection of Joan, he pleads, 'Give us peace in our time, O Lord' (Epilogue, p. 207). But he at least has made one startling discovery:

> If you could only see what you think about you would think quite differently about it. It would give you a great shock . . . for I am not cruel by nature, you know.
>
> (Epilogue, p.201)

This perhaps is Shaw's message to the audience. People who are not malevolent by nature contribute to the world's disasters through want of imagination and understanding as to the social and political consequences of the way they think.

For Shaw, Joan is a visionary, a light-bringer, an agent of the life force. The play dramatizes the propensity of humanity to destroy the instruments of its advance. The play ends on a compelling note. Joan is left alone on the stage. A circle of radiant light isolates her from the surrounding darkness which encompasses the audience. Joan raises her voice in supplication and we are left with her haunting question:

> O God that madest this beautiful earth,
> When will it be ready to receive Thy saints?
> How long, O Lord, How long?

> (Epilogue, p. 208)

An examination of the play's treatment of history thus reveals its deep regard for historical truth and its extreme fidelity to the original documents though Shaw does not merely lift from his source passively. The material is transformed through the extraordinary force of the Shavian mind and imagination and it is all brought home in terms of contemporary relevance. In *Saint Joan* the audience is taken beyond the emotional situation and made to function on an intellectual plane because Shaw did not want them emotionally swamped, unable to bring their critical faculties to bear. But a fine balance had to be achieved if Joan's suffering was not to be minimized. Shaw achieves this with extraordinary effect. The play is an ingenious blend of the serious and the jocular. Shaw continually brings situations to the verge of farce, yet the humour never jarrs or turns grotesque. Though we enter into the humour, we are never unconscious of the tragic nature of what is taking place. The laughter contains the horror, enabling us to remain detached enough to engage with issues on a mental plane, but there are also moments when the emotion is allowed to build to supremely moving heights.

As Chesterton has said, Shaw was a humorist who hated to see man look absurd. His apprehension of the wearisome pattern of human history did not allow him a detachment from it. He had to try to change things in order to live. His wit and humour are a reflection of his unease and underlying them is a passionate moral concern. 'My way of joking,' says Keegan in *John Bull's Other Island*, 'is to tell the truth. It's the funniest joke in the world' (Act 2, p. 418). 'Every dream is a prophecy: every jest is an earnest in the womb of Time' (Act 4, p. 452). Shaw has much of Keegan in him – something of the dreamer, the mystic, and the earnest jester – and in treating history in *Saint Joan* these qualities take on a prophetic force and intensity.

3

Three Plays of the 1930s: Reginald Berkeley, *The Lady with a Lamp*; Clifford Bax, *The Rose without a Thorn*; Gordon Daviot, *Richard of Bordeaux*

The plays considered in this chapter, Reginald Berkeley's *The Lady with a Lamp*, Clifford Bax's *The Rose without a Thorn* and Gordon Daviot's *Richard of Bordeaux* demonstrate the meeting and crossing of two traditions, the Romantic and the Shavian. Both the old and new ways of apprehending history can be seen coming together in these popular plays by popular playwrights of the 1930s. They exemplify the kind of narrowly realistic theatre in vogue at the time with its concentration on the obvious exterior world. These particular plays have been selected for attention because, though none attain that power and penetration which is the hallmark of the best dramatic writing, they merit criticism on a more serious vein than most plays of the period. They go beyond the domestic concerns that preoccupied so many stages of their day and achieved considerable success when first produced, reflecting the tremendous pressure exerted by public taste. Whereas, a great playwright like Shaw is creative in his approach to drama and a powerful shaping force in himself, a minor playwright merely registers the various influences determining the nature of drama in his age.

In these plays two strains appear dominant – the lingering penchant for romance and the immediate impact of Shaw. The trend in the eighteenth and nineteenth centuries was towards a more romantic treatment of history. Puff in Sheridan's play, *The Critic* (1779), declares that 'it is a received point among poets, that where history gives you a good heroic out-line for a play, you may fill it up with a little love at your own discretion; in doing which, nine times out of ten, you only make up a deficiency in the private history of the times' (Act 2, Sc. 1, ll. 15–19). Nineteenth-century writers generally entertain a similar outlook. Romance plays an essential part in the historical novels of Walter Scott who has had an immense influence on Western historical literature. Bulwer Lytton claims that Scott 'employed History to aid Romance'. He himself was engaged in the 'humbler task' of employing 'Romance in the aid of History.'[1] Such plays of his as *The Lady of Lyons* (1838) and *Richelieu* (1839) are built around romantic melodramatic situations. Similarly other dramas treating history in the period such as Dion Boucicault's *Louis XI* (1855) include a 'love interest' which is the focus of dramatic sympathy.

This romantic tradition can be seen asserting itself in *The Lady with a Lamp, The Rose without a Thorn* and *Richard of Bordeaux*. Even while trying hard to be modern, these plays have a soft romantic angle in common. Their central situations are based on facts, but these are romantically interpreted and their characters are conceived in a rather sentimental light. Unable to shake off the old Romantic tradition, these playwrights also could not resist the inescapable impact of Shaw in plays like *Saint Joan* and *Caesar and Cleopatra* where he led the way for a very different kind of historical theatre. His plays are weightily discursive while theirs are much more lightweight, but they all attempt to approach history after the Shavian manner. All three evince an awareness that mythical saints or monsters die hard and seek to put their characters in a rational credible framework. It is probably due to Shaw that both Berkeley and Daviot register a reluctance to take over uncritically a received version of history. Then again they all break away from the Romantic tradition and link up with the Shavian in the movement away from verse to prose – the use of modern colloquial idiom – and in the attempt to interpret the past in terms of contemporary issues and concerns. Thus, interestingly, two traditions can be seen meeting in these plays as both the Romantic and Shavian impulse find expression.

The expectations of audiences and critics of the day for a realistic kind of theatre also exerted considerable pressure which playwrights found hard to deny in spite of the works of Shaw and Brecht. Brecht was writing plays from 1918 yet the English theatre was oblivious of the impact he was making. Shaw and Brecht continually shatter the illusion of reality, incorporating a sense of a larger dimension of time and an awareness of different possible views of an event. Most playwrights of this period were devoted to scrupulously maintaining the illusion of reality. The play was set up to be regarded as a slice of life and the audience was invited to lose all sense of artifice and disbelief for the moment. Plausibility of thought and action, credibility of the bare explicit kind was sought, for to 'ring true' was the general measure of a play's worth. Thus, as has been pointed out, 'even history plays started pretending hard to be 'real' in the period', since writers were committed to the pretence that the play has no audience; is not a play at all but history as it happened, the real thing'.[2] The audience is placed in the role of overhearer and not participant in the collective experience that is the theatre. Essentially it is a closed world that is presented as the play's thought and action do not spill over to assert their reality in direct and present relation to the audience.

The chief limitation of this narrowly realistic mode is that the realism tends to be skin-deep. When a playwright is committed to creating and sustaining an impression of outward realism it is often at the expense of a deeper reality. Chekhov observes that naturalism of this sort 'tends to destroy the inner profound emotions in its effort to mirror their outward manifestations'. In the plays of Berkeley, Bax and Daviot considered in this chapter an outward social reality is presented, but the inward drama of being is little more than hinted at. We are given some apprehension of the personal conflicts of Richard II, Katheryn Howard, Henry VIII and Florence Nightingale, but we do not plumb the depths of their individual dilemmas. A drawing room view of the proceedings is presented for these plays treat experience from an external rather than an internal frame of reference. It is the social process that takes focus and we are kept on the outside looking on. This tends to be artificial and distancing at times.

These plays also share a certain outlook which reflects their time. All three can be found exalting the feminine viewpoint. Gordon Daviot (a pseudonym for Elizabeth Mackintosh, whom I shall be referring to as Gordon Daviot since her play is written under this name) presents a distinctly feminine angle on the peace issue dealt with in *Richard of Bordeaux*. Anne of Bohemia, Richard II's wife, is given great prominence in the play. She is Richard's mainstay and very much an equal partner in their relationship. Berkeley and Bax in their plays reveal a marked sympathy for the feminine position. Florence Nightingale breaks out of the strait-jacket imposed on women by the society of her time to realize a great personal destiny. Katheryn Howard symbolizes the new drive in women for freedom to satisfy their capacity for joy and self-expression.

This emphasis in the plays points to one of the dominant concerns of the 1930s. There was a ferment of interest in Women's Rights springing from the suffragette period. The long bitter fight for suffrage had resulted in Great Britain giving women the vote at the end of the First World War. The following year America also capitulated, granting women suffrage in 1918. During the ensuing years the struggle for feminine emancipation in all areas of human endeavour gained ever-widening attention and support. Many previously accepted ideas and values were vigorously questioned. The impact of this new awareness is reflected in these plays which were all first published by Victor Gollancz who was known for his progressive publications.

Then again, the abhorrence of war or social violence legalized in any form is noticeable in these plays, mirroring the troubled mood of the interwar period in which they were written. The intense suffering of the wounded at the military hospital in Scutari is registered in *The Lady with a Lamp*. The senseless loss of young life is felt in *The Rose without a Thorn* as Katheryn Howard falls victim to the executioner's axe. *Richard of Bordeaux* celebrates the young king's spirited efforts for peace, and the play's pacifist angle won it tremendous popularity in its time.

The threat of another even more devastating war had stimulated an upsurge of interest in pacifism. Peace societies burgeoned and flourished everywhere. The Fellowship of Reconciliation was formed in response to the war and other older established societies, like the Women's International League for Peace and Freedom, gained widespread support. The League of Nations Union was an influential body in post-war British politics especially in the conduct of foreign affairs. A World Anti-War Congress was held at Amsterdam in August 1932. It was attended by representatives from thirty thousand organizations from twenty-seven countries. The peace movement gathered such overwhelming support that it seemed for a time in the mid-1930s there was a strong impulse towards absolute pacifism.[3] This intense feeling of disquiet and concern for the preservation of society is registered in these plays with their robust stand against social violence and insistence on a high regard for life, beauty and culture.

Since they share a common background, it is not surprising to find a similarity in theme and treatment. All three plays deal with the transforming power of a dream or vision, highlighting both its positive and negative aspects. Florence Nightingale's ideal soars pure and incorruptible yet it is realized at considerable human cost. Henry VIII's dream of youth and Katheryn Howard's dream of love are vital and rejuvenating, but they spring from a capacity for naivety and self-delusion. Richard II and Anne share a vision of peace which invests their life with meaning and purpose, but since it goes against the grain of public taste and interest, its pursuit results in bitter personal suffering and disillusionment.

These plays concentrate essentially on providing stirring character portraits and present unconventional views of their protagonists. In *Richard of Bordeaux* it is not the weak self-indulgent monarch that is dramatized but the idealist, the visionary. Henry VIII in *The Rose without a Thorn* is not the hardened philanderer, but the romantic, the dreamer. And in *The Lady with a Lamp* the focus is upon the woman of steel rather than the angel of mercy. Actors were drawn to these plays because of the star parts they offered. A dominating stage presence or certain versatility was required for the main roles and actors felt they could benefit from them. Thus they drew such actors and actresses as Edith Evans, John Gielgud, Frank Vosper and Gwen Ffrangçon-Davies.

Yet these plays were obviously written to be read as well as acted. Like Shaw, Berkeley and Daviot provide mental pictures of their characters in lengthy stage directions. Unlike more modern playwrights who are extremely theatrical in their approach, these writers tend to convey their ideas mainly verbally. Climactic moments are expressed in emotive speeches rather than in bold theatrical terms. There is little reliance on effects peculiar to the theatre – dumb physical forms of expression, stage metaphors, masks, music, song, dance – as an integral part of the drama. Characters provide information and are over-explanatory of themselves. Ideas and feelings are made a little too conscious and explicit, introduced as topics of conversation instead of more imaginatively. The leaning towards statement rather than suggestion and evocation is strongly felt. Thus the style of these playwrights fails them dismally when they try to go inwards and register the subconscious life.

There is also the pull towards an over-refined treatment of character and event. Tragic elements are deliberately made more palatable. Death and disease are handled delicately as these playwrights shun presenting harsh events directly. We are given the merest glimpse of Florence Nightingale actually attending to the wounded in Scutari. Even this is treated romantically as a dying soldier turns out to be her lover, Harry Tremayne, and the dramatic focus shifts to their emotional plight. Katheryn Howard is shown going through a rehearsal of her execution rather than the event itself so the audience is shielded from a direct confrontation of death. Daviot also tried to make the fact of death less stark. The sickness and death of Queen Anne was a moment which stubbornly refused to come out right in performance. Initially the stage directions dictated that Anne should be carried from the stage, leaving Richard alone in despair. But it was found in rehearsal that the spectacle of grief was impossible to sustain with the object of it gone. So the scene had to be rewritten to portray the doctor discovering that Anne was dying of the plague and the curtain falls as the royal couple express shock and grief at the disclosure.[4]

Though these plays never attain any great dramatic force and concentration, they had enough human interest and imaginative appeal to bring them alive to audiences of their time. Despite their inability to register the inwardness of their characters with conviction, they present an engaging picture of men in society, coping with the cut and thrust of circumstance, and provide a sense of the practical realities of history. History obviously held a fascination for these playwrights. They each turned to history more than once as a source of inspiration for their plays, and also wrote biographies or historical novels. This suggests that they enjoyed exploring the region between history and fiction, that mysterious, nebulous area where history passes into fantasy and back again.

Of the three, Reginald Berkeley is the most socially conscious and active, thus his interest in historical occurrences close to his own time. He can be seen to follow in the tradition of Shaw, motivated as he is by a similar concern to give a platform to urgent contemporary issues. His efforts for the stage and screen were often the subject of controversy. His sociological play, *Machines*, produced by the Arts Theatre in 1930, was rejected by the British Broadcasting Company as too political and 'of a propaganda nature'. Essentially it deals with the threat of machines to modern life. But it also presents Berkeley's views regarding what he felt should be the whole trend of modern industrial thought, which was towards substituting a status of partnership for the status of employment.[5] Berkeley was after radical changes in the social and economic structure, and this concern finds expression in *The Lady with a Lamp* where discussion takes place over such issues as the value of work and the possibility of a new relationship between labour and capital.

In the play a rather distinguished group can be seen gathered on the terrace of Embley Park, the principle countryhouse of William Nightingale, debating the value of Carlyle's book, *Past and Present* which questions the ease and indolence of the life of the gentry class into which Florence Nightingale was born. Sidney Herbert, lately Secretary at War in Sir Robert Peel's administration, defends Carlyle's ideas:

Herbert: But that isn't what he means at all, Mrs Nightingale: He thinks everyone ought to do something useful. He thinks that Labour has a soul –

Mrs N.:   We've all got souls, Mr Herbert, at least I hope so.

Palmerston: Nobody grudges Labour a soul. The danger is, if you'll forgive the pleasantry, that it may develop a *heel* – and learn to use it.

Herbert: Of course. That's exactly Mr Carlyle's point. Unemployment has been so bad; and yet the country is so rich. He seems to think that they may combine. . . . In fact he urges them to combine.[6]

(Act 1, Sc. 2, pp. 202-3)

Through the conversation we derive a sense of the new ideas infiltrating society with a view to upsetting the established order.

Past and Present, published in 1843, is a social tract, severely critical of the conditions of its time. It was extremely influential, arousing both great praise and great anger. Within a year it received a review by Emerson and an extensive interpretation by Friedrich Engels. Florence Nightingale was deeply impressed by the book. In June 1843 she writes in a letter to Julia Smith:

Carlyle's new *Past and Present*, a beautiful book. There are bits about ''Work,'' which how I should like to read with you! ''Blessed is he who has found his work: let him ask no other blessedness. He has a work, a life-purpose: he has found it and will follow it . . .''.[7]

The book foreshadows developments to come in time, of which Florence Nightingale is to be a pioneer, especially in the marking out of new spheres of influence for women. Berkeley allies himself with these forces for change, seeking to bring about greater social awareness through his plays.

Like Shaw, Berkeley believed in the social function of art. His play, *The White Château* sets out 'to reinforce the determination to abolish war'. The subject of the play is 'not the war between A and B but War, the hideous Giant Despair of our times'.[8] This theme re-emerges in a biographical novel, *Dawn* which celebrates the heroism of Nurse Edith Cavell, executed for protecting her countrymen from the German invader. For her, however, nursing knew no frontiers. She was committed to helping the sick and helpless of either side for she served a higher goal than patriotism. Berkeley sees her actions as a 'revolt against the war machine'.[9] His film on the subject was first banned by the censor. Berkeley was obviously drawn to heroic women with a supreme commitment to a high cause. Thus we find him turning to the subject of Florence Nightingale, another woman with a burning vision, in *The Lady with a Lamp*.

This play was his most notable dramatic achievement. It was first published in 1929 by Victor Gollancz both separately and in a collection – *Famous Plays of Today*. The numerous reprintings it has received are a measure of its success. It was reprinted by Samuel French in 1929. In 1933 it was reissued by Gollancz in another collection, *Plays of a Half-Decade*, and subsequently published separately by Longmans, Green and Company in 1948 in 'The Heritage of Literature Series' and in 1949 in the series called 'Essential English Library'. The play was first produced at the Arts Theatre on 5 January 1929. It was received with enthusiasm and transferred to the Garrick Theatre on 24 January of the same year. Edith Evans co-directed the production with Leslie Banks and played the title role. It required special versatility from the actress who had to break herself down from a young eager girl to an extremely old lady because of the enormous span of years the play covers. Even to supporting actors and actresses the play offered attractive parts and Gwen Ffrangçon-Davies played Elizabeth Herbert, Leslie Banks played Harry Tremayne, Ellie Norwood, Lord Palmerston and Neil Porter, Sidney Herbert. The play was greeted in *The Daily Telegraph* as Berkeley's 'best play'. It was about a 'living woman' whom it was possible to admire wholeheartedly, 'a great woman, with the defects of her qualities and no mere bloodless myth'.[10] The *Theatre World* magazine acclaimed it as 'one of the most remarkable productions of the season'.[11]

The play stimulated considerable public discussion as revealed by correspondence in *The Times*. As a matter of interest, a reader sent in for reproduction a letter of 1854 from Sidney Herbert to Sir James Y Simpson defending Florence Nightingale from accusations of espionage directed against her at the time. Mr Shore Nightingale wrote in to make it known that neither the executors of the will of the late Miss Nightingale nor any member of her family were in any way responsible for the production of *The Lady with a Lamp*, nor had they been consulted with regard to it.[12] Berkeley was quick to retaliate, asserting that he was 'unaware of any obligation on a writer to consult the executors of the wills of historical personages before a noble life is reverently shown to the public'. The complaint that no member of her family was consulted was equally illegitimate, 'even if it were grounded in fact'. However this complaint was 'without foundation'.[13]

From this we gather that Berkeley did indeed take the trouble to consult a member of the Nightingale family regarding his play. He wished to place 'reverently' before the public his dramatization of a 'noble life'. However, in keeping with the trend of Shaw and the new breed of biographers that had arisen, he sought to present no saintly ethereal figure, but the very real and formidable human personality behind the myth. In popular Victorian iconography Florence Nightingale is enshrined as a model of feminine virtue, an angel of mercy. The play shatters this soft angelic vision of female gentleness, replacing it with the sterner, yet even more extraordinary, image of a woman of steel and the relentness driving will that lay behind her vast achievements.

It has been noted that when Lytton Strachey saw the production of *The Lady with a Lamp* in 1931, 'he recognized it as coming straight out of *Eminent Victorians*'.[14] There is strong internal evidence that Berkeley was influenced by Strachey though I have not been able to discover any external evidence of this. The play gives the distinct impression of coming under the Strachey view. After the Strachey manner, it cuts down the popular image of Florence Nightingale, yet nevertheless comes through with an image that is no less heroic. It develops as its essential theme Strachey's central point:

The Miss Nightingale of fact was not as facile fancy painted her. She worked in another fashion, and towards another end; she moved under the stress of an impetus which finds no place in the popular imagination. A Demon possessed her.

The inexorable force that drove her, the force that created, was also the force that destroyed.

Strachey emphasizes the destructive side of ambition especially when it affects personal relationships. According to him, to deny love as Florence Nightingale had, was to deny 'the most powerful and the profoundest of all the instincts of humanity'.[15] Berkeley dramatizes this notion in his play though rather sentimentally. Florence rejects the suit of the man she loves, Harry Tremayne, in answer to a higher call. Tremayne protests:

Florence, I tell you that your call is a delusion. My call is the voice of Nature. The call that is as old as Creation. The call that sounds in the forests and the prairies; among the mountains and on the plains. That is older than the human race and wider than the human race. . . . The forefather of humanity and its ultimate end. The beginning and the purpose of life. The call of Race.

(Act 1, Sc. 2, p. 221)

In turning her back on love and marriage, Lytton Strachey sees Florence Nightingale as denying her womanhood and suppressing her erotic life. As a biographer of Strachey points out, this aspect of his portrait of her is controversial because he 'hints at her perverted sexual compulsion which he presents as responsible for her actions'.[16] The erotic love she sacrifices finds another expression in her ruthless commitment to work and in the power she exerts, especially over men. Strachey claims that her desire for work could 'scarcely be distinguished from mania'. He sees her as working herself and others to death. Men became totally enslaved, their lives spent in her service, but it is chiefly in her relationship with Sidney Herbert that Strachey projects the terrible consuming force of her dominating will:

She took hold of him, taught him, shaped him, absorbed him, dominated him through and through. He did not resist; his natural inclination lay along the same path as hers; only that terrific personality swept him forward at her own fierce pace and with her own relentless stride.[17]

Berkeley takes exactly the same line. At forty-one Florence Nightingale is described in stage directions as 'in the prime of her mental powers'. 'Seven years rigid repression of sex' had 'clamped her features into an ascetic mask, fixed the lines of her mouth in a hard line, and soured her sense of humour into an acid irony' (Act 1, Sc. 1, pp. 206–7). She has devoted disciples in men like Dr Sutherland who expend their lives in her service, but it is in her relationship with Sidney Herbert that we see the destructive side of her inexorable slave-driving energy. Sidney Herbert reveres her for her 'amazing vision and capacity' and finds her devotion to her work 'magnificent' (Act 1, Sc. 1. pp. 206–7). He becomes the political instrument through which she works her will.

Where Berkeley departs from Strachey and from the facts is in his depiction of Sidney's wife, Elizabeth. She was in reality a warm admirer of Florence, but Berkeley introduces a deep antagonism between the two women to bring out their keenly opposed natures. She is representative of most social ladies of the time who were content to live drawing-room lives, and if they figured in world affairs at all did so merely as extensions of their husbands' careers. In sharp contrast Florence is an individual in her own right, self-defining and fulfilling. Through the figure of Elizabeth, Berkeley injects the play with an element of dramatic tension and dialectic. In the first production, Gwen Ffrangçon-Davies as Lady Herbert was 'a perfect foil to Edith Evans',[18] and one reviewer even thought that her performance in its subtlety overshadowed every other of the evening.[19]

In his handling of Sidney Herbert's illness and final dealings with Florence Nightingale, Berkeley shows clear indication of having been influenced by the Strachey account. With his penchant for melodrama, Strachey describes this last meeting by converting two passages from Florence Nightingale's correspondence into a theatrical event. Sidney Herbert, forced to give up the fight to reform the War Office due to ailing health, faces the moment when he has to tell Florence Nightingale the news with dread. His fear is justified:

'Blessed are the merciful!' What strange ironic prescience had led Prince Albert, in the simplicity of his heart, to choose that motto for the Crimean brooch? . . . it was not in mercy that she turned upon her old friend. 'Beaten!' she exclaimed. 'Can't you see that you've simply thrown away the game? And with all the winning cards in your hands! And so noble a game! Sidney Herbert beaten! And beaten by Ben Hawes! It is a worse disgrace . . .' her full rage burst out at last, ' . . . a worse disgrace than the hospitals at Scutari.'[20]

There is no documentary evidence that Florence Nightingale in a bitter tirade openly taunted Sidney Herbert about having been beaten by Ben Hawes, as Michael Holroyd points out.[21] But in a letter to Sir John McNeill she wrote:

What strikes me in this great defeat, more painfully even than the loss to the Army is the triumph of the bureaucracy over the leaders – the political aristocracy who at least advocate higher principles. A Sidney Herbert beaten by Ben Hawes is a greater humiliation really (as a matter of principle) than the disaster of Scutari.

Though there is no record of her saying this directly to Sidney Herbert, in a letter to Harriet Martineau, she does recall a meeting when they had spoken of Cavour whose death Sidney deeply mourned. 'And I, too was hard upon him', she writes:

I told him that Cavour's death was a blow to European liberty, but that a greater blow was that Sidney Herbert should be beaten on his own ground by a bureaucracy. I told him that no man in my day had thrown away so noble a game with all the winning cards in his hands. And his angelic temper with me, at the same time that he felt what I said was true, I shall never forget.[22]

The way in which these sentiments are expressed in the letters moderates them somewhat. In Strachey's account she is severely castigating, the words flung out in bitter rage and contempt.

The play follows the Strachey version in that Florence Nightingale gives vent to her fury in a similar confrontation but between her and Elizabeth Herbert:

Elizabeth: Florence. It's time someone told you the truth.

	You've a lust for power! If things don't go your way you make a grievance of it. . . . Dear – it isn't reasonable! Let Sidney get his health back, and perhaps later on he'll be able to pick up the threads.
Florence:	(fiercely) Pick up the threads! How can he ever recover his prestige after running away, sick, from his permanent officials? What a state affairs! What a commentary on democratic Government! The elected tribune of the people driven to a rest cure by the bureaucracy he's elected to control. Sidney Herbert beaten by Ben Hawes! It's a worse disgrace than the hospitals at Scutari. . . . Can't you see how he's letting everyone down, Elizabeth? Throwing away the game with all the winning cards in his hand.

(Act 3, Sc. 5, p. 269)

Even when Elizabeth tells her that the work is killing Sidney, Florence is implacable. 'Suppose it did kill him – or me – or you – or any of us,' she replies, 'What does that matter compared to the results?' There is undoubtedly something chilling in that she is impossible to reach even on very personal grounds. It is as if she functions on a different plane – noble, but also remote. Her very selflessness makes her almost inhuman. When Sidney Herbert comes to face her with his failure, it is clearly one of the saddest moments of his life. He is plainly very ill but she is too blind to see it. When he predicts that he will be 'dead in a month', she is gentle but disbelieving: 'Is that doctors's orders too? Cheer up, Sidney. They've said the same to me for years. But I manage to jog along.' He leaves, a broken man, and she is left to contemplate the wreckage of five years (Act 3, Sc. 5, p. 273).

From the close parallels between the two versions, it is clear that Strachey's *Eminent Victorians* is the chief source of inspiration behind Berkeley's play. Strachey has a strong visual sense. For his closely wrought biography he selected particular intriguing aspects of Florence Nightingale's life and personality. In the preface he states that he 'sought to examine and elucidate certain fragments of the truth which took [his] fancy and lay to [his] hand'.[23] He is hyperbolic and dramatic in his handling of history as can be seen from his practice of collating documentary evidence and presenting it as a dramatic event. It is interesting indeed to find a history play coming into the theatre through a historian who approaches history in almost theatrical terms.

But though the dominant view presented is Strachey's, *Eminent Victorians* is not Berkeley's only source because he does not make the errors Strachey makes, trivial though they may be. For example Strachey writes of Florence as a young girl putting her pet dog's paw in splints when it was actually a shepherd's valuable working dog which she treated by applying ordinary hot-water fomentation. Then again he describes her in later years, lying in a 'shaded chamber' upstairs in South Street while downstairs a constant flux of visiting dignitaries could be found come to beg an audience. But in fact the room was not gloomy but full of light, the walls were painted white; and visitors came only by appointment and were rarely kept waiting.[24] Berkeley gets all these details right which indicates a careful study of the facts.

He most probably read Sir Edward Cook's official biography of Florence Nightingale, *The Life of Florence Nightingale* (1913), which first traced a path through the enormous collection of private and official letters left by Miss Nightingale at her death. Berkeley has obviously drawn from this correspondence. It is not likely that he had direct access to these letters since the executors of Miss Nightingale's will claimed they were not consulted. Cook quotes profusely from this voluminous correspondence and seems the most probable source.[25]

Berkeley also seems to have been influenced by Cook's account of a serious emotional attachment in Florence Nightingale's life which called for a difficult choice:

> She was asked in marriage by one who continued for some years to press his suit. It was a proposal which seemed to those about her to promise every happiness. The match would by all have been deemed suitable, and by many might have been called brilliant. And Florence herself was strongly drawn to her admirer. . . . Yet when the proposal first came, she refused it; and when it was renewed, she persisted. . . . She turned away from a path to which she was strongly drawn in order to pursue her Ideal. . . . It was not a sacrifice which cost her a little.[26]

Berkeley places great emphasis on this incident in Florence's life. He gives the suitor (whose name is not mentioned by Cook) the fictitious name of Harry Tremayne and makes him rich and successful. Cecil Woodham-Smith, a later biographer, identifies the man as Richard Monckton Milnes who waited for Florence for nine years before his engagement to someone else.[27] Berkeley makes more of this relationship and romanticizes the whole episode. He tries to bring out Florence's deep unrest at being conscious of needs that will not find fulfilment in the socially acceptable institution of marriage. But his style fails him here for it is conceived in a very artificial manner. Alone on the terrace of her home by moonlight, Florence speaks her innermost thoughts to the fountain in the foreground:

> Fountain! Why are we given conflicting natures? Why can't we all be simple and straightforward like you? Spirted through a silver jet and falling in beautiful uniform curves. . . . How pleased your mother must be! . . . You say it is sweet to be loved and sought in marriage . . . But is the love of men and women to be compared with the service of God? You say that a lover's kiss is the centre-lock of the universe, the very heart of God himself. . . . Fountain, you have been dallying with the Night. You have been listening to the tales of lovers' joys and you are bewitched . . .
>
> (Act 1, Sc. 2, p. 217)

We see here that Berkeley is quite unable to convey the subconscious. His artificial device of the fountain to facilitate the expression of inner thoughts and emotions is an egregious blunder. The scene comes through as false and mawkishly sentimental. It gets even worse when Harry Tremayne appears and the couple communicate through the pretended medium of the fountain:

> Tremayne: Fountain, there is a woman. . . . And she is so noble and her thoughts are so lofty that I am almost afraid to approach her . . .
>
> Florence: The Fountain says: What do you know of her nature?
>
> Tremayne: Fountain, it shines in her eyes; it glows upon her face; it proclaims itself in every inflexion of her voice.
>
>   . . .
>
> Florence: (moving away) Fountain, will men never understand

that women can want something more than passion
and luxury? That they want the same freedom as
men to direct their own lives and use their own
brains? That however much they desire a mate they
can be conscious of higher purposes than mating?

(Act 1, Sc. 1, pp. 218–20)

The scene ends with Florence rising transfigured to a vision of
'multitudes of people struggling with Death'. She sees her place in
the midst of them and offers the sacrifice of their love in a prayer
while Tremayne, dropping to his knees beside her, says 'Amen'
and bends over her hand as to a saint. The scene failed miserably
in production. As one reviewer comments, the dialogue:

aiming at fanciful symbolism, comes perilously near to baby-
talk. And after that, while her lover, kneeling says Amen – he
does really say 'Amen' – to her refusal of him, Miss Nightingale
hears her 'call' and sees visions of Crimean hospitals, until you
want to shut eyes and ears and pray for the curtain.[28]

Though Berkeley allows the infiltration of maudlin sentimentality,
there is a historical basis for the stance Florence takes with regard
to marriage. Cook records that in autobiographical notes which she
preserved in relation to this episode, Florence rationally explains
her refusal to marry:

I have an intellectual nature which requires satisfaction, and that
would find it in him. I have a passional nature which requires
satisfaction, and that would find it in him. I have a moral, an
active nature which requires satisfaction, and that would not
find it in his life . . . I could be satisfied to spend a life with him
combining our different powers in some great object. I could not
satisfy this nature by spending a life with him in making society
and arranging domestic things. . . . To be nailed to a continua-
tion and exaggeration of my present life, without hope of
another, would be intolerable to me. Voluntarily to put it out of
my power ever to be able to seize the chance of forming for
myself a true and rich life would seem to me like suicide.[29]

Berkeley fails to convey the depth and intensity of Florence
Nightingale's feelings and attitude regarding the matter, but he

reveals his sympathy for the feminine viewpoint in emphasizing a woman's need for a rich fulfilled existence and a greater purpose in life than just marriage. He attempts to present a vision of a woman with a supreme vocation who by nature demands a life of epic scope and vision.

Her appointed time comes when she is asked to lead a corps of nurses to the base hospitals in Crimea. The scene at the military hospital at Scutari is very effective. It testifies not to the ministering angel of mercy but to the woman of iron will and determination. She performs no less than a miracle. Berkeley demonstrates how only a person of stupendous force of character could have brought order and sanity out of the quagmire of filth and confusion, of gross ineptitude and mismanagement. Unintimidated in a field of male predominance, she rises to the exigencies of the situation, cutting through the paralyzing red tape which is preventing efficiency and 'putting a premium on stupidity and death.' She is remorseless in her dealing with the entrenched stupidity of petty officials. Once again we see the male governed by a slavish bondage to rules:

Florence: So you think it's better for the wounded to die in accordance with regulations than be kept alive by proper attention.

Cumming: (impatiently interrupting) No, no –

Florence: . . . Or perhaps you think: according to regulation they oughtn't to die. Therefore they can't be dead.

Cumming: (savagely) No, I don't think anything of the sort. That's the whole vice of introducing women into the public service. They drag in a long string of irrelevant repartees whenever you try to get them to understand how the system works. What I must beg you to understand –

Florence: I'm not going to argue anymore . . . (Turning on Bamford) Have those blankets been delivered, Mr Bamford?

Bamford: (trying to be self-confident) No, madam.

Florence: Then in fifteen minutes I send this telegram to Lord Palmerston. And I return to England; and I publish my experiences out here. And if one single head of a department remains in his post it won't be my fault.

(Act 2, Sc. 4, pp. 251-2)

Throughout the scene we are presented with a demonstration of the 'Nightingale power' and we see in action the administrative genius, the stern disciplinarian, the uncompromising professional. In production this scene came through with impact.[30] One critic wonders if it could be bettered:

> On the stage move nurses and doctors, officials whose air of self-importance masks their incompetence, and orderlies bringing in the wounded, while over and through it all the spectator sees the dominating figure of the Lady-in-Chief, admonishing, insisting and controlling.[31]

Only at the end the picture widens to encompass the legendary image of the 'lady with a lamp'. In spite of extreme exhaustion, she 'can't disappoint the men' and goes to the door to watch the last batch of wounded being brought in from the boats. One of the men has been asking for her and it is Harry Tremayne who had joined the army after the years of rejection by her. He is fatally wounded but has held out for a last moment with her and now dies in his lover's arms, comforted by the knowledge that she loves him, and will love him and long for him 'to the end of her wretched life' (Act 2, Sc. 4, p. 259).

The influence of the Romantic tradition is evident in Berkeley's inability to resist building up a strong love interest in his play. But there is also a concern to be accurate for there is firm basis for his vision in historical fact. He thus cannot be dismissed as shallow and frivolous in his approach to history. In the first place he tries to be accurate through a careful study of the facts. Then we can see both the impact of the Romantic tradition and that of Shaw and Strachey since the play registers at moments the romantic popular image even while it attempts to sceptically cut it down and present us with a vision of the heroic in credible human terms.

The play closes with a glimpse of Florence Nightingale in her old age, helpless and bordering on senility. Yet she is not reduced in stature. She is to receive the Order of Merit for her vast achievements and when the apple-cheeked, benign old lady of eighty-seven is wheeled in to take her place at the investiture, the room becomes the 'audience-chamber of a queen'. Great tributes are paid to her. 'Florence Nightingale's service to humanity', declares the Secretary of State, 'are such as no one has yet been able to assess or measure. By her unresisting diligence she has stirred up a spirit of compassion that, please God, will never die . . .'. 'She is an international possession', says the President of the American Red Cross. 'She belongs to the world: and the world is very proud of her saintly daughter . . .'. Though conscious of some honour being bestowed upon her, Florence is not fully comprehending. Her nurse attends to her as one would a child. The play ends with Florence saying brightly as she is wheeled out, 'They were so kind. So very kind. I don't know what they were talking about. . . . We must ask Dr Sutherland' (Act 4, Sc. 8, pp. 294–8). There is a touch of extreme irony and poignancy here as we see the dominating mind and personality reduced to such puerility and childlike dependence. And yet, strangely enough, this in no way takes away from the stature of a figure who cannot be seen apart from her work. The Lady is a legend in her lifetime.

French's acting edition of the play contains an alternative ending. This was Berkeley's original ending which he decided to omit on the advice of James Agate.[32] The play is definitely stronger without it. Florence is shown in a febrile state of mind taking stock of her life in her last moments:

> . . . My life suddenly plain – like a picture. . . . On all charges. . . . Often foolish and exacting. I make no concealment or excuses . . . but the work had to be done. . . . Yet, still – if I had strength. . . . Ah! . . . the death of Sidney Herbert – and my mismanagement of him. . . . Nothing could be too severe for that. . . . And many cruel things said in anger. . . . And pride – and intolerance. . . . Only that I have honestly tried to work for other people. And I have striven to find out what is right . . .[33]

This comes through as artificial and totally unconvincing because it is so clear cut and highly conscious. The scene ends on a lame sentimental note and once again we see the definite pull towards romanticism. A choir is heard in the background rehearsing *The Dream of Gerontius*, a dramatic poem written by Cardinal Newman and set to music by Elgar. It celebrates a vision of the Last Things revealed to Gerontius just before his death. This creates the supportive mood for Florence's dying vision of Tremayne and their reunion in Paradise. The play thus concludes on a note of maudlin sentimentality. Without this scene the play was found ending 'with a scene of magnificent irony and almost intolerable pathos'.[34]

Both the Romantic and the Shavian traditions, the old and new ways of apprehending history, can be seen coming together in *The Lady with a Lamp*. The play fulfils the demands of my definition of a history play because it reveals a serious regard for historical truth. There is a definite attempt to base the play in documented fact. Berkeley follows in the path of Shaw in his concern to highlight contemporary issues and to present us with a heroine who is first and foremost a vital human being. But even while trying hard to be modern, the play has a soft romantic angle and sentimental moments which reveal the continuing influence of the Romantic school.

We turn now to a self-declared Romantic who strove to bring back 'beauty of emotion and beauty of language' into the theatre.[35] Clifford Bax never quite accomplished what he expected of himself as a writer, despite his prolific output on a wide range of subjects. This includes several volumes of discursive autobiography and reminiscence. He also wrote a number of biographies, but it was in the field of drama that he was most known. His early works were in verse and his first play to be produced in the commercial theatre was a comedy, *The Poetasters of Ispahan* (1912). He wrote a few ballad operas and a great many full-length plays, turning increasingly to historical subjects. Due to his style and treatment, his plays are more conducive to being read than performed. A case in point is *Socrates*, produced by the Stage Society in 1930. Sir Lewis Casson gave a memorable portrayal of the great philosopher. Based on the Socratic dialogues, the play is Bax's most serious and substantial offering, but it is almost totally devoid of physical action. The life of the drama resides too heavily in the force of ideas discussed and the play received only a couple of performances. His other plays on historical subjects are more light and romantic. These include *The Venetian* (1931), *The Immortal Lady* (1931), *The House of Borgia* (1935), *The King and Mistress Shore* (1936) and *Golden Eagle* (1946). The most successful was *The Rose without a Thorn* (1932).

Bax's work as a whole reveals a certain eclecticism of interest. He had a definite leaning towards the mystical and was drawn at different times to occultism, spiritualism, palmistry, yoga and astrology. In 1907 he was made chairman of the Theosophical Art Circle, a mystical art movement which aspired to give a new spiritual impetus to the arts. Travelling widely to places as far east as China and Japan, he was intrigued by oriental philosophies. In 1947 he wrote a dramatized version of Buddha's life and beliefs which was produced by the BBC and subsequently published. While most young men of the period were avid disciples of Shaw and Fabianism, Bax was taken up with the ideas of men like George Russell and Arnold Bennet.

The First World War shocked him deeply. He called it the 'most horrible war in the history of man'.[36] Concerned to prevent the recurrence of war, he edited a book of articles on the subject entitled *Never Again*! Bax had no time for the socialistic, communistic trends of his day. He believed in a privileged class if it could give back to society 'something of value – taste, manners, intellectual energy and political wisdom'. Taste would be 'the morality of the future'.[37] The preservation of beauty and culture was for Bax of paramount importance. He worshipped beauty in all forms and linked to this was his great admiration for beautiful women.

Like Berkeley he was drawn to famous women figures in history, but Bax was more captivated by notorious women who had caused a sensation in their time. He wrote an account of Nell Gwyn, *Pretty Witty Nell* (1937) and biographies of Vittoria Accoramboni, *The Life of the White Devil* (1940) and Bianco Cappello, *Bianco Cappello* (1927). Fascinated by such reckless, exotic women, he defines female genius, as consisting 'chiefly of a power not to make this or accomplish that but to live life effectively, to "take the stage," and to subdue the will of other persons by unaccountable fascination'.[38] Though his attitude can be seen as patronizing and reductive, it really ties in with his romantic slant on life. Bax had a definite sympathy with the feminist movement and in the envoi to an anthology of poetry by women poets he compiled with Meum Stewart, *The Distaff Muse* (1949), he salutes 'the brains, the sensibility and fine artistry of women poets,' hoping that the book will help destroy some of the absurd existing prejudices against women.[39]

A self-styled romantic, Bax felt himself trapped in a 'narrowly rationalistic period', doped by a trivial and materialistic society.[40] The Romantic, he says, 'relishes a world in which a millionaire may fall desperately in love with a tanner's daughter, or King Charles with Nell Gwyn, and he hopes the Rationalist will never achieve a society of complete equality'.[41] Bax's feeling of misplacement extended to the theatre where the intelligent theatre-goer 'was less excited by the conflict of human emotions' than by 'the blueprints of the Socialist Utopia or by the morality of taking rents from bawdy-houses'.[42] He reacted strongly against what he called the 'soulless and fifth-form "brilliance"' of Shaw who embodied these new trends.[43]

It was for a superficial motive that he turned to historical subjects. He felt that language had become impoverished in the theatre and people would still allow him 'a modicum of eloquence, of poetry, of passionate expression, if they knew his characters had lived a long time ago'.[44] History offered Bax an escape from the trammels of an everyday setting. It provided a more plausible climate for exotic romance, pictorial splendour and the kind of 'grand' passion and 'lofty' dialogue he valued. Thus his great admiration for the romantic, melodramatic verse plays of Stephen Phillips who has been called the 'rose-and-rapture dramatist'.[45]

But despite his natural leaning towards this type of play with the ringing tone and spectacular effect, Bax was unable to remain unaffected by the conventional taste for realism. His plays fail to do more than present an outward social reality. He wished to give back to theatre a religious drama, but his works never attain that deep poetry and high seriousness to which he aspired, and remain rather lightweight and sentimental. He refused to recognize the genius of Shaw and denied his influence, yet he moved from verse to prose as a dramatic medium and *The Rose without a Thorn* registers a certain modernity of outlook after the Shavian manner.

The Rose without a Thorn lay dormant for three years before it was produced by a company of amateurs at Bristol. Bax had almost lost hope of the play being produced by professionals when he met Nancy Price, director of the People's National Theatre who decided to produce it. Frank Vosper played Henry and Angela Baddeley took the part of Katheryn Howard. The play was produced on the 10 February 1932 at the Duchess Theatre where it ran for 113 performances. It was such a success that Nancy Price produced it again the following year at the Duke of York's Theatre where it ran for 128 performances. 'Perhaps no play,' she comments in 1962, 'has been honoured by so many repeat visits of royalty.'[46] This could have been due to Frank Vosper's extremely compelling performance as the King. John Gielgud asserts that his Henry VIII 'could hardly have been bettered'.[47] Ernest Short recalls Vosper's Henry as 'one of the most highly-wrought character studies in the thirties,' comparable with 'Laughton's remarkable effort in the film – "The Private Life of Henry VIII."'[48]

Critics were impressed by the play, especially as historical drama. Allardyce Nicoll writing in 1932 calls it 'one of the most important and beautifully constructed historical dramas of our time'.[49] J. C. Trewin in 1953 predicts that 'when theatrical recorders do their work in years ahead, the historical dramatist of our time will be Clifford Bax, author of *Socrates* and *The Rose without a Thorn*'. Yet what was popularly regarded as the 'true historical play' was one which was essentially a character study, 'neither too factual nor too coloured',[50a] a play which was carefully shaped and balanced, where there were no awkward incongruous elements that jarred and destroyed the historical illusion.

This figures in direct contrast to the type of history play written by a playwright like Brecht who reacted against plays which concentrated on providing an interpretation of character because they conveyed the notion of a basic human character or situation which he rejected. According to his view of history, man is subject to change and he shows man creating and being created by his social conditions. He deliberately shatters the illusion of reality and uses history to distance the action and pin it down as relative to a particular time and place. Though Brecht had been writing almost continuously from 1918 and had produced his important theory of an 'epic' form of theatre in 1931, the English theatre had not fully awoken to his presence; and minor playwrights like Berkeley, Bax and Daviot were unable to resist the tremendous pressure exerted by popular expectation for the conventional 'portrait-play'.

Clifford Bax is superficial in his treatment of history in *A Rose without a Thorn*. His principal source appears to be the biography by Francis Hackett, *Henry the Eighth*, published in 1929 about the time the play was written. Hackett, an Irish sociologist and novelist, was attracted to historical subjects, but his work is not seriously regarded by historians. G. Constant writing in 1934 refers to Hackett's *Henry the Eighth* as 'more amusing to be read than trustworthy'.[50b] From the close parallels between Bax's play and Hackett's account it seems evident that Hackett was Bax's main source. Hackett introduces his chapter on Katheryn Howard with the quote 'The Rose without a Thorn',[51] and explains in the course of the chapter that the phrase was the tribute Henry had inscribed on one of the countless jewels he gave to Katheryn. Hackett is taken up with this image and returns to it continually in his account. Significantly Bax chooses this phrase for the title of his play and adopts it as his central theme.

Hackett romanticizes the figures of Katheryn and Henry, providing an extremely sympathetic interpretation of their characters.

It was in 'amiable egotism that Henry enjoyed Katheryn Howard. He renewed his youth and set him on the straight and narrow path to beauty'. She was 'sensual in the grand English pre-puritan sense – "endowed with feeling"'.[52] The play presents us with a similar perspective. Katheryn is full of spontaneous kindness and Henry thinks of her as England's 'very symbol – like a rose in the morning' (Act 1, Sc. 1, p. 953)[53]. She is celebrated as a child of nature, epitomizing for Henry the almost sacramental beauty of the English countryside with its gentle subtle depths and rejuvenating qualities. It is as if his dream of renewed youth is symbolized by his marriage to Katheryn. She takes him back 'almost to twenty' (Act 1, Sc. 1, pp. 953–4).

In the light of his innumerable marriages and their most often disastrous outcome, Henry is usually thought of as a hardened philanderer. Bax presents him as an idealist, a dreamer. He always expected 'so much of love' (Act 2, Sc. 1, pp. 952). This again closely follows Hackett's portrayal of Henry as a man of deep feeling, 'who had accepted someone unquestioningly'. When Katheryn's betrayal of him was proved, he heard this revelation not as a man of power, but as 'a very simple human being'. 'It was a long time before Henry could utter his sorrow. He sat there, feeling old, his heart "pierced with pensiveness".' And finally 'he began to cry', opening 'the heart that had been wounded'.[54] Bax's dramatization of the episode strikes the same romantic note. There is the same emotional build-up to the point where Henry breaks down and weeps. His first reaction to the news of her infidelity is outraged disbelief. On its confirmation he astonishes the gathered assembly by 'burying his face between his arms and sobbing desperately' (Act 3, Sc. 1, p. 996).

Henry's intense anger and grief at being betrayed has a basis in history. In a letter to Francis I, Marillac wrote that the King had:

> changed his love for the Queen into hatred and taken such grief at being deceived that of late it was thought he had gone mad, for he called for a sword to slay her he had loved so much. Sitting in Council he suddenly called for horses without saying where he would go. Sometimes he said irrelevantly that that wicked woman had never such delight in her incontinency as she would have torture in her death. And finally he took to tears regretting his ill luck in meeting with such ill-begotten wives, and blaming his Council for this last mischief.

The Queen was officially accused of having led an 'abominable, base, carnal, voluptuous, and vicious life'. She had 'led the King by word and gesture to love her' and had 'arrogantly coupled herself with him in marriage'.[55]

Both Hackett and Bax portray Henry's response to Katheryn's infidelity without scepticism. There is no attempt to come to terms with the strange contradictions, the deep complexities, of his emotional make-up, or the tough political side of his character. They present events entirely from the angle of the personal relationships involved and take an extremely soft romantic view of the situation. It is all seen in very superficial terms and Bax goes in for the strident tone and the broad effect. He tries to register Henry's inner sensations at being betrayed:

> I am poisoned . . . there are men who care little what a woman does with her body, and preach a foul doctrine that such matters are of no account in a brief life and a hurrying world. Are they men at all? Are they my betters? Am I a savage to put so much value upon chastity? Or is it that I am a man through and through, while they are mere halfmen who are left high and dry, little stagnant pools in the rocks by the great tides of passion that have made mankind the first of God's creatures and the conquerors of the earth?
>
> (Act 2, Sc. 1, p. 983)

Like Berkeley, Bax's style fails him when he attempts to go inwards. The emotion is verbalized in language that is extremely stilted. Bax turned to history because he felt it gave him the the poetic licence to resort to an impassioned language he considered proper to the theatre, but here we see that it is fanciful and contrived to the point of absurdity. The play is punctuated with exaggerated, overworked speeches like this, but most of it is written in the racy colloquial idiom that reflects the influence of Shaw. The mixed quality of the play's language is an indication of the conflicting trends, the Romantic and the Shavian, from which Bax could not quite escape.

Bax elevates the rather sordid, clandestine affair between Katheryn Howard and Thomas Culpeper to the level of high romance. Thomas Culpeper is cast in the role of the reckless hero who risks life and limbs for a few precious moments with his beloved because without her 'the world's rubbish' (Act 2, Sc. 1, p. 966). When

the truth of their love is revealed, they both accept the consequences heroically in the knowledge of their undying devotion to
each other. In the face of impending death, Katheryn displays a
courageous and generous spirit. Acknowledging the justice of her
sentence, she is more upset that her actions have cost the lives of
others like Manox and Derham with whom she was accused of
engaging in sexual misdemeanours before her marriage to Henry:
'Poor wretched fellows! We little thought it would end like this.
We were young and wild, that was all' (Act 3, Sc. 1, p. 999).
According to the records, however, Katheryn hardly showed such
equanimity. Thomas Cranmer reports to Henry that when he went
to interrogate her he found her in 'such lamentation and heavi-
ness' and 'far entered toward a frenzy'. She tried 'to excuse and to
temper' the actions she had confessed to and said 'that all that
Derame did unto her was of his importune forcement, and, in a
manner, violence, rather than of her free consent and will'.[56]

Bax portrays her in a romantically enhanced light as representative of a new generation of women with a desire for self-expression
and a rich capacity for life. This is reflected in the Earl of Hertford's
defence of her to Henry at the end:

> We live, sir, in an age of upheaval. The new ideas from Italy
> have gone, like wine, to our heads. We no longer look upon life
> as a series of pitfalls devised by the Devil with a hope that he
> may prevent us from coming at last to heaven. We look upon it
> as a challenge to our capacity for delight, and we most honour
> the man who, like yourself, is able to extract from it the highest
> measure of joy. What wonder, then, if women have caught
> something of that new spirit, and if they too are eager not to go
> through the world as if they were deaf and blind?
>
> (Act 3, Sc. 1, p. 992)

Bax's own rather modern sentiment is expressed here because in
Katheryn's time her fate was seen as well-deserved.

In the play Katheryn is depicted as selfless and heroic in the
manner she faces her end. She is frightened 'not of dying but of
dying badly'. With childlike openness and simplicity, she requests
that the execution block be brought to her prison cell, so that she
can go through the motions of what she will have to face. It is
brought in and set before her and she stares in horrified fascination
at this monstrosity which 'makes one feel like an animal' (Act 3, Sc.

2, pp. 1001–2). Katheryn, enacting what she will be put through, must bring home a very real sense of the horror of legalized violence and this moment came across with considerable edge in the theatre.[57]

Katheryn's thoughts are full of Culpeper at the end. In a last interview with Cranmer she begs him to give Culpeper her love. As he leaves, she exclaims, 'I believe I had it in me to be happier than most people. That can't be helped. . . . Oh, I shall die as the Queen of England, but I wish I had lived as the wife of the man I loved!' (Act 3, Sc. 2, pp. 1000–2). Here again Bax can be seen following Hackett who describes Katheryn's end in the following terms:

> A large number of people had gathered at the scaffold. She spoke a few breathless words. A Spaniard heard them and wrote them. "Brothers, by the journey upon which I am bound, I have not wronged the King. But it is true that long before the King took me, I loved Culpeper, and I wish to God I had done as he wished me, for at the time the King wanted to take me he urged me to say that I was pledged to him . . . I would rather have had him for a husband than be mistress of the world, but sin blinded me and greed and grandeur; and since mine is the fault, mine also is the suffering, and my great sorrow is that Culpeper should have to die through me." At these words she could go no further. She turned to the headsman and said, "Pray hasten with thy office." He knelt before her and begged her pardon. She said wildly, "I die a Queen, but I would rather die the wife of Culpeper . . .[58]

There is however no evidence that any of this took place and considerable proof to the contrary. Culpeper denied his guilt to the last and was hardly the noble-minded hero of chilvaric romance. He persistently attempted to pin the blame on Katheryn, insisting that he had met her secretly only at her demand and she had then told him that she was dying for his love.[59] Katheryn, on the other hand, denied that she had ever loved Culpeper. She had granted him those dangerous illicit meetings merely to humour him because he had begged for a few precious moments. She made an abject confession of her guilt at the end, but this did not extend to acts of infidelity after marriage. She did not declare at her death that she would rather have died Culpeper's wife.[60] Hackett derives his narrative of these events from the *Chronicle of King Henry VIII of England: Being a Contemporary Record of some of the Principal Events of the Reigns of Henry VIII and Edward VI* by an unknown Spanish chronicler who, according to a modern historian, sparked off the 'romance' of Katheryn Howard within a generation of her death with his 'delightful and sympathetic, if singularly inaccurate, account of her career'.[61] Bax must have read Hackett's version rather than the original chronicle because he uses the details quoted in Hackett and does not follow other aspects of the Spaniard's account.[62]

Bax obviously found in Hackett an interpretation of character and event that was personally appealing and its reliability as history does not seem to have been questioned. He exercises no critical judgement, passively accepting the view of his source, for his work reveals no further reading or independence of thought. It therefore is not a history play according to my definition since Bax displays no serious regard for historical truth. His whole approach to history is shallow and opportunistic. He goes to history for subject and theme, and for the distance of time which he thinks allows him the freedom to indulge his penchant for flamboyant language and romance. But the records reveal neither grand passion nor glowing heroism. As a modern historian states, 'Katheryn's life was little more than a series of petty trivialities and wanton acts punctuated by sordid politics.'[63] Katheryn's behaviour acquires historical significance only within the context of family ambition, party rivalry and the practice of royal absolutism which renders an individual socially inferior and politically helpless. In the play Katheryn's situation is not seen in political terms and the official side of Henry is rarely emphasized. The deliberate omission of politics and the imposition of a soft romantic angle wrecks the play as a genuine historical drama.

Where Clifford Bax is quite content to take over a version of history unquestioningly, Gordon Daviot is much more critical and searching in her approach to history. Born in 1896 at Inverness, Gordon Daviot (Elizabeth Mackintosh) underwent training as a physical instructress and taught physical tranining at various schools in England and Birmingham before she had to return home to look after an invalid father. In contrast to Berkeley and Bax, she was extremely retiring by nature and shunned involvement in public life, living more or less the life of a recluse. *Richard of Bordeaux* brought her considerable fame in its time; her later dramatic ventures never attained quite the same success.

Her writings reveal a keen interest in history. She wrote history plays like *Queen of Scots* (1934) and *Dickon* (1955). Her last work, *The Privateer* is an historical novel based on the life of Henry Morgan. Daviot approached history in the manner of a crusade. She considered it practically a duty to help vindicate much maligned figures in history. In the preface to her biography of Claverhouse she refers to the false popular conception of '"Bloody Clavers"' as a noxious weed that requires 'a constant sprinkling of acid if it is to be burned out'.[64] Her play, *Dickon* about Richard III strives to redeem from calumny a figure much blackened in history because of Shakespeare's portrayal of him as a 'self-confessed and monstrous villain'.

> For 150 years the Tudor myth had stood unchallenged, and to this day in spite of Hugh Walpole and all his colleagues in the work of vindication, nine persons out of ten not only think of Richard III as a hunch-backed murderer, but are unaware that there is any evidence to the contrary.'[65]

Her novel, *The Daughter of Time*, written under the pseudonym, Josephine Tey, takes the form of a detective's systematic investigation and demolition of the case against Richard III. The title, drawn from an old proverb – Truth is the daughter of time – suggests that only with time can historical characters and events be seen in perspective so that truth and balance are restored.

In treating history Daviot imposes certain restrictions on herself as artist. For she believes that:

> to write fiction about historical fact is very nearly impermissible. It is permissible only on two accounts: (a) that neither the inevitable simplification of plot nor the invention of detail shall be allowed to falsify the general picture, and (b) that the writer shall state where the facts may be found, so that the reader may if he cares, compare the invention with the truth.[66]

This is a rather narrow, limited stance since she implies that 'the truth' is singular and apparent, and confines herself to presenting a particular view of experience. In contrast a Shavian and Brechtian structure provides some idea of alternative perspectives of a situation, for complex seeing is encouraged and is an integral part of the dramatic form. A wider historical dimension is thus encompassed through the shattering of conventions of verisimilitude which more conservative playwrights like Berkeley, Bax and Daviot pay deference to because these complied with popular taste in their time.

Richard of Bordeaux was a resounding success. Produced originally by the Arts Theatre Club for two special performances in 1932, it was subsequently presented on 2 February 1933 at the New Theatre where it played to enthusiastic audiences for over a year. The play was received, states one reviewer, 'with a full-throated roar such as the West-end seldom hears in these sophisticated days. . . . It now ranks as the best history play that has been written of late years, after *Saint Joan*'.[67] The play became one of the most popular spectaculars in London. People went thirty and forty times to see it.[68] The *Theatre World* magazine issued a special supplement consisting of seven pages of photographs of scenes from 'the play of the moment'. *Richard of Bordeaux* had 'justly been acclaimed by critics and playgoers as the outstanding event of the theatrical season'.[69]

These photographs reveal the production to have been a visual feast, and indeed it has been noted that a factor which contributed to the play's tremendous success was 'the décor by Motleys, a feature being the ingenuity with which they made the King's dress express his changing moods, and the aging of the man as he passed from youth to manhood and from manhood to premature old age'.[70] The Motleys were three women, Elizabeth Montgomery, Audrey and Peggy Harris who made a name for themselves as theatrical costumers and scene designers. *Richard of Bordeaux* helped to establish them.

Leading actors and actresses were drawn to the play because of the star parts it offered. John Gielgud, who directed the first production and played the title role, saw it as 'a gift from heaven'.[71] 'The part of Richard,' he says, 'was written with a great sense of humour, and was a splendid opportunity – the young, impetuous, highly-strung boy growing into a disillusioned man, his wife dying of plague, and his best friend betraying him.'[72] Gielgud was able to make use of all his previous acting experience 'to give light and shade to an immensely long and showy part, blending [his] methods to display every facet of emotion in the many striking opportunities which the play afforded [him]'.[73] It was in this play, he says, that he 'won his spurs both as actor and director'.[74] Gwen Ffrangçon-Davies as Anne also contributed greatly to the play's success. 'Her comedy scenes were perfect, she was exquisitely poignant in her moments of pathos, and her appearance in the rich simple dresses which the Motleys designed for her was breathtakingly lovely.'[75]

But apart from the arresting acting and visual spectacle, another reason for the play's amazing success was the topicality of its central theme.[76] It celebrates Richard II's determined efforts for peace at a time when his country was bent on war and aggressive acquisition. Ernest Short recalls that:

in 1933 Hitler was registering his hammer blows against the democratic system in Germany; in Britain, the Conservative Die-Hards were calling for the exercise of the 'strong hand' in administration. Young Richard's peace efforts and his failure to hold the sympathy of his people seemed oddly topical, especially as the dramatist was careful that no Wardour Street dialogue interfered with the quick apprehension of her topicalities.[77]

Daviot makes no attempt to view war as it was viewed in Richard's time and the play's modern dialogue and standpoint bring it within the Shavian tradition. Drama critics immediately noted the influence of Shaw, seeing it as a 'kindred way of looking for the truth in history'.[78] Daviot projects a distinctly soft feminine view, bringing the issues alive in terms of a clash between the urge towards power, greed and aggression and the urge towards beauty, culture and the preservation of peace. The First World War had obviously affected her deeply for she spoke very bitterly of it and 'must have suffered some bereavement'.[79]

Richard of Bordeaux was originally published in 1933 by Victor Gollancz. An acting edition was published by Samuel French in 1935. The play has subsequently been reproduced by Longmans, Green and company in 1938, by Penguin Plays in 1958 and Pan Books in 1966. It was also included in a collection of Daviot's plays published in 1953 and translated into German in 1966. This provides some indication of the play's success. In his foreword to the 1953 collection John Gielgud states that Daviot on two occasions was 'unfairly accused of plagiarism. On the first occasion she was sued by the author of a historical novel about Richard II, but the case was settled out of court'.[80] As the details of this incident are not recorded, I wrote to Sir John Gielgud for further information. In his reply he discloses that the book that gave rise to the piracy accusation was *The Broomscod Collar* by Gillian Olivier, published in 1930. The arbitration of the case was undertaken by Professor Oman who 'stated that both writers had evidently founded their research on the only surviving documents of the period in the British Museum'.[81] The play obviously came across with greater edge and immediacy than the novel which indicates that a play can be more influential than a novel and so, presumably, scholarly references are more necessary.

Of the three playwrights considered in this chapter, Daviot is the most original in her handling of history because she went back to primary sources and rethought to some extent. She goes against the conventional view of Richard II as a prodigal, indolent king who does not measure up to his calling, and presents a young ruler of great promise whose noblest instincts are thwarted by the greed and tyranny of society. Daviot's portrait seems to have been built up from the accounts of various chroniclers and historians who, though they do not wholly vindicate Richard, evince a recognition of fine impulses.

The French chronicler Froissart appears to have exerted considerable influence because he makes much of Richard's commitment to peace, the central focus of the play. His impartiality as an observer is generally acknowledged, and in *The Daughter of Time* Daviot asserts that more credence can be given to a contemporary Frenchman's report than an Englishman's because of the inevitable Tudor bias of the latter.[82] Froissart stresses Richard II's courage and independence in persistently striving for peace despite fierce opposition from the nobles and commons who were quick to complain:

What is now become of our grand enterprises and our valiant captains? Would that our gallant king Edward, and his son, the prince of Wales, were now alive! We used to invade France and rebuff our enemies, so that they were afraid to show themselves, or venture to engage us; and, when they did so, they were defeated. What a glorious expedition did our king Edward, of happy memory, make, when he landed in Normandy, and marched through France![83]

In Daviot's play, members of the king's council continually glory in past military exploits. Richard's dream of peace for a better England is dismissed as 'visionary nonsense', amidst the general appetite for war and plunder, a trend set by previous monarchs. Peace is a dirty word, a 'monstrous suggestion'. Richard comments bitterly that he is not the king: 'Oh, no, I am merely Edward III's grandson. And my father's son. They always compare me in their minds with my father. 'If the Black Prince had lived, there would be none of this Pacifist nonsense.' 'War, war, war! It is all they ever think of' (Part 1, Sc. 1, p. 16–21).[84] In reference to the negotiating of a peace treaty between France and England, Froissart mentions the ordinary Englishman's obsession when it came to a question of Calais 'for the commons of England love Calais more than any other town in the world, saying, that as long as they are masters of Calais, they carry the keys of France at their girdle . . .'.[85] Similarly in Daviot's play, Calais is referred to as a particular blind-spot of the English. Robet De Vere laments the fact that Richard's counsellors had ever let him 'mention the name of that misbegotten little French village. No Englishman is quite sane on the subject of Calais' (Part 1, Sc. 4, p. 51).

Froissart recounts the details of Richard's first expedition to Ireland where the Irish kings submitted to Richard 'more through love and good humour than by battle or force'. The four kings were knighted 'with much solemnitie' and dined afterwards with Richard. They were 'much stared at' by the English who regarded them as 'strange savage creatures'.[86] In the play Gloucester, recalling the same expedition, expresses his disgust at seeing the 'King of England feasting barbarians and presenting them with gifts. Knighting traitors instead of stringing them up' (Part 2, Sc. 2, p. 76). Froissart also relates how the Archbishop of Canterbury, sent by Richard's enemies to invite the exiled Derby back from France, travels in the guise of a simple monk.[87] Daviot too has the Archbishop approaching Derby disguised as a 'sort of priest person' and this serves to accentuate his essential facelessness (Part 2, Sc. 5, p. 94). Though the language used in the play is modern colloquial idiom after the Shavian manner, there is a distinct similarity of tone and stance that links Froissart's and Daviot's accounts. Daviot thus seems to have been influenced by Froissart's picturesque narrative though of course she might have been following an historian of her own time who followed Froissart, the original source for some of these incidents.

In the play Richard and Anne are shown caught up with a dream to 'make England so rich and so beautiful'. Their predilection for fine clothes and exotic cuisine is depicted as reflective of an aesthetic sense, incomprehensible to the crude rapacious spirits of their time. They waste money 'on beauty instead of war' (Part I, Sc. 1, p. 16; Sc. 5, p. 61). Their passion for the arts, for poetry, music and colourful pageantry is seen by most as gross effeminacy, vain and gaudy self-indulgence. Daviot has a firm historical basis for portraying Richard as a man endowed with a fine artistic sensibility. A modern historian, Anthony Steel, writing in 1941, notes that:

> In literature the period is marked by the first great burst of vernacular excellence in English history; Chaucer and Langland . . . in art and architecture Richard's reign represents the last great effort of the English Middle Ages . . . Richard II, like Henry III, was undoubtedly himself a connoisseur of building, sculpture, painting, books and music, as well as of plate, jewellery and dress; there is on record plentiful, if scattered evidence of these tastes, which has never been put together.[88]

Most historians of Daviot's time, in spite of modifying Tudor versions of Richard's reign and character, tend to perpetuate the conventional notion of Richard as an effete king.[89] Among the more sympathetic are W. Stubbs and K. Vickers. Stubbs finds Richard's personal character a problem to ascertain, but acknowledges that the legislation in his reign was 'marked by real policy and intelligible purpose'. Richard was 'a peaceful king thwarted at every turn by ambitious kinsmen'.[90] Though Daviot shares this view, it is Vickers who appears to have been a major source of influence because of the demonstrably firmer parallels between their portrayals.

In the play Henry, Earl of Derby, is an obvious foil to Richard, as Mary, his wife is to Anne. Beside Richard's volatile wit and artistic temperament, Henry's phlegmatic disposition is decidedly unattractive. He is totally devoid of Richard's grace and presence. A stolid figure, he is efficient and pragmatic, but quite unimaginative and something of a boor. Richard calls him a 'tradesman', describing how as he rode through London in victory, 'he ducked to each blessing like a street singer catching coins in a hat' (Part 2, Sc. 6. pp. 104–5). An equally marked contrast is drawn between Anne and Mary. Anne is a strong enlightened individual with an alive inquiring mind and very definite views of her own. She thinks that 'the Church is too rich, and has forgotten its mission' and 'something ought to be done to make it simpler and kindlier'. Mary on the other hand is incapable of making a statement for herself. She 'should like to study these things too, but the children take up most of [her] time'. She is a placid, subservient creature, quite willing to concede that 'men understand these matters of State' better than women ever can (Part 1, Sc. 3, pp. 37–8). Richard and Anne relate as equals. Their relationship is based on deep, mutual love and respect. Mary is completely under the domination of Henry, who relegates her to a fireside role and domesticity.

As with Berkeley and Bax, Daviot presents a modern outlook as to the role of women in society. Her portrayal of Anne as an extremely cultivated individual, however, has a strong historical basis. She was of a famous line, the family of Luxumbourg, and was the daughter of the emperor, Charles of Bohemia, who was a great lover of the arts and founder of the University of Prague. Anne herself was highly educated and well versed in the scriptures. She possessed the gospels in three languages, Bohemian, German and Latin, and Archbishop Arundel is reported to have remarked that 'she studied the four gospels constantly in English, explained by the expositions of the doctors; and in the study of these, and reading of godly books, she was more diligent than the prelates themselves'.[91] James Gairdner notes that in the commission given to the English plenipotentiaries sent to conclude negotiations for Richard II's marriage to Anne, 'it is expressly stated that Richard had selected her on account of her nobility of birth, and her reputed gentleness of character. The omission of all reference to beauty is perhaps significant'.[92]

The play places considerable emphasis on the relationship between Anne and Richard, the close companionship they enjoy which is both supportive and stimulating. Anne is seen to have a salutary influence on Richard and after her death, he deteriorates in character, becoming rash and vengeful. Froissart describes Richard at Anne's death as 'inconsolable for her loss',[93] but does not suggest that this caused a crucial change in Richard which resulted in later indiscretions. In his study Vickers makes much more of this relationship, asserting that Richard's:

> impetuous nature found one healthy outlet in the love he bore to his wife, the gracious girl to whom Chaucer dedicated his "Legend of Good Women." He seldom or never allowed her to leave his side and after serving her faithfully in life, so deeply mourned her death that it marked a 'change in the fate of the

nation. . . . His happy home life had helped to carry the King through many troubles, and after he lost that comfort he seemed to have become more reckless.[94]

Daviot takes precisely this angle in the play which suggests that she was influenced by Vickers.

There are other distinct correspondences between the two accounts which point to this. Vickers observes that men grumbled at Richard's friends, 'sneering at Suffolk's commercial origin, that of a merchant rather than a knight'.[95] Contempt for De la Pole's commercial origin finds voice in the play. Richard declares that the people do not trust De la Pole because 'they suspect him of lining his pockets. They can't forget that his father was a merchant' (Part 1, Sc. 1, p. 17). Referring to the deaths of Gloucester and Arundel, Vickers comments that 'it is hard to squeeze out a tear for either victim'.[96] A definite verbal echo can be found in the play. Two commoners discuss the violent deaths of these men and one remarks, 'Well I must admit I don't approve of hole-and-corner business, but I don't feel like shedding tears over either of them' (Part 2, Sc. 3, p. 83).[97]

Vickers, however, is not a continuous source of influence for Daviot since in his overall assessment he is mixed in sympathy:

It was Richard's fate to experience a recrudescence of that feudal spirit which had puzzled Edward I and shattered Edward II, and he was not strong enough to stand against it. His appearance was too feminine, his prodigality too obviously the product of weakness. It was only by fits and starts that he could concentrate his attention, for he was ever fonder of pomp and display than of the business of Government. More especially he neglected the control of the members of his household, who brought their master into disrepute by their arrogance and rapacity. His principles were, so far as we can gather, generous, and his career suggests a sympathy for the poor at every turn.[98]

Daviot does not follow Vickers blindly. In fact she seems to have exercised a certain independence of judgement and gone against the general view of contemporary historians in her portrait of Richard as a king who is deeply concerned with the affairs of government. A loyal and courageous individual, he is supported for the most part by true and wise counsellors. But he is gradually embittered by the purblind nature of society, its frustrations of his noblest endeavours and judicial murder of his friends. We are confronted by a picture of great possibilities atrophied.

The controversial character in the play, as in history, is Robert de Vere, Earl of Oxford, who has been called Richard's evil genius.[99] Though Richard created him Marquis of Dublin and Duke of Ireland, he was no lowborn upstart as Froissart asserts.[100] He was from an ancient line of noble descent, and as Earl of Oxford ranked high in the kingdom, but there were those, envious of the prominence Richard gave him, who saw him as a favourite of the Gaveston type.[101] In the play he is an enigmatic figure and we are never sure quite what to make of him. Richard is drawn to him because they share similar qualities of mind and spirit. But there are salient differences. Despite the king's rich fund of humour, he is intense when it comes to matters that touch him deeply. While Robert can sit back and laugh, Richard cannot because he cares, cares 'dreadfully' (Part 1, Sc. 1, p. 17). Richard is unable to distance himself from events. He is slowly torn apart by all that happens. In the hour of his worst catastrophe, Robert can say, 'And, strange as it may seem, life is still desirable' (Part 1, Sc. 2, p. 31). Richard wishes he had Robert's 'Olympian view,' but one is kept always in doubt whether his ability to keep removed is a strong vantage point or an escape from commitment.

Richard is one of those who has to live for something larger than himself. He begins his reign with a vision which had seemed worth realizing but the constant battle with a hostile public is a soul-destroying experience. His disillusionment with society is profound at the end. The Archbishop of Canterbury, come to lead Richard into captivity, falls victim to his scorn. He wishes to deceive Richard's party into believing that he has come from Flint with only two others, but Montague, catching sight of glints of light in the distance, demands an explanation:

Canterbury: I really don't know. The sun is shining on something bright, I expect.

Montague: Yes, the sun is shining on something bright! Do you think we are fools? That is the sun shining on helmets and spear-points. You and your two followers!

Richard: Come, come, Montague. Let us not be hasty. We can hardly accuse the Archbishop, who is not only

an ambassador but also a holy man of God, of
deliberately concealing the truth. We must take his
word for it that the points of light are merely –
points of light, my lord?

(Part 2, Sc. 6, p. 102)

Richard's scepticism is complete. In the final scene, when Henry
and his supporters come to pressure him into signing the deed of
abdication, he reduces them all to size through the mordant nature
of his wit:

Richard: I know that I am your prisoner, Henry. But it might
have been more graceful to announce your arrival.
You should learn from the Archbishop how to do an
evil thing gracefully. (To Canterbury) Good day, my
lord. Are you ambassador today, or do you for once
represent the Archbishop of Canterbury? (To York)
Good day, my lord. I am glad your son is safe. Will
you tell him so from me?

York: You must believe me, sir, when I say how inexpress-
ibly painful all this is for me.

Richard: (soothing) Yes, yes. It is a little painful for me too.

(Part 2, Sc. 6, p. 106)

There is historical support for Daviot's portrayal of Richard as
humorous in defeat. In the official account of the deposition in the
roll of Parliament, Richard is described as showing a cheerful
countenance (*hilari vultu*) to the lords who visited him in prison.[102]
Daviot turns this to good effect in the play. Richard is shown to be
buoyant in spirit yet acid in his humour. Here Daviot strikes a
different note from Shakespeare, and it was this that attracted
Gielgud to the role. 'Shakespeare's Richard,' he says, 'although a
wonderful part for an actor, has no humour and can be monot-
onously lyrical.'[103] Richard's humour was winning on the stage
and one reviewer talks of the relish Daviot gives to the king's
character in his preserving of 'irony and wit in the face of
disaster'.[104]
Richard scans the deed of abdication before signing it:

"Insufficient and useless." "Unworthy to reign." It is not a
generous document, is it? "Tyranny." Have I ever been a tyrant.

At least no tyrant has shed less blood. Nor been so tolerant of others. I have never persecuted anyone for his own good. I leave that to you, Henry. What the towns will save in feasts for the King they will spend on the burning of heretics.

(Part 2, Sc. 4, p. 107)

Daviot keeps close to history in emphasizing these grounds for the deposition of Richard II. He was indicted on account of his evil government and he had to confess to 'being altogether insufficient and unfit to rule'. One of the principal charges against him was that he 'imposed great Taxes upon his Subjects whereby he did excessively oppress his subjects and impoverish the Kingdom'.[105] Daviot's portrayal of Richard as profoundly disillusioned with his people in the end also has a basis in history. A contemporary chronicler, Adam of Usk, reports that he himself heard the following words of Richard as he lay a prisoner in the Tower: 'A wondrous and fickle land is this, for it hath exiled, slain and destroyed, or ruined so many kings, rulers and great men and is ever tainted with strife, variance and envy.'[106]

Richard's capacity for humour, his royalty of bearing, his concern for the safety of his wife and child and his servant, Maudelyn, in his darkest hour make him a moving figure at the end. Gielgud states that he 'nearly always enjoyed acting the last scenes of the play' because he found a way of playing them, excercising complete control of his emotions, while the audience 'became more and more affected, to the point of tears'.[107] Maudelyn's anguish at being separated from his beloved master borders on sentimentality, but the play ends on a satirical note. Richard, stripped of title, family, and friends, is brought to a state of utter isolation. He learns just before Maudelyn leaves him that the Commons have been complaining about Henry's extravagance. The curtain falls as Richard, staring after the retreating Maudelyn, then at the empty room, savours the irony of this. Amusement slowly returns to his face as he says to himself, 'Extravagance! How Robert would have laughed!' (Part 2, Sc. 6, p. 111).

A. Steel, in his book, *Richard II*, published in 1941, sees the need for modern specialized research to attempt a re-examination of the king but of 'a different kind from the blind sentimental vindication and romantic modernization of Richard to be found in the works of certain historical novelists and in that successful play, *Richard of Bordeaux*' Sentimental and romantic though it may be in tone and treatment, Daviot's play fulfils the conditions of my definition of a history play because it is well grounded in documented fact and seriously concerned with the question of historical truth. Steel himself endorses the view it presents when, pointing out various aspects of Richard's character, he states:

> There is the passionate and loyal friend and husband of early manhood, corrupted into bitterness and cynicism by personal insult and the judicial murder of his companions. There is the defender of the church, orthodox and sincerely religious to the last, yet strangely averse from the newly-fangled idea of burning his subjects when they happened to be heretics. There is the unbalanced widower, half-hearted autocrat and pitiful neurotic of later years.[108]

Interestingly, Daviot appears to anticipate the views of historians writing more recently. R. H. Jones in 1968 agrees that the conventional notion of Richard II requires substantial correction:

> De la Pole's administration did not escape criticism, but modern verdicts have generally commended both his policies and his integrity . . . Richard himself had responded very favourably to the teaching of his mentors. His attachment to de Vere and his impulsive fits of temper were his most conspicuous weaknesses. Neither was in itself serious. He developed the high sense of dignity of his own position which was necessary to an exalted conception of the royal prerogative. Consistently, even courageously, he defended his ministers and his partisans from criticism and abuse. At the same time he demonstrated on more than one occasion a degree of independence which proved him to be no mere instrument in the hands of others.[109]

A. Tuck, writing in 1973, talks of Richard's 'strong and bitter sense of personal loss' at the removal of his friends of the 1380's, his 'considerable political shrewdness and skill in using the strengths of his position to place his power on new, and perhaps firmer, foundations'. He stresses the confused and often contradictory attitudes of 'the various sections of English society to the prospect of an end to war', for there were many who stood to lose if peace were contracted, who would have preferred Richard to be a 'more opportunist and warlike king'.[110]

In *Richard of Bordeaux* Daviot clearly sets out to challenge the

image of Richard II established by Shakespeare, which has dominated the popular imagination for centuries. In fact Shakespeare's
Richard II was playing at the Old Vic in 1929. Daviot is said to have
seen Gielgud in the part of Richard, and therefore had him in mind
for the role in her play.[111] E. Martin Browne recalls that Gielgud:

> was already famous for his Hamlet and many other Shakes-
> pearan parts at the Old Vic; perhaps foremost among them was
> Richard the Second. To portray the same character in a modern
> play was in itself enough to arouse interest in Gordon Daviot's
> new reading of this piece of history.[112]

Spectators were thus immediately alive to the contrast between her
Richard's and Shakespeare's. Gielgud's representation of Richard
II in Shakespeare's play 'presides over the present stage like a
beautiful ghost', states one reviewer of *Richard of Bordeaux*.[113]

Shakespeare wrote according to his own lights and situation. His
concerns were Elizabethan, thus the explosive question of the
divine right of kings assumes predominance in his play. The
profound implications of this for the man and for the nation is
Shakespeare's focus. The historical Richard's crisis sprang partly
from an intrinsic concept of royal authority. Shakespeare brings
this alive not as a mere theory of sovereignty, but as an integral
part of the man and his dilemma. The belief that the king is God's
own deputy is a faith that both elevates and oppresses Richard. We
experience the sacred awe and mystery of the royal office through
the complex, inward state of the man who has lost his kingship,
but not his sense of kingship. Shakespeare draws attention to
Richard's deficiencies as king, but the real pressure of the play is to
bring us to an imaginative apprehension of the singular catastrophic nature of the act of abdication through the agony of the
man who is king by right but not by fact. In Shakespeare's play
Richard's tragedy is the tragedy of the deposed king. Its concern is
with the universal rather than the particular, and its treatment of
history is poetic.

In *Richard of Bordeaux* the emphasis is on the particular man and
individual. Daviot views events from the perspective of her own
time. Against the turbulent militaristic tendencies of his society,
Richard's struggle for peace is seen as fine and ennobling. The play
focuses on the external social conflict rather than the inward man.
Its treatment of history is narrowly realistic. Unlike Shaw, Daviot is

not great enough a playwright to challenge an image of Shakespeare's and impress her own upon the modern consciousness. The image she projects is for her own generation only. In spite of her attempt to present a corrective to Shakespeare's view and the vindication of Richard II by contemporary historians, Shakespeare's image of the king continues to dominate the human imagination.

Of the playwrights dealt with in this chapter, Gordon Daviot is the most original in her treatment of history. The overall view she presents of Richard II is arrived at without the aid of contemporary historians and she can be found anticipating the stance of much later historians. Reginald Berkeley is the most socially conscious writer of the three, motivated as he is by the active concern to bring about social change. Clifford Bax is the most romantic and superficial in his approach to history. He allows romance and sentiment to take over to such an extent that his play cannot be regarded as a genuine history play.

Interesting facts about the kind of drama in vogue in the period have emerged from a consideration of these plays and their writers. They all followed fashionable ideas of the time, with their exaltation of the feminine viewpoint, their reaction against war and violence and insistence on beauty, culture and the arts of peace. It was a period of transition between the old and the new way of apprehending history, thus we see the intrusion of a soft romantic angle even while they are striving to be modern. Characters are conceived in a rather romantic light because audiences were still eager for this kind of theatre. Functioning on the edge of the Romantic tradition, they also experienced the powerful impact of Shaw with his startling modern idiom and perspective. Thus a rather intriguing blend of two contrasting traditions can be seen in their plays. These writers were also affected by the tremendous pressure exerted by popular taste for a realistic true-to-life portrayal which required concentration on a single dimension of time and experience. Now it is not possible to write plays of this nature any more. Everything is different because of Brecht who was also influenced by Shaw. The following chapter traces the Shavian/ Brechtian influence as it operated in a far more alive and conscious artist who was able to fuse it into his own style and come through with a unique powerful offering of his own.

4

T. S. Eliot: *Murder in the Cathedral*

In striking contrast to the minor playwrights dealt with in the previous chapter, who waver unconsciously on the edge of two traditions, the Romantic and the Shavian, we see in T. S. Eliot's *Murder in the Cathedral*, the forging ahead of an independent spirit. Acutely conscious of traditions, old and new, Eliot draws inspiration from these, but merges them into his own style. He breaks right away from the naturalist theatre of his time, as is evident from the stylization and formal design of the piece. Moving into a much more direct, physical form of theatre, he presents us in 1935 with a charged emotive ritual which in many ways prefigures future trends.

Eliot returns to poetry as the form of language on the stage, but departs radically from the tedium of nineteenth-century blank verse. Poetry is used in a fresh compelling way to create and sustain dramatic tension with its startling changes of pace and tone, its mixture of the solemn rhythms of medieval verse with the liveliness of modern colloquial prose. Various features of the play anticipate much later theatrical fashions: the resurrection of the Greek chorus, the exploration of the theatrical possibilities of mime, music and body movement, and the brilliant use of ritual to link past and present and to express the secret inner world of the anguished self. Then again the preoccupation with the complexity and precariousness of personality, and Beckets' consciousness of role are very modern.

There is also the unsettling break with stage illusion at the end when in a sudden switch from high emotion the Knights come forward to address the audience in the manner of a public debate. It is a moment of Shavian irony intended to shock the audience out of over-emotional empathy to consider the situation as it relates to them. Eliot goes even further than Shaw because the audience is not allowed to hide in the dark, to reside in a sense of physical isolation, through this very direct confrontation of them by the

Knights. Indeed right through the play Eliot can be found continually distancing the audience from the surface of the action in order to involve it on a rational plane. Becket himself reveals a certain detachment from his role and can often be found commenting on it. Eliot is not averse to making the audience aware of its own identity and the fact of performance.

The explosive impact of Brecht on the modern stage comes immediately to mind, and the question arises – it is rather surprising it has not been posed before – of Eliot's connection with Brecht. Brecht was very much in the air, and the good creative artist is very quick to pick up and exploit new influences. Could Eliot have been influenced by Brechtian ideas and techniques? Brecht had been writing from 1918 and before the first production of *Murder in the Cathedral* on 15 June 1935, he had written numerous works, including *Baal* (1918/20), *The Threepenny Opera* (1928), *Mahagonny* (1928/29), *St Joan of the Stockyards* (1929/30), *The Seven Deadly Sins* (1933) and *Threepenny Novel* (1934). Eliot could very well have had knowledge of Brecht's writings and productions in Berlin. He was functioning as editor of *The Criterion* from 1922–39 and there would have been the influx of all kinds of information about literary and theatrical happenings abroad. Though I have not found any specific reference to Brecht in Eliot's signed and unsigned articles in *The Criterion*, it is no proof that Eliot was not aware of Brecht just because he gives no explicit indication of Brecht's influence.

We can see this with regard to Shaw. Eliot is extremely grudging in his acknowledgement of the influence of *Saint Joan* upon *Murder in Cathedral*. He says of the scene where the Knights confront the audience after the murder, that he might, for all he knows, have been 'slightly under the influence of *Saint Joan*',[1] when Shaw's impress is so glaringly apparent that most critics refer to the scene as Shavian. As previously indicated, Eliot makes very slighting remarks about Shaw's Saint Joan, describing her as 'one of the most superstitious effigies which have been erected to that remarkable woman'. She is perhaps 'the greatest sacrilege of all Joans', for Shaw 'has turned her into a great middle-class reformer, and her place is a little higher than Mrs Pankhurst'.[2] But in *Murder in the Cathedral* Eliot adopts the same anti-heroic approach and modernity of perspective. Like Shaw, he does not allow the spectators an emotional escape from rational consciousness, but attempts to engage them in a conflict of opinions so that they are forced to grapple with the issues for themselves. Like Shaw, he brings in a sense of multiple layers of time by allowing his characters of foreknowledge of subsequent events in history and creating an awareness in the audience of alternative views of the situation presented. Eliot therefore owes much more to Shaw than he admits. So he might well have known of Brecht's works and ideas even if he does not express an awareness of them. And of course Eliot and Brecht had a common model in Shaw. Brecht greatly admired Shaw and his concern to get the audience critically involved, wrestling with social problems and their possible solutions. Shaw, he says, 'unhesitatingly appealed to the reason' and delighted in 'dislocating our stock associations.' His world is one that arises from opinions. He created a play 'by inventing a series of complications which gave his characters a chance to develop their opinions as fully as possible and to oppose them to our own'.[3] Brecht himself was committed to this aim of involving the audience as thinking beings so that they might come to rational conclusions which could form the basis for social action outside the theatre. Shaw therefore is definitely a link between Eliot and Brecht – both have acknowledged his influence and there is no questioning their major debt to him.

There is also another firm connection. Auden and Isherwood were great admirers of Brecht and they were very close to Eliot in terms of time and theatrical practice. Their plays were written for the Group Theatre, formally organized by Rupert Doone in 1932. Eliot took a keen interest in the activities of this theatre because he sympathized with its prime objective, which was to correlate speech, mime and music in drama. Auden was in Berlin in 1928/29 and describes his stay in Germany as a crucial experience: 'I was awakened in that for the first time I felt the shaking of the foundation of things.'[4] German poetry and theatre, particularly that of Brecht, made a tremendous impression on him. He saw *The Threepenny Opera* when it was first produced and later collaborated on English translations of several of Brecht's plays. Both Auden and Isherwood have acknowledged the immense impact Brecht had on their dramatic works.[5] Isherwood has said that the plays he wrote with Auden, especially *The Dog Beneath the Skin*, owe an enormous debt to German expressionism and to Brecht's *The Threepenny Opera* and *Mahagonny*. In 1939 he wrote that if poetic drama had a rebirth in England the movement would be largely German in inspiration and origin.[6] Critics too have singled out Brecht as the dominant influence on Auden and Isherwoods's plays. F. Buell talks of Auden as the English equivalent of Brecht[7] and Eric Bentley refers to the extravaganzas of Auden and Isherwood as the 'best imitations of Brecht'.[8]

Auden and Eliot could well have influenced each other's work because their plays appeared in print almost side by side in the 1930s: *Sweeney Agonistes* (1926/27), *Paid on Both Sides* (1930), *The Dance of Death* (1933), *The Rock* (1934), *Murder in the Cathedral* (1935), *The Dog Beneath the Skin* (1935), *In the Frontiers* (1938), and *The Family Reunion* (1939). Eliot was certainly most familiar with Auden's work because Auden had a contract with Faber and Eliot was at the editorial desk at the time. It was Eliot who considered Auden's works for publication. He was impressed by what he read and commissioned Auden to write for *The Criterion*. After a dinner party with Auden in the 1940s, Eliot wrote to a friend that Auden was one of the younger poets for whom he had 'the highest hopes' and with whom he felt 'the closest sympathy'.[9] Auden in turn respected Eliot highly both as a poet and a man.[10] He dined occasionally with the Eliots in the early thirties, so they were on friendly terms even then.[11] It seems highly likely that Brecht would have come up in conversation since Auden was so taken up with his ideas. Even if Brecht was not openly discussed, Eliot definitely came into contact with Brechtian theories through Auden's work.

In 1928, while he was in Berlin, Auden sent his first play, *Paid on Both Sides*, in to *The Criterion*. Eliot found it 'quite a brilliant piece of work'.[12] It first appeared in *The Criterion* in January 1930 and was published by Faber in both the 1930 and 1933 editions of Auden's early volume of poetry called *Poems*. Brecht's influence on this play is patently clear. It breaks completely with naturalist theatre. There is no attempt to create and sustain a dramatic illusion into which an audience can escape. The play operates on different levels of meaning and the emphasis is not on character and plot, but on the social situation represented. There are continual shifts in mood and tone, and the plays ends in a characteristically Brechtian fashion. The characters and audience are faced with the choice of accepting the oppressive state of affairs in their home country or migrating to another which offers the possibility of change to a better way of life. The play is a mixture of political farce and satire, irony and pathos.

Auden's *The Dance of Death*, published by Faber in 1933, even further employs Brechtian techniques of alienation. As has been noted regarding an early production of the play:

. . . an announcer mediates between stage and audience, actors are planted in the audience, the theatre manager and stage hands appear on the stage . . . the stage is bare, with actors occasionally pantomiming scenery. The Dancer's role makes ballet prominent, while the parody musical-comedy chorus does other kinds of dancing, with singing. The small jazz orchestra on stage indicates immediately the distance from conventional drama.[13]

The play uses cabaret songs for satiric effect. It is symbolic and didactic, a sort of political musical comedy and the influence of German experimental drama of the 1920s and 1930s, particularly that of Brecht, is starkly apparent. In October 1935 the Group Theatre opened a season at The Westminster Theatre and Auden's *The Dance of Death* was performed as a double-bill with Eliot's *Sweeney Agonistes*, which again reveals how closely their work was associated. Eliot would surely have seen the production and been intrigued by Auden's work since he believed strongly in the dramatic possibilities of ballet movement in drama. He would already have read the play since it was published by Faber in 1933.

In November 1934 Auden sent Isherwood the typescript of *The Chase*, which had already been accepted by Eliot for publication. Isherwood suggested a series of changes which led to a collaboration. The play was retitled *Where is Francis?* and finally renamed *The Dog Beneath the Skin* (derived from Eliot's line, 'the skull beneath the skin' from *Whispers of Immortality*) at Rupert Doone's suggestion.[14] The play is a typical Brechtian recipe, a mixing of comic revue, light verse and popular song with a serious political theme. The action does not develop but each scene exists for itself. It ends with a chorus that was lifted from *The Chase*[15] which invites the audience to thought, decision and change outside the theatre. In *Murder in the Cathedral* the audience is similarly challenged at the end to come to terms with the moral and political implications of what they have seen. Eliot had read *The Chase* in 1934 and might have been influenced by its Brechtian character and conclusion.

The Dog Beneath the Skin was published by Faber in May 1935 just after *Murder in the Cathedral* had been published. The Group Theatre produced it a year later. Eliot attended a performance and afterwards wrote to Rupert Doone that he had enjoyed it, but also commented:

What did irritate me was the chorus – not that Veronica Turleigh is not very good indeed; but these interruptions of the action become more and more irritating as the play goes on, and one tires of having things explained and being preached at. I do think Auden ought to find a different method in his next play.[16]

He was referring to the Brechtian technique of periodically interrupting the action to alienate the sympathies of the audience from the dramatic situation as opposed to the old method of dramatic concentration and involvement. Eliot himself is a specialist in alienation, exploiting its effects with subtlety and potency in his plays.

Eliot's close association with the work of Auden and the Group Theatre strongly indicates that Brecht was almost certainly a source of inspiration for Eliot. I have gone into this matter in some detail because the connection between Brecht and Eliot has not been established before; yet the Brechtian influence is strikingly evident in *Murder in the Cathedral*.

Brecht broke radically with the naturalist tradition because he felt it created a climate of emotional acceptance where the impotence of the character is transferred through empathy to the audience. He reacted strongly against plays which tempted the audience to unconsciousness, to being emotionally engulfed to such an extent that its critical faculties were drugged. Brecht referred to playwrights who based their plays on 'entering into feelings' as 'sleeplullers'.[17] He felt the audience should be above the situation dramatized, not caught up within it: 'Complex seeing should be practised. Though thinking *above* the flow of the action is more important than thinking from *within* the flow of the play.'[18] His plays encourage an overall objective response. In order to allow for critical withdrawal from character and event, Brecht continually makes the audience conscious of the reality of theatrical performance.

Brecht uses the notion of history to facilitate this distancing of the action, and to show it as relative to a particular time and place. He rejected the concept of a basic character or situation. The actor must play the incidents as if they were historical because:

historical incidents are unique, transitory incidents associated with particular periods. The conduct of the persons involved in them is not fixed and "universally human"; it includes elements that have been or may be overtaken by the course of history and is subject to criticism from the immediately following period's point of view.

'The conduct of those born before us is alienated from us by an incessant evolution.'[19] This extraordinary statement drives home the idea of an ever-widening gulf which separates the past from the present, and the present from the past. It relates of course to the Marxist view of history, its doctrine of historical determinism and the necessity of change. Things do change and must change, and we can either assist history in its relentless onward movement or be brushed aside by forces too great to deny.

Yet despite Brecht's dramatic and political theories, his best plays achieve a very fine tension between the changing and unchanging aspects of being. Some of his most famous and unforgettable characters are universal human types with whom we identify profoundly. The audience is kept both detached and involved in a flow of mixed feeling, interest, empathy and reflection. What comes through with potent effect is Brecht's provision of a complex, multidimensional vision, through his registering of alternative points of view, so that the audience is drawn in to consider a predicament from different perspectives. A world is no longer dramatized mainly from the inside. The point of reference shifts from an internal to an external consciousness, and a situation is held apart, observed and entered into from the outside.

Eliot similarly can be found distancing the audience from the action intermittently, and moving in the direction of self-conscious theatricality in *Murder in the Cathedral*. He too presents the world depicted from the outside, enabling the audience to observe and reflect, to make connections between past and present, and to see the situation depicted in terms of a wider historical reference. He also includes the sense of a historical situation being overtaken by the course of history and rendered anachronistic by subsequent developments. But Eliot does it with an eye to preventing the audience from resting in a complacency engendered by the knowledge of modern sophisticated interpretations of the event . Unlike Brecht, his concern is to force the audience to come to terms with the eternal and universal, condensed within the transitory and particular.

In an unsigned article in *The Criterion* in October 1932, Eliot comments that one of the problems of our age is that 'we are still over-valuing the changing, and ignoring the permanent.' The Permanent has come to mean Paralysis and Death. The failure to grasp the proper relation of the Eternal and the Transient has resulted in an 'over-estimation of the importance of our time.' This is natural, he says, to an age which, whatever its professions, is still imbued with the doctrine of progress. 'But the doctrine of progress, while it can do little to make the future more real to us, has a very strong influence towards making the past less real to us. For it leads us to take for granted that the past, any part or the whole of it, has its meaning only in the present; leads us to ask of any past age, not what it has been in itself, not what the individuals composing it have made of themselves, but, what has that age done for *us*?'

In *Murder in the Cathedral* the audience is tempted by the Knights at the end to fall into precisely this trap – to see what Becket has accomplished in relation to their own time and values. Eliot sees this as part of the modern crisis:

> The notion that a past age or civilization might be great in itself, precious in the eye of God, because it succeeded in adjusting the delicate relation of the Eternal and the Transient, is completely alien to us. No age has been more egocentric, so to speak, than our own; others have been egocentric through ignorance, ours through complacent historical knowledge.[20]

Eliot sought to highlight the universal truths embodied in a historical situation, but his task was made more difficult because he was working against the tide of contemporary thought and feeling. In an age of scepticism when science seemed steadily bent on disenchanting the universe, Eliot was pointing to its inscrutable mystery, the eternal present in time and the continual possibility of the numinous experience in the midst of the everyday. In a world distrustful of saints, the general tendency, as has been seen in the preceding chapter, was to shatter the myth and find the human being behind the saint. *Murder in the Cathedral* explores the possibility of the saint within the man.

In reaction to the tendency of nineteenth-century writers and historians, like Mommsen, to romanticize their heroes and pronounce facile moral judgements, the succeeding generation was apt to be very wary. It often went to the opposite extreme, reducing uniqueness to mediocrity and hesitating to take any ethical values as fixed in the fear that moral judgements might be no more than a matter of social taste or fashion. In the 1920s Brecht was already opposing the idea of the individual as the focus in history and drama, when against a universe of events he appeared so small and narrowly bound by his time and circumstance. The emphasis in his plays is on social relations, man as a variable of his environment and the environment as a variable of man. The historical process becomes the point of reference, the generator of values, the source of character.

Brecht's stance is related to the Marxian view that history produces the individual. By this Marx does not mean that men do not make their own history, but that they make it 'under circumstances directly encountered, given, and transmitted from the past'.[21] As Keith Dickson points out, Brecht 'follows Marx in urging that historical analysis is not only a means of understanding the present in terms of the past, but an instrument for changing it'.[22] Brecht's shift of focus is essential to his idea of a society-changing theatre as can be seen from the contrast set up in his play, *Galileo* (1938): 'Unhappy is the land who has no heroes.' 'No, unhappy is the land who has a need for heroes.'

In Shaw's view of history the great individual is extremely important since he or she points the way of historical progress, but, like Brecht, Shaw's main aim is to bring society into focus since he too is concerned to generate social awareness and change. Thus in *Saint Joan* he takes very deliberate steps to shift the audience's attention away from Joan's martyrdom to the kind of world that destroys the instruments of its advance: 'O God that madest this beautiful earth / When will it be ready to receive Thy saints? / How long, O Lord, how long?'

Eliot is also interested in getting the audience critically aroused by the social and moral issues surrounding an historical event, but his emphasis is on the individual as a spiritual being, a universe within himself, and on martyrdom as a source of spiritual renewal and growth. Eliot's focus is not the social or the particular. It is the absolute incarnated in the particular that he is concerned to illumine, what holds true for all time, despite the progression of history which might render its particular form and expression an anachronism. The individual is the centre, and it is the value of the individual life and the tradition of significant individual lives that is affirmed. The timeless value of the present is asserted over and above all social and historical process, all evolutionary or revolutionary movement.

The idea that these three playwrights are connected in some ways is intriguing, considering their varying positions: Shaw, an agnostic socialist, with his belief in creative evolution; Brecht, a Marxist and materialist, with his contempt for religion; Eliot, an Anglo-Catholic, with his faith in Christ and the Church – a strange assortment, divided in their philosophies yet united in their appeal to reason and to history as the basis for their beliefs.

Eliot's concept of history is essentially the Christian concept. Religious thought is inextricably bound up with historical thought, for Christianity is a historical religion, in the very particular sense that its religious doctrines are at the same time historical events or interpretations. Belief in the Incarnation, the Crucifixion, and the Resurrection of God in Christ, present questions which must transcend the apparatus of the scientific historian, but provide certain bearings for the interpretation of the whole human drama on earth and the scheme of things in time. History is the process of divine disclosure, and the central point in history, the point which gives meaning to human existence, is the Incarnation:

> Then came, at a predetermined moment, a moment
>   in and out of time,
> A moment not out of time, but in time, in what
>   we call history; transecting, bisecting
>   the world of time, a moment in time but not
>   like a moment of time,
> A moment in time but time was made through that
>   moment: for without the meaning there is
>   no time and that moment of time gave the
>   meaning.

> (The Rock)

Here the 'impossible union of spheres of existence is actual', the past and future are conquered and reconciled'. The divine incarnates itself in time, therefore the eternal manifests itself within the temporal. 'History is a pattern of timeless moments.' 'But to apprehend the point of intersection of the timeless with time is an occupation for the saint' (*Four Quartets*). The saint relates time and

eternity and a martyrdom is an affirmation of timeless reality, of timeless value in time. Thus in *Murder in the Cathedral* Becket preaches in his last sermon that 'a martyrdom is always the design of God, for His love of men, to warn them and to lead them, to bring them back to His ways' (Interlude, ll. 65–7).[23]
Nevil Coghill points out that:

no modern historian can accept Eliot's postulate that a 'martyrdom is always the design of God' because historians wish their art to approximate as nearly as possible to a science, and obey the laws of terrestial evidence like other sciences. If historians allowed the idea that God from time to time made unaccountable interferences in the course of events, history would cease to be scientific and so abandon its special discipline.

But, he continues, a 'poet is under no obligation to accept the limitations that historians impose on themselves.'[24]
This is undoubtedly true. The academic historian must perforce concern himself with what can be established by concrete external evidence, bringing out the things which must be valid, irrespective of creed or philosophy. But the historical playwright is not confined by the same limits and is free to carry the issues over into the sphere of the prophet, the philosopher or the theologian. Contemplating history, it is natural to be driven into ultra-historical realms. For an interpretation of the human drama the writer is ultimately thrown back on his own most private beliefs and experience. Thus we find in *Murder in the Cathedral*, Eliot projecting the turmoil of his inner state. There is a sense of terrible personal anguish in the play which suggests an emotional experience of an excruciating kind.
Murder in the Cathedral is a tremendously powerful play related to Christian history, yet it also explores a psychological interior condition which could have connections with Eliot's own at the time. Originally written for the Canterbury Festival and produced in the Chapter House of Canterbury Cathedral, itself rife with very live associations with Becket, the audience is under pressure to see it in historical terms, to put the emphasis on the external historical aspect. Yet very prevalent is the obscure psychological conflict going on in Eliot himself. This psychological conflict is subterranean, but it accounts for what is powerful in the play.

This interior aspect was brought out forcefully in Terry Hands's production of *Murder in the Cathedral* in 1972 at the Aldwych Theatre. In her review of it Katharine Worth vividly recalls:

the impressionistic set by Farrah, its pillars and arches tremulously fading in and out with each change in the stage light, its properties – white altar, huge cross – carried on by priests seeming to be deliberately setting a scene for martyrdom. It created an exotic, insubstantial world which insidiously suggested itself, Genet style, as a creation of the troubled mind, a projection of an inner landscape which the male characters – the priests, and above all, Becket – needed desperately to establish as protection against a double terror. First a mysterious sexual nausea was brilliantly indicated by an athletic female chorus, dancing and miming the acts of sex as an accompaniment to horrific images of animality - huge and ridiculous scaly wings, the taste of putrid flesh in the spoon. Then came the terrible vision of the "void" hypnotically delivered by priests in a chillingly flat monotone: "no objects, no tones / No colours, no forms to distract, to divert the soul / From seeing itself, foully united for ever, nothing with nothing."

The play became a 'modern drama of self-consciousness in which the nausea and dread were related to troubling divisions in Becket's own nature'.[25] This production brought out the fact that the play allows for a very modern psychological interpretation and treatment.

Eliot wrote the play during an extremely traumatic time in his life. In 1933 he left his wife who was suffering from a serious psychological disturbance. She had been under medical treatment for years. The effect of her illness and heavy financial pressures on Eliot was very harrowing. He considered himself 'emotionally deranged' and it had been a 'lifelong affliction'. He too had undergone medical treatment for his neurosis.[26] Dredging the subconscious for truths about the self is an agonizing experience and Eliot's writings during this period reflect this painful self-consciousness. His unhappy marriage caused him a nightmare of anxiety and self-doubt, reinforcing the feeling of sexual guilt and horror of women mirrored in his early work. As Lyndall Gordon observes in her sensitive study of Eliot's formative years, 'There is no denying that many of Eliot's early poems suggest sexual problems – not lack of libido, but inhibition, distrust of women, and a certain physical queasiness.'[27] Another biographer, T. S. Matthew, also indicates that Eliot's sense of sin and guilt seems to have been centred 'on two peculiar obsessions which he stated as general truths: that every man wants to murder a girl; that sex is sin is death'.[28]

These feelings of sexual dread and recoil emerge strongly in the dramatic works Eliot wrote during this time of intense personal stress caused by the break-up of his marriage. In addition was the overwhelming guilt which accompanied the terrible decision to leave his wife. He felt perhaps that he was abandoning her. It was done in a rather cruel fashion. In February 1933, while he was away in America on a lecture tour, he had his solicitors serve a Deed of Separation on his wife. Attached to it was a letter from him, explaining what he was doing. She did not accept the enforced separation quietly, but endeavoured for years to get him back, often attempting to attract his attention in wild uncontrollable ways. Eventually she entered a mental home where she died in 1947. On leaving her, Eliot was hounded by dreadful remorse. His friend, Wyndham Lewis, describes him as looking like a 'harassed and exhausted refugee, in flight from some scourge of God'.[29]

The inner torment Eliot suffered is registered in the plays he wrote during this period. *Sweeney Agonistes* (1926), *Murder in the Cathedral* (1935) and *The Family Reunion* (1939) are all explorations into the interior and follow a strikingly similar pattern. All three deal with phantoms in the mind and a state of acute self-consciousness. There is the same grappling with a subterranean nightmare world to do with sex, women and violence. In *Murder in the Cathedral* the sexual nausea in the verse strongly conveys a sense of contagion and shuddering physical distaste. This feeling of physical revulsion is also expressed by Sweeney in *Sweeney Agonistes* and Harry in *The Family Reunion*:

> Sweeney: Birth, and copulation and death.
> That's all, that's all, that's all.
> Birth, and copulation and death.
> . . .
> Birth, and copulation, and death.
> That's all the facts when you come to
> brass tacks:

Birth, and copulation, and death.[30]

Harry: . . . You do not know
The noxious smell untraceable in the
    drains,
Inaccessible to the plumbers, that has
    its hour of the night; you do not
    know
The unspoken voice of sorrow in the
    ancient bedroom
At three o'clock in the morning . . .
. . . I am the old house
With the noxious smell and the sorrow
    before morning,
In which all past is present, all
    degradation
Is unredeemable.[31]

An overwhelming sense of guilt and contamination related to sex is what all three protagonists seem to be fighting to free themselves of.

In *Sweeney Agonistes* Eliot brilliantly realizes a realm of dark anxieties and obsessions. Through it all runs the all-compelling drive towards murder:

I knew a man once did a girl in
Any man might do a girl in
Any man has to, needs to, wants to
Once in a lifetime, do a girl in.[32]

That Sweeney is going to murder Dusty in the end is implicit from the whole movement of the action. *The Family Reunion* similarly deals with dark drives in the subconscious. After being kept abroad for years by an unhappy marriage, Harry returns home clearly suffering from some sort of nervous breakdown caused by the death of his wife, who either fell from the deck of an ocean liner or was pushed overboard by her husband. Truths are unearthed about the family's closely hidden past and Harry learns that his father had been similarly obsessed with an urge to kill his own wife. The decision Harry finally makes to leave home, to come to terms with his sense of being haunted by hereditary sin and guilt, results in the death of his mother. As with *Sweeney Agonistes* and *Murder in the Cathedral*, there is in *The Family Reunion* the preoccupation with murder and the struggle to escape an all-constraining bond: 'One thinks to escape / By violence, but one is still alone / In an over-crowded desert, jostled by ghosts.' Harry, like Sweeney and Becket, is a lonely, tormented, extremely self-conscious being. He is deeply aware of troubling divisions within himself, and hounded by spectres of the avenging Furies.[33]

In *Murder in the Cathedral* Becket suffers from the same over-whelming sense of being hunted down – 'All my life they have been coming, these feet.' He is continually dogged by threats of violence and visions of his own martyrdom. There is a real connection here with the 'murder' obsession of Sweeney and Harry. The essential action of the play, as Eliot himself sees it, is: 'A man comes home, foreseeing that he will be killed, and he is killed.' A very personal nightmare is involved. Eliot says that he 'wanted to concentrate on death and martyrdom'[34] and the whole drive of the play is towards this cardinal event. There is a similar drive within Becket himself. He is caught up with the dominating sense of this particular destiny, but there is a narcissistic tendency in his urge towards martyrdom. It is this rooted egotism that has to come to birth in Becket's consciousness and so find expurgation. The word 'martyr' as we so often use it today implies an element of the self-inflicted. The distinction between suicide and martyrdom is a fine one, and it is a line Eliot explores in his play. There is an extremely personal trauma behind it all. Eliot deliberately dehumanizes the characters and situation to distance them from himself, but much of the torment, the withdrawal into self, the shrinking from sex and women that can be found in *Murder in the Cathedral* may relate to his own marital problems at the time.

Perhaps Eliot's conversion to Christianity in 1927 was an attempt to find an inner peace and reconciliation in his dilemma. A biographer states that 'Eliot's passionate purpose in becoming a declared Christian was to turn his back on Hell and his face toward Heaven.' He once expressed to an old friend, Paul Elmer More:

his incomprehension of those people who did not feel the emptiness at the core of life; and confessed that it was his own awareness of this central nothingness that had driven him to accept the partial panacea of Christianity. Further: that Hell exists, and for those who do not believe in life after death, Hell establishes itself here on earth; that people go to Hell of their own choice, and cannot change themselves sufficiently to make the attempt.[35]

Murder in the Cathedral powerfully realizes this fear of void, of nothingness, at the heart of existence, and the hell people can create within themselves. A struggle towards inner peace is the central experience of the play. The sense of wrestling with an inner world of nightmare is continually brought home through the hypnotic effect of rhythm, chant and ritualistic movement, and the lines often suggest an unbearable affliction that springs from guilt:

> In the small circle of pain within the skull
> You still shall tramp and tread one endless
>   round
> Of thought, to justify your action to
>   yourselves
> Weaving a fiction which unravels as you weave,
> Pacing forever in the hell of make-believe
> Which never is belief . . .

> > > > (Part II, ll. 606–11)

As established in the introduction, the writer of a history play may use intensely personal experience for his interpretation of history as long as there is a basis for his vision in historical fact. Eliot may delve deep into the intimate recesses of his private life in his realization of the theme of death and martyrdom, but he is in no way indifferent to historical realities. There was much in history that served his personal needs. In Becket he found a character with whom he could identify profoundly in many respects. Both had the unmistakable stamp of greatness, possessing extraordinary gifts of which they could not help but be aware. They were both haunted by a sense of past guilt for different reasons – Eliot because he had left his wife, Becket because of former worldly compliance. They were both extremely withdrawn individuals – there was about them a certain reserve, an inner tension, even repression. They both hid their deepest personality, meeting others on a different level.

A distinguished modern historian, David Knowles, writes of Becket in 1963:

In all the mass of biographical material there is scarcely a reference to personal affection being given or received. . . . The only two human beings (apart from his mother) who are recorded to have loved him are the two masters, Theobald and the king, whom in different ways he strove to please by concealing his real self, and it is worth noting that both were, though in different ways, disillusioned at the last.[36]

Becket had a very worldly side which he hid from Archbishop Theobald, his spiritual father, and a deeply spiritual side which he hid from Henry, his secular lord. Thus there was a certain contradiction in his make-up and, like Eliot, he must have suffered at times from an acute sense of self-division.

Both Becket and Eliot went through a phase of terrible mental and moral strife, resulting in illness. Knowles describes the archbishop before the critical meeting with the king at Northampton in October 1164:

He was face to face with pain, imprisonment, perhaps even death, and that not for a principle but in a feudal, personal quarrel; he would pass into oblivion and pope and king would pick up the threads of their old life while he lay in prison or in the grave. His mental agony was joined to physical fear such as the battlefield had not brought, and that in its turn brought on an illness that was possibly the result of the mind's attempt to escape from its dilemma.

It is impossible to be certain whether Becket's illness was psychosomatic, but as Knowles states 'the fact of its frequent recurrence and its sudden disappearance would suggest a psychological element, and all agree that it was brought on by anxiety.'[37] Eliot thus has very strong historical support for placing such emphasis on a torn anguished interior state. In so doing he anticipates the views of modern historians who acknowledge the psychological dimension as a very real part of Becket's predicament. In the play we find ourselves caught up in conflict on different levels. Eliot is scrupulous in his regard for the external world of events, but the play is immensely inward as well, and the true field of battle is the inner one.

Murder in the Cathedral was written for the Canterbury Festival of 1935 after Eliot was approached by George Bell. It is Eliot's only history play. The historical sections of *The Rock*, 'a pageant play' presented in 1934 were written by E. M. Browne and Eliot only contributed the choruses. These are oppressively didactic, dominated by the concern to drive home the Christian message. Eliot himself refers to them as written in the voice of the poet 'addressing – indeed haranguing – an audience'.[38] This tone is transcended in *Murder in the Cathedral* where the Chorus expresses a profound state of consciousness, a state of mixed spiritual hope and fear. The play has undergone many minor textual alterations in the course of successive editions. A special Canterbury edition was printed locally to be sold at the Festival and went out of print. The first edition of the play to be published was the Faber edition in 1935 which was the text without the benefit of production experience. Its variations from the Canterbury version have been aptly illustrated by E. M. Browne who shows that the later editions of the play, which may be taken as final, follow the Canterbury text closely and are merely a tauter version of it.[39]

Eliot shows a deep regard for historical truth. Like Shaw, he goes back to primary sources to gain a first-hand knowledge of available documentary evidence and then proceeds to present a distinctly modern vision. Like Shaw, he is keen to make it known that his play is founded on historical fact. When Nevil Coghill was asked by Eliot to prepare the 1965 Faber edition of *Murder in the Cathedral*, one of the features Eliot wanted brought out was 'how the action and dialogue were based in authentic contemporary records and were faithful to historical truth'.[40] In this edition Coghill includes translations of brief extracts from the primary source, the Rolls series of *Materials for the History of Thomas Becket, Archbishop of Canterbury* edited by J. C. Robertson and J. B. Sheppard (1875–85).

This work contains a vast accumulation of material about Becket written in Latin by his contemporaries and writers of the next generation. It superceded the collection made by J. A. Giles, *Sanctus Thomas Cantuariensis* (1845–6). Its seven volumes are devoted mainly to contemporary biographies of the archbishop and the extensive contemporary correspondence which refers to him. Eliot knew Latin and might have referred to this enduring work in the British Museum, or he could have used available translations of material from this work such as J. A. Giles's *The Life and Letters of Thomas Becket* (1846) and W. H. Hutton's *St. Thomas of Canterbury from Contemporary Biographers and other Chroniclers* (1899), *The Eng-*

lish Saints (1903) and *Thomas Becket: Archbishop of Canterbury* (1910).

The contemporary source material for the history of Thomas Becket is voluminous and of unequal value. A later translation of selections from this material by D. C. Douglas and G. W. Greenway, *English Historical Documents 1042–1189* (1953) discusses the varied character of the abundant testimony and reproduces the most authoritative accounts. A comparison of Coghill's notes to the play, which show how most of its dialogue and action is based on one or other of these chroniclers' reports, and Douglas and Greenway's claim for the authenticity of their extracts, reveals that Eliot took great care to make his dramatization of events accord with the most reliable of these accounts.

From the original sources Eliot derived his controlling ideas for the play. Even his portrayal of Becket's spiritual dilemma, his need to plumb the innermost recesses of his conscience to purify his will of any impulse towards martyrdom, has historical vindication. There are numerous indications in contemporary letters and accounts of Becket's declared willingness to accept martyrdom if it came to the crunch. During his last months he became increasingly convinced that only through his death would a solution be found to the conflict between State and Church.

Edward Grim, a secular clerk on a visit to Canterbury, was present at the murder. According to Douglas and Greenway, he may be regarded as the most detached and impartial witness since he was more or less a stranger to Canterbury and his presence at the martyrdom was accidental. All the events he records are confirmed by other writers.[41] Eliot's dramatization of the murder closely follows the account of Grim who describes Becket as actually desiring martyrdom in the end:

> . . . he who had long since yearned for martyrdom, now saw that the occasion to embrace it had seemingly arrived, and dreaded lest it should be deferred or even altogether lost, if he took refuge in the church. But the monks still pressed him, saying that it was not becoming for him to absent himself from vespers. . . . He lingered for a while motionless in that less sacred spot deliberately awaiting that happy hour of consummation which he had craved with many sighs and sought with such devotion; for he feared lest, as has been said, reverence for the sanctity of the sacred building might deter even the impious from their purpose and cheat him of his heart's desire.[42]

Similarly Eliot presents Becket rejecting the priests' entreaties to seek refuge:

> Go to vespers, remember me at your prayers.
> They shall find the shepherd here; the flock
>   shall be spared.
> I have had a tremor of bliss, a wink of heaven,
>   a whisper,
> And I would no longer be denied; all things
> Proceed to a joyful consummation.

(Part 2, ll. 71–5)

Before reaching this point Becket has to pass through a painful process of consciousness in order to purge his will of any element of self-interestedness. To dramatize the profundities of mind and motive, Eliot takes us into the tremendous corridors that lie within. But there is a firm historical basis for the portrayal in Becket of an urge towards martyrdom which provides Eliot with a take-off point for his exploration of the inner man.

Another dominating idea which can be traced in the sources and shown to have some connection with the way Eliot treats it in the play is the theme of peace. The Women of Canterbury continually lament the disturbance of the quiet seasons. The Priests anxiously inquire of the Messenger – 'Is it peace or war?' 'What peace can there be found/To grow between the hammer and the anvil' (Part 1, ll. 79–81). This phrase the 'hammer and the anvil' was actually used by the Bishop of Chichester in the historical situation. He is reported to have said to Becket:

> You have shut us up in a snare by your prohibition, you have snared us, as it were, between the hammer and the anvil; for if we disobey we are ensnared in the bonds of disobedience; if we obey, we infringe the constitution and trespass against the king.[43]

Becket was continually under pressure to submit to the king. Many asserted that this was in line with his duty to provide for the peace and security of the Church and the Realm, as revealed by the following excerpt from a letter to Becket from the bishops and clergy of England (June 1160):

We do not assert that our lord the king has never erred, but we do say and assert with confidence that he has always been prepared to make recompense to God. He has been made king by the Lord to provide in everything for the peace of his subjects. It is to preserve this peace to the churches and peoples committed to his charge that he wishes and requires the dignities vouchsafed to his predecessors to be maintained and secured to himself. . . . Wherefore it is the common petition of us all that you will not by precipitate measures scatter and destroy, but provide with paternal solicitude that the sheep committed to your charge may enjoy life, peace and security.[44]

Becket was also put upon by members of his own side. Herbert of Bosham, a close friend and adviser of Becket, narrates how, after the failure of the conference at Montmarte (18 November 1169), one of their company went up to the archbishop and said, 'This day the peace of the Church has been discussed in the chapel of the Martyrdom, and it is my belief that only through your martyrdom will the Church ever obtain peace.' Becket replied laconically, 'Would to God she might be delivered, even by my blood.'[45] Becket was hedged around with threats, but he was not alone in his attitude regarding this question of peace. The same chronicler reports the pope to have said to Becket that:

> the cause the archbishop was advocating was the cause of justice and of the Church, and that, if peace was to be made, it must be at one and the same time the peace of the Church and the peace of justice. For the Church, whether in peace or without peace, it was precious to yield one's life, and for the archbishop more precious than for others.[46]

Eliot must have been intrigued by the way this issue of peace continually preoccupied characters in the historical situation, especially since peace was an equally pressing concern in his own time. It was a period of growing tension and unease due to the menacing nature of the international political scene. Robert Sencourt observes that in the year Eliot was completing *Murder in the Cathedral*, 'Mussolini had come out with the prophecy that if the nations of Europe persisted in their current mentalities, there would be general war by 1939.'[47] The play was produced in 1935, just two years after the advance of Hitler to power. The questions posed by

Becket in his final sermon must have come across with particular edge and immediacy to audiences of the first production:

> Now think for a moment about the meaning of this word 'peace'. Does it seem strange to you that the angels should have announced Peace, when ceaselessly the world has been stricken with War and the fear of War? Does it seem to you that the angelic voices were mistaken, and that the promise was a disappointment and a cheat?
>
> (Part 1, ll. 20–7)

From history Eliot derives the biblical text on which Becket's last sermon is based. William Fitz Stephen records that before the High Mass on Christmas day which the archbishop celebrated, Becket:

> preached a splendid sermon to the people, taking for his subject a text on which he was wont to ponder, namely, "on earth peace to men of good will." And when he made mention of the holy fathers of the church of Canterbury who were therein confessors, he said that they already had an archbishop who was a martyr, St. Alphege, and it was possible that in a short time they would have yet another . . .[48]

In the play Becket also ends his sermon with this prediction of his own death. According to E. M. Browne who directed the first production, the sermon has always been 'the best-remembered scene of the play,' mainly because 'the author was exactly right in calculating that when the hero reveals his heart in saying farewell to his people, he will win maximum response'.[49] But it might have had such impact for audiences of the original production because the theme of peace was of such urgent relevance to their time.

During his sermon Becket questions whether the peace Christ himself promised his disciples ('Peace I leave with you, my peace I give unto you') was as we normally think of it, 'the kingdom of England at peace with its neighbours, the barons at peace with the King, the householder counting over his peaceful gains, the swept hearth, his best wine for a friend at the table, his wife singing to the children?' Christ's disciples knew no such peace for they went on to suffer torture, imprisonment, disappointment and, eventually, death by martyrdom. 'So then, He gave to his disciples peace, but not peace as the world gives' (Part 1, ll. 30–40). Eliot sets up the notion of two kinds of peace, which, though not necessarily mutually exclusive, have to be kept separate in order to resolve the conflict – 'The peace of man is always uncertain unless men keep the peace of God.' The peace of God is an inner peace which springs from being in harmony with God's will.[50] Thus Eliot very carefully integrates the exterior world of events and the interior world of the spirit in *Murder in the Cathedral* so that one of the most inwardlooking of playwrights, he is also one of the most scrupulous in his respect for the outward plane of concrete historical action.

Various criticism has been devoted to Eliot's treatment of historical material. J. T. Boulton studies Eliot's use of original sources in realizing a theme which, he says, 'concentres everything in the play – the clash between the values and attitudes of Secularism and those of religion'.[51] He illustrates how Eliot often relies on contemporary narrative for the detail, the general tone and the order of speeches. The minor changes he makes are usually in the direction of impersonalization, to extend the conflict beyond the individuals concerned. It becomes a conflict between State and Church, the law of man and the law of God. P. M. Adair's reading of the sources suggests that Eliot 'deliberately sacrificed the warmth and vitality and ironic vigour of the Thomas his contemporaries knew, in subjugation to his religious conception of sainthood and martyrdom'.[52]

These could be partly Eliot's motives, but he could also be using this impersonality as a mask, a way of distancing himself from himself, and of covering up involvement of a very personal kind. The Becket he presents is an icon-like figure – lone, austere, remote. He makes no attempt to invest Becket with flesh and blood or to convey a living relationship between him and his fellow priests. He is his own counsellor, and the priests look to him from a distance removed, as creatures to be led, whereas the records tell us that, though he inspired admiration and loyalty rather than affection, Becket had intimate advisers like Herbert of Bosham and John of Salisbury, who felt very free to speak their minds in agreement or opposition.

These two historical characters appear by name in Eliot's manuscript notes, as E. M. Browne shows, reproducing excerpts from pages of the original manuscript preserved in the Houghton Library, Harvard. 'They have clearly been sacrificed to the formal pattern', Browne comments:

In the printed cast list, no characters are given names: even the
Knights who kill Becket and whose names are well known are
listed as First, Second, Third and Fourth. This is the terminus of
the process by which history, though its sources are treated with
the most careful respect, is subjected to theme; the human action
is subordinated to the divine, the action in time to the timeless
movement of God's will.[53]

But it is significant that Becket at the end does actually refer to one
of the knights by name as he turns to face them, which suggests a
certain intimacy with his murderers. The doubling of the parts of
the Knights and the Tempters, as has become theatrical practice,
also drives home their relation to vital aspects of Becket's personality. The exclusion of Henry from the play is again extremely
significant. Henry, because of his key role in history and sheer
force of personality, would have figured as too much of a separate
entity. Eliot dramatizes a complex state of consciousness and all
the other characters can be seen as inextricably linked to Becket
himself, part of the mind's dialogue with itself.

There is also the curious male/female dichotomy in the play,
with Becket, the Priests, the Tempters and the Knights on one
side, and on the other, the Chorus of Women, a strangely one-sex
congregation over which Becket achieves mastery and transcendence. There is the same sort of male/female division in *Sweeney
Agonistes* where Doris and Dusty unite against the male threat of
Sweeney and Pereira – 'A woman runs a terrible risk'. Thus the
formal design of *Murder in the Cathedral* need not merely relate to its
religious theme, as most critics suggest, but to a hidden psychological struggle going on in Eliot himself. By making the characters
and situation a little abstract and inhuman, Eliot is able to use
private experience and guard it behind an ambiguous impersonal
facade.

Thus there are compelling human aspects of the historical situation which he leaves out. Edward Grim, whose account of the
murder Eliot follows very closely for the most part, stood by Becket
to the last and had his arm nearly severed in his effort to ward off a
blow at the archbishop's head. This moving feature is omitted. It is
as if Eliot deliberately steers clear of all aspects of character and
event that might arouse a rush of sympathy for his protagonist and
bring home his full humanity. He continually takes the action

away from the personal, breaking up connections that are known and familiar, presenting us with a haunting phantasmagoria of multiple faces and voices which suggest forces both without and within.

Becket's isolation is emphasized. This isolation could be partly the isolation of the priest. It intensifies Becket's predicament, faced with a decision that involves his pastoral commission. There is a struggle to discern what is right action and what is merely an extension of his own will. Yet, as Katharine Worth points out, 'the isolated elements are meant to coalesce, Chorus and Saint to come together in the redemption of one by the death of the other'. However the Chorus are 'not involved in any human relationship with Becket real enough to move belief in his having power to affect their lives'.[54] Actors too have felt this a problem. Robert Speaight, who has played the part of Becket more than a thousand times, confesses that he has 'never felt near to him as a man. He remains a figure on a tapestry or an effigy on a tomb – imposing, important, intransigent, undoubtedly heroic, but not very intelligent and with not much to say to the modern world . . . '.[55]

It is again this removed quality that leads Helen Gardner to state that Becket's 'sanctity appears too near to spiritual self-culture' and 'there is more than a trace in the Archbishop of the "classic prig"'. 'There is a taint of professionalism about his sanctity; the note of complacency is always creeping into his self-conscious presentation of himself.'[56] Undeniably there is in Becket a capacity for self-absorption and self-dramatization, but this is precisely what Eliot is focusing upon as central to Becket's spiritual dilemma. Eliot's instinctive sense of what might have been a principal weakness of Becket cannot be dismissed for, as Robert Speaight acknowledges, 'There was a self-dramatizing side to his character – as the chroniclers record it for us – which might well have tempted him to do the right deed for the wrong reason.'[57] It was certainly a temptation known to Eliot.

The fact that Becket comes across as a dehumanized figure to a large extent, and that Eliot fails to establish a viable relationship between priest and people, so essential to his theme of Christian redemption, is probably due to a desire to remove the situation from himself. The poet, he believes, must preserve a necessary impersonality. He should go through a 'process of depersonalization.' For:

Poetry is not a turning loose of emotion, but an escape from emotion; it is not the expression of personality; but an escape from personality. But, of course, only those who have personality and emotions know what it means to want to escape from these things.[58]

The play unites both the public world of history and the theatre with the private world of the individual and the poet, the exterior world of physical action with the interior world of spiritual happening. It is precisely this capacity to suggest both dimensions simultaneously that Eliot sees as the distinctive feature of poetic drama:

It is possible that what distinguishes poetic drama from prosaic drama is a kind of doubleness in the action, as if it took place on two planes at once. In this it is different from allegory, in which the abstraction is something conceived, not something differently felt, and from symbolism (as in the plays of Maeterlinck) in which the tangible world is deliberately diminished – both symbolism and allegory being operations of the conscious planned mind. In poetic drama a certain apparent irrelevance may be the symptom of this doubleness; or the drama has an underpattern, less manifest than the theatrical one.[59]

Eliot was preoccupied with the poetic medium as a powerful force for suggesting that area of feeling and experience beyond the 'nameable, classifiable emotions and motives of our conscious life', a part of life which he felt prose drama was wholly inadequate to express. The proper aim of dramatic poetry, he says, 'is to go as far in this direction as it is possible to go, without losing that contact with the ordinary everyday world with which drama must come to terms'.[60]

It is thus not surprising that Eliot moved right out of the realist tradition, the mainstream of the theatre in the 1930s, with its concentration on the obvious exterior world. Eliot recognized the limitations of this tradition of narrow realism, asserting as early as 1922:

The realism of the ordinary stage is something to which we can no longer respond, because to us it is no longer realistic. We know that the gesture of daily existence is inadequate for the stage; instead of pretending that the stage gesture is a copy of reality, let us adopt a literal untruth, a thorough-going convention, a ritual. For the stage – not only in its remote origins, but always – is a ritual, and the failure of the contemporary stage to satisfy the craving for ritual is one of the reasons why it is not a living art.[61]

Eliot saw realistic drama as 'drama striving steadily to escape the conditions of art'.[62] He stressed the importance of form – harmonious design, musical rhythm, ritualistic action. It was partly the coherent simplicity and beauty of design, and the perception of an order in life it elicits, that Eliot so greatly admired in *Everyman*. Eliot has acknowledged that he kept in mind its versification while writing *Murder in the Cathedral*.[63] He saw *Everyman* as a model play and wanted English drama to go back to that drama of medieval ritual which deals with permanent elements of humanity and essential religious emotions. In *Everyman*, he says:

the religious and the dramatic are not merely combined, but wholly fused. Everyman is on the one hand the human soul in extremity, and on the other any man in any dangerous position from which we wonder how he is going to escape . . . [64]

In *Murder in the Cathedral* Eliot achieves the same poetic balance in form and fusion of the religious and the dramatic in theme.

He presents us with a central conflict – the individual against the world and the individual divided against himself. The play opens plunging us into an atmosphere of impending doom. Dramatic tension is created by the Chorus, the Women of Canterbury, a curiously one-sex congregation set in opposition to an all-male priestly caste who are quick to rebuke and restrain these women. Dimly perceptive of the Archbishop's return, the Chorus expresses strong foreboding. They are the common people who have suffered 'various oppression,' but left mostly to their own devices, prefer 'to pass unobserved' (Part 1, ll. 26–9). Camouflaged by the anonymity of their existence, they would rather avoid accountability of any great sort. Yet already they are being involved by something larger than themselves:

> Some presage of an act
> Which our eyes are compelled to witness, has

> forced our feet
> Toward the cathedral. We are forced to
> bear witness.

(Part 1, ll. 6–8)

The Christian theme of an inexorable will behind the scheme of things is introduced. An eternal design runs through the temporal and human action is subordinate to the divine:

> Destiny waits in the hand of God, not in the
>   hands of statesmen
> Who do, some well, some ill, planning and
>   guessing,
> Having their aims which turn in their hands in
>   the pattern of time.

(Part 1, ll. 44–6)

The idea of the wheel of time is foreshadowed here, with the suggestion of an all-controlling centrifugal force. Throughout the play runs the image of the universe, half-formed, in a state of becoming, groaning in travail. The New Year 'waits, breathes, waits, whispers in darkness'. 'Destiny waits in the hand of God, shaping the still unshapen.'

Waiting is a central theme in the play. The Chorus labours us with this sense of waiting in anguished expectancy: 'What shall we do in the heat of summer / But wait in barren orchards for another October?' The passage of time is emphasized:

> Seven years and the summer is over
> Seven years since the Archbishop left us.

These lines are repeated by the Priests on their entry. They have 'had enough of waiting from December to dismal December' (Part 1, ll. 38–48). Thomas himself waits in tense anticipation, foreseeing the nature of his death long before it actually occurs. In the waiting of all these characters is the same kind of deep apprehension of something alien and menacing that we are made to feel in *Sweeney Agonistes*, as Doris and Dusty wait in dread of the shrilling of the telephone or the knock upon the door in fear that it might be 'Pereira'.

The Chorus dread the Archbishop's return, but they are not a 'spiritless lot' who only 'regain some spiritual stature under the guidance of Thomas', as N. Coghill comments.[65] They have the keener intuitive sense of women and a capacity for spiritual insight – 'I have seen these things in a shaft of sunlight' – which make them aware that something cataclysmic is about to happen. The Second Priest reproves them for their 'craven apprehension' and dismisses them as 'foolish, immodest and babbling women'. Yet there is an element of extreme naivety about his response to the news of the Archbishop's return:

> The Archbishop shall be at our head,
>   dispelling dismay and doubt.
> He will tell us what we are to do, he will
>   give us our orders, instruct us.

> (Part 1, ll. 127–36)

His glib assurance is tempered by the utterance of the First Priest who fears for the Archbishop and the Church. He saw Becket

> as Chancellor, flattered by the king,
> Liked or feared by courtiers, in their
>   overbearing fashion,
> Despised and always despising, always isolated,
> Never one among them, always insecure;
> His pride always feeding upon his own virtues . . .

> (Part 1, ll. 114–22)

This is Becket in the days of his chancellorship, but it points to a capacity for cold, inhuman pride and detachment, and a solitariness that is self-serving. Before the archbishop's entry we are given this strong image of a man with an impulse towards self-absorption, a man able to turn in on himself, isolated partly by his own nature.

The Third Priest, who is the most spiritually percipient, is for allowing the pattern of events to take their course:

> For ill or good, let the wheel turn.
> For who knows the end of good or evil?
> Until the grinders cease
> And the doors shall be shut in the street,
> And all the daughters of music shall be
>   brought low.

(Part 1, ll. 137–43)

His words allude to a famous passage in Ecclesiastes which seems
to be an eschatological foreshadowing of the end of all time when
'God will bring every deed into judgement with every secret thing,
whether good or evil' (Ecclesiastes 12:14). Biblical phrases and
allusions are frequently included in the play and they lend a
ritualistic tone, suggesting a timeless dimension of being.

The Chorus continues to build up expectancy of a moment of
universal reckoning from which none can escape. They register the
'strain on the brain of the small folk' asked to bear witness to
reality in all its starkness. They are not without courage and
resilience for they have had their 'private terrors', their 'particular
shadows,' yet they have gone on 'living and partly living' in their
'humble and tarnished existence'. But this is a fear of a different
nature, 'a fear like birth and death, when we see birth and death
alone / In a void apart'. The inexorable cycle of earthly life, the
machine-like inevitability of the passage of time, is driven home in
their depiction of ordinary existence, and reinforced through the
relentless rhythm of the verse:

> One year is a year of rain,
> Another a year of dryness,
> One year the apples are abundant,
> Another year the plums are lacking.
> Yet we have gone on living,
> Living and partly living.

(Part 1, ll. 161–8)

Mind and spirit are partially anaesthetized by the rhythms of
day and night, work and rest, life and death, a pattern underlined
by the cycle of the seasons and the whole natural world. There is a

kind of dreadful automatism in existence, which is also expressed in *The Family Reunion*:

> In a thick smoke, many creatures moving
> Without direction, for no direction
> Leads anywhere but round and round in
>   that vapour –
> Without purpose, and without principle
>   of conduct
> In flickering intervals of light and
>   darkness . . .[66]

It is a terrible nightmare that is conveyed – the idea of history without spiritual direction. Life is a meaningless cycle of matter, a perpetually recurring pattern, with no fixed aim. Nothing leads anywhere but all goes round and round in a circle. Eliot was certainly subject to this nightmare, but it is also surely central to the modern mind – there is no God; all is chance; we are alone in the universe produced by chemical accident. The aeons of universal history and the natural world are inhuman, alien, rendering human action and suffering meaningless. The Women of Canterbury would rather not be brought up short to face the ultimate meaning of it all for 'human kind cannot bear very much reality'. They register powerfully the pain of consciousness and a condition of spiritual lostness which is central to the play:

> And our hearts are torn from us, our brains
>   unskinned like the layers of an onion,
>   our selves are lost lost
> In a final fear which none understands.

> (Part 1, ll. 188–9)

The superior stance of the Second Priest who chastises them for their cowardice is cut down by Becket who enters at this point:

> They speak better than they know, and beyond
>   your understanding.
> They know and do not know, what it is to act or
>   suffer,

> They know and do not know, that action is
>   suffering
> And suffering is action. Neither does the agent
>   suffer
> Nor the patient act. But both are fixed
> In an eternal action, an eternal patience
> To which all must consent that it may be willed
> And which all must suffer that they may will it,
> That the pattern may subsist, for the pattern is
>   the action
> And the suffering, that the wheel may
>   turn and still
> Be forever still.

(Part 1, ll. 107–17)

Becket's calm entrance and air of imperturbability contrasts sharply with the extreme agitation of the Chorus. The conflict for him, he thinks, has been transcended. This cryptic paradoxical pronouncement conveys the idea that he has arrived at some kind of revelation regarding the meaning of human action and suffering in time. Time and eternity are interrelated. A divine pattern underlies the temporal. The action and the suffering are fixed in 'an eternal patience to which all must consent that it may be willed'. To move in harmony with the divine will requires the surrender of the human will, which is both an active and passive state of being, a total attitude of living receptively, of living a Passion.

And yet Becket appears very much more director than directed. He is always a little above the action, and prepares the audience for it almost like an omniscient narrator:

> For a little time the hungry hawk
> Will only soar and hover, circling lower,
> Waiting excuse, pretence, opportunity.
> End will be simple, sudden, God-given.
> Meanwhile the substance of our first act
> Will be shadows, and the strife with shadows.
> Heavier the interval than the consummation.
> All things prepare the event. Watch.

(Part 1, ll. 247–54)

Through the theatrical imagery the audience is made conscious of performance and kept a little detached. These words coming from Becket in relation to his own situation may reflect a certain prescience, but also a certain consciousness of role and capacity for self-dramatization. In the Brechtian mode Eliot has Becket unfolding his own history and commenting on it from time to time.

The 'strife with shadows' suggests an internal struggle which Becket's confrontation with the Tempters can be seen to represent. Browne in his productions tended to interpret them 'as exteriorizations of Becket's inner conflicts, past or present'.[67] But there are sufficient touches to allow us to see them as representing external forces as well. The doubling of their parts with the four Knights, as is most often done in production, adds to their protean character. They are highly individual, clear-cut cameo sketches in themselves. And there are other echoes of history in the imitation of medieval and earlier verse styles. The First Tempter bows himself in glibly:

> You see, my Lord, I do not wait upon ceremony:
> Here I have come, forgetting all acrimony,
> Hoping that your present gravity
> Will find excuse for my humble levity
> Remembering all the good times past.

> (Part 1, ll. 255–9)

He tries to fill Becket with nostalgia, to convince him that bitterness can be overcome and friendship recovered along with all the worldly pleasures of the past. Becket dismisses this with some contempt: 'You talk of seasons that are past. I remember / Not worth forgetting.' The Tempter changes his tone, slipping into a modern colloquial idiom which suits his assumption of a conspiratorial air of easy familiarity:

> My Lord, a nod is as good as a wink
> A man will often love what he spurns.
> For the good times past, that are come again
> I am your man.

> (Part 1, ll. 291–4)

When Becket reads his meaning instantly and parries him in the same manner, the Tempter allows an ugly, hostile note to intrude:

> Be easy, man!
> The easy man lives to eat the best dinners.
> Take a friend's advice. Leave well alone,
> Or your goose may be cooked and eaten to the
>   bone.

> (Part 1, ll, 303–6)

Eliot very effectively uses startling changes of rhythm and speech-style to break up moods or step up tension, and to connect past and present. There is often considerable cut and thrust in the exchanges between Becket and the Tempters, the pushing of punchy statements, questions and answers, back and forth:

> Second Tempter: Power is present, for him who
>   will wield it.
> Thomas: Who shall have it?
> Second Tempter: He who will come.
> Thomas: What shall be the month?
> Second Tempter: The last from the first

> (Part 1, ll. 361–4)

The precise meaning of this sort of dialogue is not so important as the underlying feeling – the sense of inner turmoil and of a tenacious struggle between intractable forces that can only be ended by the capitulation or annihilation of one of them. Eliot's use of pace and tone in language to express strain, hostility and aggression brings to mind Pinter's use of words as a weapon in *The Birthday Party* when Stanley is broken down.

The element of pride constantly evident in Becket's replies to the first three Tempters reminds one of his extraordinary achievements during those seven years at Henry's court, and points to the multiple sides to a single personality of no common mould. It is to the Becket of the past that these three Tempters appeal, to old friendships, values and ambitions. The Fourth Tempter is unexpected because it is to the Becket of the present that he appeals, the Becket who has surrendered his life to the Church and begun to show signs of possible sainthood. His temptation is to a loftier ambition for 'what is pleasure, kingly rule' to 'general grasp of spiritual power?' (Part 1, ll. 504–7) Becket's confrontation with the Fourth Tempter brings strongly to mind the temptation of Marlowe's Dr Faustus seduced by his own fantasies of power and glory. Both protagonists are extremely self-conscious individuals, split by conflicting impulses and endowed with an extraordinary sense of the dramatic. There is the same luxuriant spinning out of a consuming vision. The situations are in reverse though, for while Faustus dreams of unlimited power exercised for a limited time on earth, Becket dreams of an enduring power held from beyond the grave. At the heart of both *Doctor Faustus* and *Murder in the Cathedral* is a tremendous spiritual struggle.

Eliot could well have been influenced by Marlowe's play when he wrote *Murder in the Cathedral*. He showed a recurrent interest in Christopher Marlowe during these years. From 1919 to 1934 he wrote on Elizabethan dramatists and considered them also in performance for in the 1920's he attended the Phoenix Society presentation of Elizabethan, Renaissance and Restoration plays, referring to it in *The Criterion* as 'a wholly commendable enterprise'.[68] In 1927 he reviewed Una Ellis Fermor's book on Christopher Marlowe and found it particularly good on *Doctor Faustus*.[69]

Eliot had a high regard for Marlowe both as a poet and a dramatist. In an article on Marlowe in 1919, he comments on Marlowe's breaking up of the line to gain intensity in the last soliloquy in *Doctor Faustus*, and of his development of 'a new and important conversational tone in the dialogue of Faustus and the devil'.[70] Eliot employs the same conversational tone in Becket's confrontation with the Tempters. There is furthermore a distinct verbal echo in Faustus being urged by his good and bad angels – 'Sweet Faustus, think of heaven and heavenly things' 'No, Faustus, think of honour and of wealth' (Sc. V, ll. 21–20) – and Becket being exhorted by the Fourth Tempter:

> But think, Thomas, think of glory after death
>
> . . .
>
> Think, Thomas, think of enemies dismayed,
> Creeping in penance, frightened of a shade;
> Think of pilgrims, standing in line
> Before the glittering jewelled shrine,
> From generation to generation

> Bending the knee in supplication,
> Think of miracles, by God's grace
> And think of your enemies, in another place.

(Part 1, ll. 528–40)

Like Shaw, Eliot gives a forward perspective to the situation, referring to known future events. The canvas is widened immeasurably. Becket is seen not merely at the centre of his own stage in history, but against the much larger backdrop of universal history. The Fourth Tempter tells Becket 'that nothing lasts, but the wheel turns', that 'the shrine shall be pillaged, and the gold spent / the jewels gone for light ladies' ornament'. And a time will come

> When miracles cease, and the faithful desert you,
> And men shall only do their best to forget you.
> And later is worse, when men will not hate you
> Enough to defame or to execrate you,
> But pondering the qualities that you lacked
> Will only try to find the historical fact.
> When men shall declare that there was no mystery
> About this man who played a certain part in
>   history.

(Part 1, ll. 547–60)

This immediately involves the spectators because the action on the stage is seen spilling over into a continuum of events which ultimately links up with their own age. Eliot very effectively short-circuits any attempt on the audience's part to evade coming to terms with the situation presented through the sense of its remoteness in time. It is also not allowed to rest secure in a complacency that might spring from a knowledge of modern sophisticated interpretations of the event. For he satirizes the tendency of some contemporary historical assessors to reduce the extraordinary to comprehensible mediocrity through their shallow academic treatment of motive and character, when each human being has unfathomable depths and is an irreducible mystery in himself.

For Becket, the Fourth Tempter stressing the ultimate insignificance of his achievement in time, the idea that 'nothing lasts, but the wheel turns', is the temptation to see it all negated and passing into oblivion. It drives home the sense of time bringing to an end the individual life and generations of individual lives. It is the inhuman time of universal history and the objective natural world, without the Christian framework of belief which attributes to it spiritual direction and meaning. It is thus alien and diminishing, rendering human action and suffering meaningless. The audience is also tempted to see Becket's stand as ultimately insignificant. To Becket, faced with the exigencies of the immediate situation, the issues might seem vital, the room for manoeuvre so small, but to the audience, with their knowledge of the larger movement of events in history, the individual and the issues appear greatly reduced.

Still more terrifying for Becket is the thought that he may be deliberately courting martyrdom for personal glory. This leads to anguished self-questioning: 'Is there no way, in my soul's sickness / Does not lead to damnation in pride?' 'Can I neither act nor suffer / Without perdition?' This is met with the ironical addressing of his own former pronouncement back to him by the Fourth Tempter:

> You know and do not know, what it is to act or
>   suffer.
> You know and do not know, that action is
>   suffering,
> And suffering action. Neither does the agent
>   suffer
> Nor the patient act. But both are fixed
> In an eternal action, an eternal patience
> To which all must consent that it may be willed
> And which all must suffer that they may will it,
> That the pattern may subsist, that the wheel may
>   turn and still
> Be forever still.

> (Part 1, ll. 591–9)

The words now come across with a new edge of meaning, accompanying the realization that one can be moving in apparent harmony with the eternal design, yet evil can be deeply imbedded in the seeds of motivation. Each person, of his own nature, is a

magnetic field that can distort reality to suit its own pattern. Where
lies certainty?

The temptation to despair is very great. Becket falls silent as the
struggle rages within him. The Chorus breaks into a lament,
expressing extreme horror and repugnance: 'What is the sickly
smell, the vapour? the dark green light from a cloud on a withered
tree? The earth is heaving to parturition of issue of hell. What is the
sticky dew that forms on the back of my hand?' The Priests and
Tempters join in what can be described as a symphony of despair.
'Man's life is a cheat and a disappointment / All things are unreal /
Unreal or disappointing.' Man passes from 'unreality to unreality,'
from 'deception to deception.' Becket is menaced on all sides, as
these three groups of nameless faces and voices assail him alter-
nately like phantasms in some awful nightmare.

The experience of being divided by self-confounding doubts and
fears is powerfully conveyed and this is built to a crescendo by the
Chorus's mounting hysteria: 'We have not been too happy, my
Lord, we have not been too happy / We are not ignorant women,
we know what we must expect and not expect.' 'We know of
extortion and violence / Destitution, disease. . . . We have seen the
young man mutilated / The torn girl trembling by the mill-stream.'

> . . . but now a new terror has soiled us,
>   which none can avert, none can avoid,
>   flowing under our feet and over the sky . . .
>   flowing in at the ear and the mouth and the
>   eye.
> God is leaving us, God is leaving us, more pang,
>   more pain than birth or death.
> Sweet and cloying through the dark air
> Falls the stifling scent of despair;
>   . . .
> O Thomas Archbishop, save us, save us,
>   save yourself that we may be saved;
> Destroy yourself and we are destroyed.

(Part 1, ll. 654–64)

The Chorus of Women appear oppressive haunting creatures
here – clinging, parasitic. The sexual imagery in the verse, the

nightmarish sense impressions work together to involve us in the experience of something monstrous and unnatural, some hidden unspeakable terror. Becket struggles to retain self-possession in the throes of an emotion that makes him queasy. He turns away from all this nausea to find refuge in a male priestly role which frees him from the emotional complexity of his own make-up. He becomes simply the man who expects to be killed and is killed:

> Now is my way clear, now is my meaning plain:
> Temptation shall not come in this kind again.
> The last temptation is the greatest treason:
> To do the right deed for the wrong reason.
> . . .
>   I know
> What yet remains to show you of my history
> Will seem to most of you at best futility,
> Senseless self-slaughter of a lunatic,
> Arrogant passion of a fanatic.
> I know that history at all times draws
> The strangest consequence from remotest cause.

(Part 1, ll. 694–700)

Becket arrives at some kind of release and liberation, but we get the distinct impression that he has not come through the conflict so much as evaded it. He finds relief in the part he seems destined to play in history.

In Martin Browne's production the temptation scene was played in private. Browne found the presence of the other characters a limitation and thought of ways to get them off the stage. Terry Hands, however, effectively exploited the fact of their presence in his production:

> The temptation scene was, unusually, played in public, with the tempters emerging from the crowd and slipping back into it while Becket stood apart as the priests robed him, turning him from a vulnerable figure in a hair shirt into the Archbishop who had finally escaped from the horror of his own multiplicity. When the Fourth Tempter, who had been sitting with his back to the audience throughout the robing scene, turned round to

reveal a mirror image of the Becket in the hair shirt, it was as if in abandoning this twin, Becket had committed a kind of self-murder.[71]

Becket in the production is robed in the Brechtian way. In the director's mind it was obviously appropriate to think of Brecht's *Galileo* where the Pope is a humane person, but, as he is robed, takes on his office and becomes dehumanized. Similarly Becket is shown subjugating self to office in the process of being robed. He takes refuge in the role, escaping the torments of a divided self.

This interpretation is not forced because Becket is shown extremely conscious of role throughout the play. There is always about him a certain attitudinizing; he is forever above the action, never quite caught up in it. This is also a theme that recurs in Eliot's plays. Characters in *The Family Reunion* feel 'embarrassed, impatient, fretful, ill at ease', like 'amateur actors in a dream', forced 'to play an unread part in some monstrous farce, ridiculous in some nightmare pantomine' (Part 1, Sc. 1, p. 22). The protagonist in Eliot's last play, *The Elder Statesman*, describes the lifelong attempt to escape a personal dilemma by seeking refuge in role:

> Has there been nothing in your life . . .
> Which you wish to forget? Which you wish
>   to keep unknown? . . .
> I've spent my life in trying to forget myself,
> In trying to identify myself with the part
> I had chosen to play.[72]

Murder in the Cathedral portrays the individual's struggle to cope with a hidden unbearable reality. The play is immensely inward, but Eliot retains balance and control by continually pointing outwards to history and current circumstance.

By continually making us conscious of history, Elliot distances the action to some degree, involving us on a rational plane. The audience is kept alert and functioning on two levels of experience. Through the figure of Becket, intellectualizing his dilemma, we function on the level of conscious thought; but the Chorus draws us in to apprehend the experience on an emotional plane. The Chorus presents the grim underside of the conflict, the inner tumult that springs from deep wells of human need that can never be totally fathomed. No matter how rational man is, the unconscious finds ways in which to manifest itself, exposing his points of greatest vulnerability. Paradoxically, although Eliot uses a form that is highly balanced and controlled, throughout the play there is the sense of something untrammelled, uninhibited, orgiastic and threatening breaking out, something raw and elemental that will go its own way despite man's attempt to rationalize and control it. Becket must strive towards disinterested right action, but he cannot trust himself. The first part of the play ends with him once more surrendering the situation to God:

> I shall no longer act or suffer, to the swords'
>   end.
> Now my good Angel, whom God appoints
> To be my guardian, hover over the swords' points.
>
> (Part 1, ll. 705–7)

The Interlude is the moment of calm before the storm. Becket preaches to his people on Christmas morning and the sermon is spoken in simple direct prose which reflects a calm acceptance of mind and spirit.

Part Two begins with the Chorus sweeping the audience back into disquiet:

> Does the bird sing in the South?
> Only the sea-bird cries, driven inland
>   by the storm,
> What sign of the spring of the year?
> Only the death of the old: not a stir, not a
>   shoot, not a breath.
>   . . .
> Between Christmas and Easter what work shall be
>   done?
> The ploughman shall go out in March and turn the
>   same earth
> He has turned before, the bird shall sing the
>   same song.
>
> (Part 1, ll. 1–20)

The cycle of the Christian year and the cycle of the natural year parallel the action. Both reflect the paradox of death and rebirth. One is continually set against the other, for, if only the sense of the controlling rhythms of nature predominates, we are faced with Sweeney's question again: 'Is it all birth, death, copulation.' The cycle of the Christian year is a cycle of momentous spiritual events, to make them present again in the minds of the people, so that they can see their lives bound up with this significance.

The play gains great ritual power through its associations with Christian liturgy which bring the centuries together, underlining the universal significance of the action through the sense of traditional worship. The dramatic force of the play is also much enhanced by the exploitation of overtly theatrical effects. For example, the entry of the three Priests, one after the other, with the appropriate banner of the feast-day each represents, signals the passage of the three days after Christmas. Their appearances are punctuated by the introits of the respective saints and each chants highly emotive lines, interwoven with phrases from scripture:

> Since St. John the Apostle a day: and the day of
> the Holy Innocents.
> *Out of the mouth of very babes, O God.*
> As the voice of many waters, of thunder, of
> harps,
> They sang as it were a new song.
> The blood of thy saints have they shed like
> water,
> And there was no man to bury them.

(Part 2, ll. 41–8)

An atmosphere of profound mystery and foreboding is created. The hypnotic quality of the incantation with its scriptural reverberations must penetrate deep feelings rooted in the religious life of the audience. The Priests point to the possibility each day holds for the moment of timeless significance:

> The critical moment
> That is always now, and here. Even now,
> in sordid particulars

The eternal design may appear.

(Part 2, ll. 60–2)

The four Knights enter and the banners disappear. The dramatic point is made with fine economy, aural, visual and ritual elements combining to provide maximum dramatic impact.

The bestiality of the Knights comes over in their confrontation of Becket. They refer to him as 'the backstairs brat who was born in Cheapside' and their tone is insolent and provocative. The virulence of their verbal attack is often underscored by half-lines or phrases picked up and bandied around, which reinforces the impression of the crude taunting and bullying of a victim before the assault:

Second Knight: Won't you ask us to pray to God
for you, in your need?
Third Knight: Yes, we'll pray for you!
First Knight: Yes, we'll pray for you!
Three Knights: Yes, we'll pray that God may help
you!

(Part 2, ll. 114–7)

After rebuking them, Becket leaves, and the Knights also depart, to return with swords. The Chorus breaks into an outpouring of terror which extends the significance of the action as well as suggests deep psychological disturbance:

I have smelt them, the death-bringers,
senses are quickened
By subtile forebodings; I have heard
Fluting in the night-time, fluting and owls,
have seen at noon
Scaly wings slanting over, huge and ridiculous.
I have tasted
The savour of putrid flesh in the spoon.
I have felt
The heaving of earth at nightfall,
restless, absurd . . .
. . .

> I have seen
> Rings of light coiling downwards,
>   descending
> To the horror of the ape.

(Part 2, ll. 205–2)

There is a peculiar fixation on the rot and decay of organic life and an obsession with oppressive evolutionary images. Identification is expressed with animal existence at the lowest level:

> I have tasted / The living lobster, the crab, the oyster, the whelk and the prawn; and they live and spawn in my bowels . . . I have lain on the floor of the sea and breathed with the breathing of the sea-anemone, swallowed with the ingurgitation of the sponge.

(Part 2, ll. 213–6)

These are the sensations of a personality experiencing deep fragmentation. A modern psychoanalyst talks of the 'rock-bottom attitude' of patients and, where so-called schizophrenic processes have taken over, this attitude, he says, is:

> expressed in strange evolutionary imagery. Total feeling becomes dehumanized, and eventually demammalized. These patients can feel like a crab or a shellfish or mollusc, or even abandon what life and movement there is on the lowest animal level and become a lonely twisted tree on the ledge of a stormy rock, or the rock, of just the ledge out in nowhere.[73]

This was an ordeal that Eliot must have experienced as part of his own personal neurosis, and he uses it here to express spiritual chaos and inward fracture, physical corruption and revulsion. We are made to feel the whole drag of the corporeal world and the deep-seated conviction of sin and contamination. A sense of universal degradation is conveyed. Everything is infiltrated and tainted. There is 'death in the rose, death in the hollyhock'. The deep inscrutable mystery of evil is felt through its imaging in the impersonal objective world of nature and in man's unconscious biological life with its heritage of imperfectly tamed instincts and appetites. It is all interlinked and interpenetrating with man's social life:

> What is woven in the councils of princes
> Is woven also in our veins, our brains,
> Is woven like a pattern of living worms
> In the guts of the women of Canterbury.

> (Part 2, ll. 229–302)

Becket's predicament is constantly set against a larger backdrop. Becket is man apart, contemplating himself and his situation. But in the choric odes the vision continually widens, to set this against the whole of creation, the human and sub-human strata of which man is a part. Becket presents history on one plane – the individual, the drama of personality, the world of social relations. The Chorus presents the substructure – the female, the unconscious, the world of nature and animality, the illimitable waste. Through the choric odes we apprehend imaginatively how deeply man himself is rooted in earthiness, despite Becket's intellectualizing of his predicament. In Becket we see highly conscious man and his choice of self-awareness, but against this we see the vast other side of the picture – man as part of the ecology in whose balance we are partly animals, because nature and history are not separable in the last resort.

The Chorus acknowledge their part in the guilt and the horror, expressing it in violent sexual terms:

> I have consented, Lord Archbishop, have
> consented.
> Am torn away, subdued, violated,
> United to the spiritual flesh of nature,
> Mastered by the animal powers of the spirit,
> Dominated by the lust of self-demolition,
> By the final utter uttermost death of the spirit,
> By the final ecstasy of waste and shame . . .

> (Part 2, ll. 237–44)

There is an echo from Shakespeare here – 'the expense of spirit in a waste of shame is lust in action'. It is significant that the idea of sin and guilt in *Murder in the Cathedral* is continually related to sex, and here it is conveyed overpoweringly through the sexual hysteria of the Women of Canterbury.

Becket, who re-enters now, tries to comfort them:

> This is one moment,
> But know that another
> Shall pierce you with a sudden painful joy
> When the figure of God's purpose is made
>   complete.

> > > (Part 2, ll. 248–51)

Sexual and religious experience are closely related in the play and these lines bring to mind, Christ being pierced on the cross, a physical death which signifies spiritual life. The play is built on paradoxes like this, where joy and sorrow, the physical and the spiritual, the temporal and the eternal, interpenetrate and find unity in the meaning of the Incarnation.

The atmosphere is further charged when the Knights re-enter the Cathedral, slightly tipsy, bent on violence. The mood they bring of a rowdy drunken brawl accentuates the peculiar horror of the violation of priest and sanctuary. Jazz rhythms in their speech are profoundly disquieting, suggesting dark primitive forces – menacing, compulsive, seeking outlet:

> Where is Becket, the traitor to the King?
> Where is Becket, the meddling priest?
> Come down Daniel to the lion's den,
> Come down Daniel for the mark of the beast.

> > > (Part 2, ll. 353–6)

Becket comes forward fearlessly: 'It is the just man who / Like a bold lion, should be without fear / I am here.'

The killing can be done ritualistically, as the slaughter of an unresisting sacrificial victim, in keeping with the theme and mood of the play. In the first production the action was slowly mimed, 'to reproduce the gestures and attitudes of the Knights as these are

represented in the medieval iconography of St. Thomas'. Robert
Speaight felt that there was a hint of affectation in this and the shock
of sacrilege was absent. In a production directed by Robert Help-
mann for the International Festival of Arts in Adelaide the Knights
converged on Becket with a bestial roar, their swords upraised,
and a pair of heavy circular doors before the altar closed in upon
them. 'An effect of sudden violence was thus secured without any
untidy realism.' [74] In Terry Hands's production the Knights were
'extremely sinister figures in black plastic and inhuman mask-like
visors'. Events took on:

> a dream-like, surrealist quality: the Knights cast monstrous black
> shadows, a white cloth came down like a pillar of cloud when
> the murder was done: red cloths were draped over the body and
> then later spread over the stage in the form of a cross, to balance
> the great wooden cross they all knelt to at the end.[75]

The murder is the climax the play has been building up to, a
moment of almost orgiastic release. The Chorus erupts ecstatically:

> Clear the air! clean the sky! wash the wind! take the stone from
> the stone, take the skin from the arm, take the muscle from the
> bone, and wash them. Wash the stone, wash the bone, wash the
> brain, wash the soul, wash them wash them!
>
> (Part 2, l. 422)

Their sorrow is expressed in haunting surrealistic images: 'A rain
of blood has blinded my eyes . . . I wander in a land of barren
boughs: if I break them, they bleed; I wander in a land of dry
stones: if I touch them they bleed' (Part 2, ll. 399–400). Continually
there is the sense of the plumbing of an inner dark of unbearable
loneliness and grief. The almost perpetual anguish of the Chorus is
its chief expression.

At this emotional summit the Knights, having completed the
murder, advance suddenly to the front of the stage and address
the audience in modern colloquial terms, turning the stage into a
public forum. Eliot intended by this 'to shock the audience out of
their complacency'.[76] There have been critics and audiences who
have found this scene a marring excrescence. Raymond Williams,
for instance, describes it as 'essentially sentimental'.[77] But it is
clearly integral to the play's form and purpose. It brings the action

firmly out of the realm of the interior, back into the external plane of history and contemporary events. D. E. Jones is also surely right in saying that it is the 'tempting of the audience corresponding to the temptation of Thomas'.[78]

The Knights step out of the twelfth century, as Becket has continually done though in a less startling fashion, and strive to win the spectators' support for their action. They project themselves as fair-minded pragmatic Englishmen with no talent for sophistry, men of action rather than of words, who have been perfectly disinterested and merely sought their country's best interest. They appeal to similar qualities in the audience, certain that they are a 'hard-headed sensible people' not to be taken in by 'emotional claptrap'. Putting forward views which may sound highly tenable to a modern audience, they refer to Henry's commendable desire for legal reform and for an ideal state through the union of spiritual and temporal administration under a central government. They attempt to engage the audience in a sense of complicity through reference to subsequent historical developments, pointing to the present where there is a 'just subordination of the Church to the welfare of the State,' due to their first step:

> We have been instrumental in bringing about the state of affairs that you approve. We have served your interest; we merit your applause; and if there is any guilt whatever in the matter, you must share it with us.
>
> (Part 2, ll. 530–4)

A modern audience with its belief in the equality of all under the law might find itself in agreement. The view that Becket shared this vision of Henry's, but, on attaining the office of Primate of all England, became a 'monster of egotism', would find sympathy with some modern historians. Many spectators have been won over by these arguments, but the brute fact of the murder lies before us, and there is the voice of political expediency in the Knights' professions with its sinister undertones of totalitarianism. And whatever the rights and wrongs of Becket's claim for the Church, the one issue on which he would have modern sentiment behind him is his refusal to yield to an overmastering central power. This is what emerged most strongly in the 1972 production of the play by the Royal Shakespeare Company. Reviewing it, Martin Esslin found the play fully vindicated' even to a generation that had not 'the slightest interest in whether the Church should be subordinated to the State or not'. What came across was 'the determination of an individual who refuses to submit to the power of the State and to the violence with which this power imposes itself on the individual'.[79]

This scene gives the play a contemporary edge and flavour. Before they leave the stage, the Knights dismiss the audience: '. . . now disperse quietly to your homes. Please be careful not to loiter in groups at street corners, and do nothing that might provoke any public outbreak'. The attention of the audience is then allowed to return to the dark church and the silent motionless form. A sense of desolation is expressed by the First Priest:

> The Church lies bereft,
> Alone, desecrated, desolated, and the heathen
> shall build on the ruins,
> Their world without God. I see it. I see it.

> (Part 2, ll. 587–9)

The Third Priest refutes this, asserting that 'the Church is stronger for this action,' 'supreme as long as men will die for it'. This leads to an ode of praise to God by the Chorus, while a *Te Deum* is sung by a choir in the distance. God's glory is displayed in 'all creatures of the earth', 'both the hunters and the hunted', for all things exist only 'in Thy light and Thy glory is declared even in that which denies Thee; the darkness declares the glory of light'. God is thanked for His redemption by blood, for 'wherever a saint has dwelt, wherever a martyr has given his blood', there lies holy ground, and 'from such ground springs that which forever renews the earth / Though it is forever denied'. The play ends with an acknowledgement of sin and a plea for forgiveness.

We have been brought with Becket from conflict to recognition, and from recognition to release and renewal. The stages of this cycle of guilt, remorse and expiation are essential movements in a purgatorial journey, an expression of Eliot's concept of the progress of sin described in the *The Family Reunion*:

> It is possible that sin may strain and struggle
> In its dark instinctive birth to come to
>   consciousness

And so find expurgation.

From the fantasies of the ego and the darkness of the will, the individual seeks release and reconciliation. History, for Eliot, is a story in which Providence is resisted by human aberration. The special role of the saint or martyr is to bring men back to God's way. This has to be done every so often, or the lure of self-sufficiency, resignation or despair proves too great. The inexorable movement of time threatens to negate the value of the individual life of significant action, and the collective tradition of significant lives. But we are brought to a point where we can look beyond that negation. Through time and beyond time runs the creative and saving design of God. This is the purpose of history, constantly active, forever achieving itself. The present itself is capable of timeless value, and the saint's role in history is to relate time and eternity

> That the pattern may subsist, for the pattern
> is the action
> And the suffering, that the wheel may turn
> and still
> Be forever still.

Through the actualities of a case in history, Eliot realises his vision of martyrdom, dramatising the significance of such an event for humanity. The play presents us with the questions of human life and destiny that men are faced with when history becomes catastrophic. The audience is drawn in to grapple with these on a mental and emotional plane, and is carried through to a state of reconciliation by a vision of history which embraces the catastrophe and transcends the immediate spectacle of tragedy.

The play is constructed around the Christian theme of sin and redemption; however, Eliot does not really communicate the experience of spiritual reconciliation and renewal in *Murder in the Cathedral*. This assurance, for Eliot, lies some way off. There is more of nightmare in the play. A horror of void, of the abyss, predominates. Through a profoundly disturbing under-pattern, feelings of intense anguish, isolation, and disorientation are registered. The play dramatizes a condition of acute self-division and self-consciousness, a state of alienation and withdrawal from women and the world, which must have accorded with Eliot's own feelings at the time. Ultimately one's interpretation of the human drama is conditioned by one's most private experience of life and stands merely as an extension of it. But Eliot is in no way unmindful of history, as is evident from his careful integration of interior experience with external historical detail. Thus his achievement emerges as a peculiarly fine and subtle balance between inner and outer reality.

5

Three Plays of the 1960s: Robert Bolt, *A Man for All Seasons*; Peter Shaffer, *The Royal Hunt of the Sun*; John Osborne, *Luther*

The three plays dealt with in this chapter – Robert Bolt's *A Man for All Seasons*, Peter Shaffer's *The Royal Hunt of the Sun* and John Osborne's *Luther* illustrate different concerns and different levels of imagination in approaching history. Bolt and Shaffer can be seen going to history merely for a source. They provide examples of two popular treatments of history. In Thomas More, Bolt finds a protagonist of compelling stature around whom to build a play that is essentially a character study. Shaffer, on the other hand, is attracted to the historical phenomenon of the mysterious Inca world with its sun king conquered by rapacious Spanish conquistadors, because of the opportunities it affords for romance, sensation and exotic spectacle. History is used in a rather shallow way for, having found a source conducive to their purpose, these two dramatists do not go much further. They figure in sharp contrast to playwrights like Shaw, T. S. Eliot and Edward Bond, who are highly conscious of the far-reaching implications of their subjects, and register a sense of both the deep undercurrents and broad sweep of events in history.

Yet there are elements that make both these plays interesting and worthy of attention. There is the moving quality of the character portrait in *A Man for All Seasons*.[1] Bolt presents us with a man of sympathy, integrity and deep convictions who stands for the possibility of being real in an inhuman environment. However for all More's idealism there is an extremely practical side to his nature, and there are points of lively interchange in the play, as he strives to evade disaster by every legal trick his subtle mind can employ. Bolt conveys with effect the swift build-up of events which strip More of every legal safeguard and bring him to a point of ultimate commitment.

What is compelling about Shaffer's *The Royal Hunt of the Sun* is the dazzling visual spectacle, the ability to create atmosphere and generate excitement in the theatre through bold physical action. The audience's introduction to the Inca world is a wonderful moment. As one reviewer of the original production describes it:

> The stage bursts into glorious life when the Spaniards finally reach the Inca capital, and a huge golden motif backstage suddenly opens out, petal by petal, like a great sunflower, to reveal the immobile form of Atahuallpa, the Inca Sun King, a scintillating figure in white and gold.[2]

Another riveting theatrical happening is the much-awaited meeting between the Spaniards and the Inca royal court. The audience is hit by an explosion of sound and colour as the Peruvian Indians make their majestic ceremonial entry. The stage cascades with exotic costumes and fantastic head-dresses, ablaze with vibrant colours. This is accompanied by pulsating drum beats and strange plaintive music from reed pipes, cymbals and giant maraccas. The music builds to a violent crescendo as the Spaniards sound the call for battle and the Indians scatter in hysterical confusion. Wave upon wave, they are cut down by the relentless Spanish troops and a gigantic bloodstained cloth finally billows out over the stage to signify a great massacre (Act 1, pp. 36–9).[3]

In striking contrast to these two plays which illustrate the putting over of history in a popular way, John Osborne's *Luther*, a play of much greater force and weight, provides an irreverent controversial treatment of a famous historical figure. Luther is presented in anything but noble, edifying or exotic, romantic terms. The play is audacious and challenging. Fraught with tension and anxiety, Osborne's anarchical, obsessive Luther is physically and spiritually racked by a daemon of truth and doubt. The physical and spiritual crises he experiences are shown to be inextricably linked. His anguished struggle for spiritual truth relates directly to the physical torment to which he is subjected by violent fits and chronic constipation. The climax of an attack is often the moment of spiritual doubt or revelation. Thus Luther's first outburst of protest occurs during a religious service when he is hurled to the ground by gagging convulsions and strangled words are forced out by him: 'Not! Me! I am *not!*' (Act 1, Sc. 1, p. 23).[4]

This intensely private interior conflict is placed against a wide backdrop – the social religious world Luther helped to overturn. Osborne draws in broad sweeping lines here. Historical characters like Tetzel, the notorious hawker of indulgences, and Pope Leo X are lively caricatures. The scatological invective indulged in by both sides, is balanced by arguments of considerable weight, marshalled in support of individualism and the private conscience on the one hand, and catholicism and the unity of the Church on the other. The play focuses on the individual of remarkable stature who is both prime mover and victim of social and religious forces. It is a forceful rhetorical piece moving towards expressionism and a more poetic and violent form of theatre.

All three plays dealt with in this chapter reveal a distinct preoccupation with the question of selfhood and identity. In a sense a person's view, irrespective of its rights or wrongs, is the person himself, his claim on existence, the fact that he *is*. Luther in Osborne's play is driven to the point where he is impelled to cry, 'Here I stand; God help me; I can do no more' (Act 3, Sc. 1, p. 85). The Inca king, Atahuallpa, when he accuses the Spanish commander, Pizarro, of having no word to pledge, stands for selfhood in the same way. For Bolt too, Thomas More became 'a man with an adamantine sense of his own self. He knew where he began and left off, what area of himself he could yield to the encroachments of his enemies, and what to the encroachments of those he loved'.[5]

The predicament of the individual within the context of a complex society, is how to give meaning to his existence, with his overwhelming sense of the severely limited area for exercise of will, conscience, reason and identity. Thomas More is blessed with a feeling of wholeness of being which contributes to a positive self-concept. What is focused in the play is the conflict that arises when a world of violence and unrest is set against him. Pizarro and Luther possess no such self-assurance. In them is projected the human personality rent by schism. Shaffer and Osborne both show a distinct interest in the psychological domain, the pivotal role of childhood in the transfer of positive or negative emotions, and the way in which adverse childhood experience can breed deep guilt and mistrust towards the universe. Shaffer's perception, however, is much more limited than Osborne's, and his imaginative treatment of this dimension is crude and superficial in comparison. Osborne registers in a deep way the profound human agitation resulting from the sense of fracture within. Shaw's influence can be seen in all three plays in that their characters are psychologically out of their own age, and a twentieth-century consciousness is openly brought to bear.

All three playwrights reveal a common interest, in their various ways, in religious motivation. It is religious experience, not history, that predominantly engrosses them. This certainly separates them from Brecht, in whose terms critics usually consider them. Yet, unlike Brecht, they subordinate social and political issues to historical personalities whose private religious needs are of central dramatic interest. They also differ from T. S. Eliot in that they do not work from a basis of religious belief and are unable to profess faith in an 'intelligible heaven', to use Sartre's phrase. They suffer from the characteristic dilemma of numerous twentieth-century writers whose works, as H. F. Smith observes, reflect a metaphysical awareness, but an awareness which 'is no longer sustained by positive faith or intellectual conviction, so that it survives only as a *feeling*, something which can be undeniably sensed, but no longer confidently affirmed'.[6] Bolt and Shaffer, however, are unable to provide more than a surface impression of spiritual unrest, while Osborne, a playwright of much greater calibre, is able to convey deep undercurrents of existential anxiety and disquiet. A collective neurosis is expressed in Luther's anguish at the weight of a metaphysical loneliness: 'I am alone. I am alone, and against myself. . . . How can I justify myself? . . . How can I be justified?' (Act 1, Sc. 1, p. 20).

Of these three playwrights, Bolt, who graduated from Manchester University with a degree in history, has shown a recurrent interest in historical subjects. In 1962 he wrote the screenplay for *Lawrence of Arabia*. *Vivat! Vivat Regina!* (1970) focuses on the conflict between Elizabeth I and Mary, Queen of Scots. He wrote a screenplay on *Lady Caroline Lamb* in 1972, and *State of Revolution* (1977) dramatizes the role of Lenin in the Russian Revolution. Bolt has said, on more than one occasion, that he goes to history because it enables him to make his characters 'theatrically big without embarrassment'. History is 'just Dutch courage, it enables you to write in a grand manner'.[7] It is 'both a pledge of actuality and a release from it'.[8] This is a rather shallow reason for turning to history. It also reflects a certain diffidence in the playwright. After the revolutionary impact of Brecht and Shaw it is indeed surprising that Bolt should feel that he needs historical distance in order to be blatantly theatrical. Limited in scope and perception, Bolt is basically a conventional playwright. He is aware of what is going on in the theatre and his plays reflect the influence of various fashionable trends, but he lacks the artistic ability to be boldly creative in his own right and produce drama of the first rank. In his approach to history, Bolt shows a scrupulous regard for the facts and has definite views on the subject. Though the playwright does not have to bind himself to anything 'constructed of cast iron' when he binds himself to history, he is 'obliged to be as accurate, historically, as he can'. This is because he has

> borrowed not only his story but some of his emotion from actual people who actually lived. He is in debt to them for their virtues and vices, imaginatively energized by the actual energy they expended. He owes them the truth and is a kind of crook if he doesn't pay up. Then too, the audience brings a special credulity to a history play. . . . Because everyone in the audience knows that Joan of Arc really was executed the playwright can take her to her death with an authority and an appearance of inevitability which he would otherwise have to work for. He can only honour this double debt to his character and to his audience by sticking to the facts.[9]

This debt is undoubtedly honoured in *A Man for All Seasons*, the first of Bolt's plays to be set in the past, and by far his greatest popular success. First broadcast on radio in a condensed form in 1954, it was then televised in 1957, and subsequently produced at the Globe Theatre, London, on 1 July 1960, with Paul Schofield in the title role; it was published in the same year. The first production met with outstanding success. It was hailed as a 'most accomplished drama',[10] and ran in London for almost a year. Then it was taken to New York where it ran for 637 performances and was equally acclaimed. 'In conception and execution it is a masterpiece, a splendid tribute to the author, to Noel Willman who directed it both here and abroad, and the excellent Anglo-American cast.'[11] It is a 'drama of stature and absorbing interest, which deserves the triumph here it had in England, and Mr Schofield is one of the best actors in the world'.[12]

One of the reasons for the play's overwhelming success was the superb performance by Paul Schofield, a powerful actor who was able to realize intelligence and nobility, a deep humanity and luminous charm in the role. He gave a 'hypnotic performance'.[13] A whole range of emotion was communicated through his controlled delivery and remarkably expressive face. 'In the calm yet forceful and stubborn portrayal of the part by Mr Schofield, there is the suggestion of human frailties, of a sly humor, a simplicity which adds belief to his sincere dedication to his god. Here is an actor of truly noble stature.'[14] As a result of the play's success on the stage, it was made into a film in 1966 and won six academy awards. The play has since been produced in many countries, and frequently revived in Britain, but without anything like the original impact.

Bolt's principal historical source for the play appears to be R. W. Chambers's biography, *Thomas More* (1934). In an interview with Ronald Hayman, Bolt cites Chambers in support of a historical point which is sure evidence that he was familiar with Chambers's work.[15] Considering both portrayals, the strong parallels between the two indicate clearly that Chambers was the key influence on Bolt's play. Bolt's rendering of historical personalities closely follows Chambers's reading of their characters. For example, Chambers sees William Roper as a trifle forward and pompous, a rather awkward young man to have about the house, whose writings reveal him as not 'quite understanding the man whose memory he later grew to revere'.[16] This is exactly how Roper is depicted in the play.

Chambers's own comments on certain historical incidents also feature in the play at various points. He relates how, after resigning the Chancellorship, More was reduced to such poverty that he was forced to resort to burning great bundles of bracken, for lack of other fuel. Chambers remarks that one can imagine Mistress Alice Shore shivering over the embers of Chelsea bracken, reflecting that her husband had refused a sum from the Church for his writings which would have placed them all in luxury.[17] Bolt dramatises precisely such a situation in Act 2 of the play with Alice sitting wearily on a bundle of bracken, demanding to know 'why a man in poverty can't take four thousand pounds' from the Church when the money was 'charity pure and simple!' (Act 2, pp. 172-3). Another instance relates to More's trial during which Richard Rich perjures himself. Chambers reflects that if Rich had really trapped More into uttering the incriminating words, 'Rich would have instantly called upon Southwell and Palmer to witness them.'[18] Bolt uses this comment, presenting it as one of the points which More makes in denial of the incident having happened:

> If I had really said this is it not obvious he would instantly have called these men to witness?
>
> (Act 2, p. 203)

Chambers also quotes Robert Whittinton's encomium on More, from which Bolt derives the title of his play:

> More is a man of an angel's wit and singular learning. I know not his fellow. For where is the man of that gentleness, lowliness, and affability? And, as time requireth, a man of marvellous mirth and pastimes, and sometime of as sad gravity. A man for all seasons.[19]

Characters and events are naturally severely telescoped in the play. More's family life is represented in his relationships with Dame Alice, Margaret and William Roper, though his actual household was much larger. Bolt is justified in emphasising More's happy home life which was renowned, as well as his legal astuteness and impartiality. At one point in the play Roper accusingly declares that More would even give 'the Devil benefit of law!' (Act 1, p. 147). This is not an exaggeration for Bolt obviously derived the idea from an actual statement of More's that 'if the parties will at my hands call for justice, then, all were it my father stood on one side, and the Devil on the other, his cause being good, the Devil should have right'.[20]

The influence of Shaw is evident in Bolt's merging of historical detail with an overtly modern perspective. 'The action of the play,' Bolt says, 'ends in 1535, but the play was written in 1960, and if in production one date must obscure the other, it is 1960 which I would wish clearly to occupy the stage.'[21] The language is modern and colloquial for the most part. 'Nice boy . . . terribly strong principles though,' remarks More of his prospective son-in-law (Act 1, p. 126). Yet Bolt often blends More's own words with his dialogue, a common practice among modern playwrights which reflects the much greater demand in our time for documentary evidence in support of a view.

Inevitable comparisons have been made between *A Man for All*

Seasons and Brecht's *Galileo* which was produced with great success at the Mermaid Theatre, opening two weeks before *A Man for All Seasons* on 16 June 1960. Bolt invites the comparison, aiming at Brechtian effects through his use of an episodic structure, brief summaries of historical events through the device of the Common Man, a wily humorous character who acts as commentator on the action and who assumes many roles: steward, boatman, jailer, foreman of the jury, executioner. He also helps to change and set the scene, fishing out relevant items from a huge property basket which he pushes conspicuously about the stage. The original production had 'bits of scenery and noticeboards descend on the stage and rise again quite in the Brechtian manner'.[22] Bolt himself described the style he used as a 'bastardized version of the one most recently associated with Bertolt Brecht'.[23]

The play was found to suffer in comparison with *Galileo*. 'It takes a Brecht to be Brechtian', states T. Milne. 'Brecht very firmly ties the issues involved in Galileo's denial of his own discoveries to the state of society' and it is a limitation in Bolt's play that we are not told why More refuses or what 'effect this will have on the growing Tudor State and its people'.[24] K. Tynan asserts that Bolt 'looks at history exclusively through the eyes of his saintly hero' while 'Brecht's vision is broader: he looks at Galileo through the eyes of history.'[25]

But Bolt is surely not bound to approach his subject in the manner of Brecht, and though his play has Brechtian features the borrowings are a matter of superficial externals. The play is not Brechtian in essential spirit and concern. Its interest is not in social process or conditions, but in a historical personality who is the centre of the play. As Bolt himself says:

> What first attracted me was a person who could not be accused of any incapacity for life, who indeed seized life in great variety and almost greedy quantities, who nevertheless found something in himself without which life was valueless and when that was denied him was able to grasp death.[26]

Bolt concentrates on the private man rather than the public figure, and is preoccupied with religious experience rather than historical development. This greatly distances him from Brecht. Even the Common Man, overtly a Brechtian alienation device, 'is intended to draw the audience into the play, not thrust them off it'. Rather

than encourage critical detachment, he is meant to directly involve
the audience by inviting recognition, Bolt wishing him 'to indicate
"that which is common to us all"'.[27]

A ubiquitous, protean figure, the Common Man is a versatile,
economical instrument since he serves many purposes. He introduces the various characters, indicates the passage of time and
facilitates the swift setting and changing of scenes. He also brings a
touch of humour, sometimes comic, sometimes ironic, into the
proceedings. The play opens with him. When the curtain rises, the
set is in darkness except for a single spot which descends vertically
upon the Common Man, who stands in front of a large property
basket. He is clad from head to foot in black tights which delineate
a pot-bellied figure. He addresses the audience:

> It is perverse! To start a play made up of Kings and Cardinals in
> speaking costumes and intellectuals with embroidered mouths,
> with me. If a King, or a Cardinal had done the prologue he'd
> have had the right materials. And an intellectual would have
> shown enough majestic meanings, coloured propositions, and
> closely woven liturgical stuff to dress the House of Lords! But
> this! Is this a costume? Does this say anything? It barely covers
> one man's nakedness! A bit of black material to reduce Old
> Adam to the Common Man. Oh, if they'd let me come on naked,
> I could have shown you something of my own.
>
> (Act 1, p. 109)

Backing towards the basket, he says, 'Well for a proposition of
my own, I need a costume.' He takes out and puts on the coat and
hat of a steward, announcing his role – 'Matthew! The Household
Steward of Sir Thomas More!' The lights come swiftly on. From the
basket he takes out five silver goblets and a jug with a lid with
which he proceeds to furnish a table. A burst of conversational
merriment is heard off-stage. Pausing, he indicates: 'There's company to dinner.' He finishes laying the table and then declares:

> All right! A Common Man! A Sixteenth-Century Butler! (He
> drinks from the jug) All right – the Six – (Breaks off, agreeably
> surprised by the quality of the liquor, regards the jug respect-
> fully and drinks again). The Sixteenth Century is the Century of
> the Common Man. (Puts down the jug) Like all other centuries.
> And that's my proposition.
>
> (Act 1, p. 110)

The Common Man, who slips in and out of innumerable little roles like this one, is reflective of the general facelessness of the times. He is a likeable rogue who knows how to adapt himself to his environment and look after his own interests. Shrewdly pragmatic, he is not averse to compromising his integrity in little ways, but, acutely sensitive to danger, he knows exactly where to draw the line. The great thing, he tells the audience, is 'not to get out of your depth. . . . Oh, when I can't touch the bottom I'll go deaf, blind and dumb' (Act 1, p. 113). Audiences have found him an engaging figure. A reviewer of one production of the play comments that:

> it is this character – or rather George Rose's assumption of it in place of Leo McKern, who created it – which has drawn us once again to see *A Man for All Seasons*. It is a rewarding role for the actor, and George Rose plays it with no less relish than its creator, with a natural clown's humour and with a most endearing air.[28]

The sixteenth century, straddled between the medieval and modern world and assailed by revolutionary currents, was a period of uneasy flux. The form of the play reinforces the mutability and amorphousness that is the texture of the times. Each act is broken up into little episodes which dissolve and blend into each other, registering the impression of life as nebulous. For instance, in Act One, after a midnight interview during which Wolsey has failed to gain More's support for his efforts to secure a papal dispensation to enable King Henry to divorce Queen Catherine, More turns to go when Wolsey calls after him, 'More! You should have been a cleric!' More looks back, amused, and replies, 'Like yourself, your Grace?' He leaves, and Wolsey is left staring after him in contemplation. Then he too exits with candle, taking most of the light from the stage as he does so. The whole rear of the stage now becomes patterned with webbed reflections thrown from the brightly moonlit water, while a strip of light descends along the front of the stage to provide the acting area for the next scene, where More is hailing a boatman to take him home up the river (Act 1, p. 121). In such ways, lighting is skillfully used to effect swift cinematic shifts of time and place with lines blurring and merging to provide an unsettling sense of impermanence.

The passage of events is suggested with great economy. Wolsey's death, for example, is portrayed symbolically. The stage is dimmed, and then a bright light descends below. Into this light from the wings are thrown the great red robe and hat of the Cardinal. The Common Man enters from the opposite wing and roughly piles them into his basket. Taking a pair spectacles from his pocket and a book from his basket, he then proceeds to read:

> Whether we follow tradition in ascribing Wolsey's death to a broken heart, or accept Professor Larcomb's less feeling diagnosis of pulmonary pneumonia, its effective cause was the king's displeasure. He died at Leicester on 29 November 1530 while on his way to the Tower under charge of High Treason.
>
> (Act 1, p. 128)

Here we find a playwright actually quoting a historical source to the audience.[29] Bolt like Shaw and T. S. Eliot continually shatters the illusion of reality and keeps the audience conscious of the presentation of history. A future perspective is also sometimes provided. When More is about to be interrogated in the Tower by Cromwell, Norfolk, Cranmer and Rich, the Common Man as jailer, expresses commiseration for the prisoner: 'I'd let him out if I could but I can't. Not without taking up residence in there myself. . . . You know the old adage? "Better a live rat than a dead lion," and that's about it.' An envelope descends swiftly before him. He opens it and reads out aloud:

> With reference to the old adage: 'Thomas Cromwell was found guilty of High Treason and executed on 28 July 1540. Norfolk was found guilty of High Treason and should have been executed on 27 January 1547 but on the night of 26 January, the King died of syphilis and wasn't able to sign the warrant. Thomas Cranmer.' (Jerking thumb) That's the other one – 'was burned alive on 21 March 1556.' (He is about to conclude but sees a postscript.) Oh. 'Richard Rich became a Knight and Solicitor-General, a Baron and Lord Chancellor, and died in his bed.' So did I. And so, I hope (pushing off basket) will all of you.
>
> (Act 2, p. 183)

The notion of time rolling inexorably forward and catching up with all concerned is conveyed with the accompanying sense of the ephemeral nature of people and events in history, forcing the audience to contemplate the ultimate meaning of human action and suffering.

For More, the issue finally is not support for any political cause or religious institution, but what he stands for in himself, the very ground of his being. As he tries to explain to his anguished daughter who pleads with him to swear to the Act of Succession:

> When a man takes an oath, Meg, he's holding his own self in his own hands. Like water (cups hands) and if he opens his fingers *then* – he needn't hope to find himself again.
>
> (Act 2, p. 161)

Bolt has apologized for treating 'Thomas More, a Christian Saint, as a hero of selfhood.'[30] This has been a target for criticism. In a talk on the BBC Third World Programme, Anthony Kenner argued that Bolt's equations of self with soul and self with the love of God at certain points in the play are unhistorical, and that Bolt uses the word 'conscience' in a sense it did not have in the sixteenth century. Ronald Hayman, in his book on Bolt, agrees, stating that:

> taken out of context, many of More's pronouncements can give the impression that he anticipated Kant in holding that the individual must make his own moral decisions, but in their context, they show that More followed Aquinas's doctrine of conscience, seeing it not as an arbiter but as an opinion about God's law.[31a]

On the contrary the historical More gives Bolt ample basis for portraying him as a hero of selfhood for More did believe very strongly that the individual must assume responsibility for his own moral decisions. When pressed by the commissioners on refusing to swear the oath to the Act of Succession, More declares that he leaves 'every man to his own conscience' and thinks that every man should leave him to his.[31b] More was obviously nettled at a suggestion that his obstinacy was due to the example of Fisher, Bishop of London. In a dialogue recorded in a letter to his daughter he states,'. . . I refused the oath before it was offered him [Fisher] . . .Verily, daughter, I never intend (God being my good lord) to pin my soul on another man's back, not even the best man I know this day living: for I know not whither he may hap to carry it'.[32] There are points when he does seem to equate self with soul.

In a letter to Dr Nicholas Wilson, also imprisoned in the Tower, he talks of the need to follow his own conscience, 'for which my selff muste ma(ake) answer to God'.[33]

Hayman claims that the historical More would never have said, as Bolt's More in the play:

> What matters to me is not whether it's true or not but that I believe it to be true, or rather not that I *believe* it, but that *I* believe it.[34]

But a similar sentiment lies behind the historical More's reply to Margaret, when she begs him to follow the example of so many eminent people in the realm and swear the oath. More answers her by telling her the tale of a suit between a Londoner and a Northerner which had to be settled by a jury of twelve men. The jury was made of Northerners, with the exception of one Southerner called Company, who dissented from the verdict the rest were agreed upon. Asked to play the 'good companion' and go along with them for company, he replies:

> But when we shall hence, and come before God, and he shall send you to Heaven for doing according to your conscience, and me to the Devil for doing against mine, if I shall then say to you, 'Go now for good company with me,' would ye go?[35]

To more, what a man believed was definitely less important than that *he* believed it, for his salvation rested on that ultimately:

> And this is the last poynt that any man may with his saluacion come to, as farre as I can see, and it is bounden if he see peryll to examine his conscience surely by learning and by good counsaille and be sure that his conscience be such as it may stande with his saluacion, or els reforme it. And if the matter be such, as both parties may stande with saluacion, then whither side his conscience fall, he is safe ynough before God . . . . [36]

The clinching fact is that he could finally turn round to his judges at his trial and say, 'that though your Lordships have now here in earth been judges to my condemnation, we may yet hereafter in Heaven merrily all meet together, to our everlasting salvation'.[37] Thus More does see the individual conscience as an arbiter, though it is not so much a question of it being right to do what you yourself believe is right, but that in the last resort your conscience is all you have to fall back on.

There are moments of trenchant dialogue in the play as when More faces the commission of enquiry into his case. He refuses to answer Archbishop Cranmer's questions regarding the Act of Succession:

> Norfolk: Thomas, you insult the King and His Council in the person of the Lord Archbishop.
> More: I insult no one. I will not take the oath. I will not tell you why I will not.
> Norfolk: Then your reasons must be treasonable!
> More: Not 'must be'; may be.
> Norfolk: It's a fair assumption!
> More: The law requires more than an assumption; the law requires a fact.
>
> (Act 2, pp. 185–7)

At the trial, law and justice are made a travesty of, as More's condemnation is ensured by Rich's act of perjury. All look at More after Rich has made his damning statement, but More looks at Rich:

> More: In good faith, Rich, I am sorrier for your perjury than my peril.
> Norfolk: Do you deny this?
> More: Yes! My lords, if I were a man who heeded not the taking of an oath, you know well I need not be here. Now I will take an oath! If what Master Rich has said is true, then I pray God I may may never see God in the face! Which I would not say were it otherwise for anything on earth.
>
> (Act 2, p. 202)

Bolt keeps close to the historical More's own words here for he is recorded to have said:

> If I were a man, my Lords, that did not regard an oath, I needed not, as it is well known, in this place, at this time, nor in this case, to stand here as an accused person. And if this oath of

yours, Master Rich, be true, then pray I that I never see God in the face; which I would not say, were it otherwise, to win the whole world.

He then gave his own version of what had passed and concluded, 'In good faith, Master Rich, I am sorrier for your perjury than for my own peril.'[38]

Bolt draws freely upon More's writings and recorded sayings, including them at affective points, and this lends vigour to the dialogue. A reviewer of the 1976 production of the play at the Young Vic, describes Alfred Lynch in the title role as rising 'to a fine level of dignity' when he 'has More's own words to say after his condemnation'. Part of More's speech at this point – 'I am the King's true subject, and pray for him and all the realm . . . I do none harm, I say none harm, I think none harm. And if this be not enough to keep a man alive, in good faith I long not to live. . .And therefore, my poor body is at the King's pleasure. Would God my death might do him some good.' (Act 2, p. 205)[39] - was actually spoken by the historical More at one of Cromwell's interrogation sessions in the Tower.[40] Bolt inserts these words into More's final speech at the trial where their emotional force adds to the climactic nature of the scene.

When Norfolk rises to finally pass sentence, the scene change immediately commences. The trappings of justice are flown upwards. The lights are dimmed but for two areas spotlighted to the front, and an arch at the head of the stairs which begins to show blue sky:

> Through this arch – where the axe and the block are silhouetted against a light of steadily increasing brilliance – comes the murmuration of a large crowd, formalised almost into a chant and mounting, so that Norfolk has to shout the end of his speech.

The foreman of the jury, the Common Man, doffs hat and goes to the area spotlighted on the left with Cranmer while More goes to the area spotlighted on the right. Cromwell moves to the bottom of the stairs and beckons to the Common Man, pointing to the top of the stairs. The Common Man joins him reluctantly, shaking his head and indicating in mime that he has not the proper costume in his property basket

Cromwell takes a small black mask from his sleeve and offers it to him. The Common Man puts it on, thus, in his black tights, becoming the traditional headsman. He ascends the stairs, straddles his legs and picks up the axe, silhouetted against the sky.

At once the crowd falls silent. On mounting the scaffold, More offers a few words of encouragement to the executioner: 'Friend, be not afraid of your office. You send me to God. . . . He will not refuse one who is so blithe to go to him.' He kneels and immediately there is a harsh roar of kettledrums and total black-out at the end of the stairs (Act 2, p. 205–7). Bolt does not shrink from showing the execution on stage, but, typically, he handles it in an extremely discreet conservative manner, without any ugly edge or shock to the violence.

The historical More's bearing on the scaffold is probably unique in history. He is recorded to have made many light-hearted jests, which historians give credence to since such humour was characteristic of More. As he mounted the shaky steps of the scaffold, he turned to the Lieutenant, 'I pray you, Master Lieutenant, see me safe up, and for my coming down let me shift for myself.' He is reported to have moved his beard from the block, remarking that 'it had never committed treason'. Before kneeling down at the scaffold, he embraced the executioner and then addressed the following words to him:

Pluck up thy spirits, man, and be not afraid to do thine office; my neck is very short, take heed therefore thou strike not awry, for saving of thine honesty.[41]

It is highly revealing of Bolt that he uses the tamest part of this speech and leaves out More's extraordinary humour at such a dark moment. Instead he substitutes a feeling expressed by More on various previous occasions. In his *Dialogue of Comfort against Tribulation* More writes that 'he that so loveth him (God), that he longeth to go to him, my heart cannot give me but he shall be welcome . . . '[42] Bolt waters down the event of More's execution by including this sentiment in place of the humour, so typical of More and full of period flavour, and so amazing at such a tragic moment. A playwright of stronger imagination, like John Osborne or Edward Bond, would have pounced on it. The humour that Bolt attributes to More in the play has a refined, ironic quality, but is bland and antiseptic in comparison to More's actual vital earthy brand of humour. As K. Tynan comments, Bolt has 'indulged in a lot simplification' where More is concerned, banishing 'More the scurrilous pamphleteer' and 'More the vernacular comic, whom C. S. Lewis has called "our first great Cockney humorist".'[43]

Bolt sees More as the perfect human being:

> What's amazing about More is the perfection of his behaviour – both in detail and overall. A nearly faultless performance, but without any recourse to a transcendental explanation. And his style was so good. He was a perfect gentleman – a breathtaking performance as a human being. . . . This is why people liked the play. . . . And he didn't do anything that you and I couldn't have done. St Francis talked to the birds, but anyone at his best could do what More did.

This is an extremely simplistic *reductio ad absurdum* of a complex and extraordinary person.

In his concern to make More 'a man for all seasons,' Bolt leaves out aspects of the man and the period which a modern audience might not find agreeable. More was by no means always the 'perfect gentleman', showing 'taste, wit, courtesy' and consideration on all occasions.[44] In controversy he could be coarse and virulent, as was the habit among scholars and theologians of the time. Thus More answered Luther's scurrilous attack on Henry with equal asperity and frequent lapses into vulgarity. Then again, there is More's unchivalrous treatment of the fallen Wolsey when, in his opening speech in Parliament on becoming Chancellor, he is reported to have made a bitter attack on his ruined predecessor. These features are excluded in the play which concentrates on More's endearing qualities and fails to include his disagreeable sides.

Then again Bolt tones down the religious side of More's character. He had an amazing faith and was a man of no ordinary mettle. Contrary to Bolt's view quoted above, there was most certainly 'a transcendental explanation' for More's behaviour; his Christian faith was the mainspring of his life and it enabled him to live and die as few people could. Despite his social grace and ease, and the happiness of his home life, the rigours of a monastic existence had a distinct appeal for More. In early years he seriously considered

joining the monastic order of the Carthusians, and even after
deciding against it, it was his practice to wear a hair shirt and
scourge himself, facts he revealed only to his daughter, Margaret.
These exercises were undertaken in a manner of quiet discipline
rather than morbid religiosity.

In the same spirit he took the trials of prison life as a means of
attaining a higher spiritual life. Chambers states that 'tales of
More's bearing during his last days in prison seem to show that
both his austerities and his humour were already becoming
legendary'. We are told that 'he scourged himself and meditated
upon death, wrapping a linen sheet round himself like a shroud'.
During one of Margaret's visits to her father in the Tower, More
remarked:

> I believe, Meg, that they that have put me here ween they have
> done me a high displeasure. But I assure thee on my faith, my
> own good daughter, if it had not been for my wife and you that
> be my children, whom I account the chief part of my charge, I
> would not have failed long ere this to have closed myself in as
> straight a room, and straighter too . . . Me thinketh God maketh
> me a wanton, and setteth me on his lap and dandleth me.[45]

Bolt leaves out this ascetic side to More's nature, probably
because he wishes to give his protagonist an all-round human
appeal, and these extreme tendencies might prove strange and
alienating to a modern audience. Indeed a reviewer of the first
production can be found enthusing that 'what places Thomas
More among the most human and appealing of martyrs is that he
lacked the zealot's eagerness of a Becket to welcome death as a
demonstration of his love of God'.[46] Yet though the historical More
in no way courted martyrdom, he considered it 'a happy and
blessed thing' 'for the love of God to suffer loss of goods, imprisonment, loss of lands and life also'. During the time of his retirement,
as troubles began to increase, he would say to his family that 'if he
might perceive his wife and children would encourage him to die
in a good cause, it should so comfort him that, for very joy thereof,
it would make him merrily run to death'.[47] In his concern to make
More a popular hero, Bolt dilutes the unique vital quality of More's
faith, suppressing elements which would have provided depth
and complexity to his portrayal of this remarkable human being.

Ronald Hayman is the only critic who has devoted a whole book to Bolt. Major critics have not been drawn to him and few have dealt with him substantially. For, as one critic comments:

the extreme limits of his style are marked at one end by the complete realism of *The Critic and the Heart* and at the other by the discreet adventure into impressionistic staging, half-Brecht, half BBC historical documentary, of *A Man for All Seasons*.[48]

Despite the surface modernity of *A Man for All Seasons* it clearly emerges that Bolt is basically a conventional playwright putting over history in a popular way.

The play considered next, Peter Shaffer's *The Royal Hunt of the Sun*, provides another example of a popular treatment of history, but where Bolt goes for the personal detail and the subdued effect, Shaffer looks for the public encounter and the glittering spectacle. Unlike Bolt, Shaffer is not often drawn to history and when he is, it is to exploit possibilities for sensation. *Amadeus*, his other play based in history, attempts to explore the nature of creative genius through the lives of Mozart and Salieri, but, casting a lurid light on these two personalities, Shaffer focuses essentially on the violent tensions between them which lead to the murder of one by the other.

The Royal Hunt of the Sun dramatizes a tale of epic adventure – the invasion of Peru by the Spanish under Francisco Pizarro. Their surmounting of awesome physical obstacles in the quest for gold eventually brings about the ruin and desecration of a great civilization. The play dwells upon the strange attraction between the aging embittered agnostic Spanish commander and the young idealistic magnificent Inca king, revered by his people as a god, the Son of the Sun. Pizarro falls under his spell and undergoes a momentary conversion, hoping to recover lost faith, innocence and the capacity for worship. However he is forced eventually to agree to the killing of his god to secure the safety of his men. The play functions on two levels. It presents the clash of two alien worlds, and also attempts to explore deep primitive religious forces in man. However it is only on the external spectacular level that the play succeeds.

It was first produced on 7 July 1964 by the National Theatre Company, and published in the same year. This production, directed by John Dexter, with Colin Blakely as Pizarro and Robert

Stephen as Atahuallpa, was a phenomenal success. 'The result of wonderful teamwork from author, director and designer, Peter Shaffer's new play had an overwhelming reception on the occasion of its première,' reports *Theatre World* magazine:

> There are many unforgettable moments of visual splendour, including the symbolic treacherous massacre of three thousand unarmed Incas, the ritual robing of the King, and the death vigil, when mourners, wearing strangely haunting golden masks, wail with growing alarm as the body of their lifeless Sun King fails to respond to the ray of the sun for his expected resurrection.[49]

Bernard Levin in *The Daily Mail* (8/7/64) called it 'the greatest play of our generation'. The play was one of the National Theatre's most outstanding popular successes. From the Chichester Festival it transferred to the London Old Vic where it ran for 122 performances over a period of three years. It opened on 26 October 1965 in New York where it enjoyed another long run of up to 261 performances. In 1969 a film version was produced with Robert Shaw as Pizarro and Christopher Plummer as the Inca.

But, as with *A Man for All Seasons*, subsequent revivals of the play have not received anything like the initial enthusiasm. This indicates that these early productions were extremely flattering to the text. They played up the spectacular element and the lack of this on the same prodigal scale in later productions, accentuated the play's defects. Reviewers of the 1973 Prospect Theatre Company production refer to the 'frail and bony structure in which the author encloses his huge themes'.[50] The encounters between Pizarro and the Inca are 'muddied with washes of pidgin English' and 'surrounded by vast frames of verbiage'.[51] The failure of the play's language is undeniable, as well as the shallowness of its thought, but it succeeds as a bold theatrical piece. Thus J. R. Taylor asserts that anyone who saw the original productions will remember, 'the extraordinary impression they created of a meeting of two worlds in a dead empty space brought to life by the magic of the theatre, long after any argument about the philosophic profundity of the words (or their culpable lack of it) has been forgotten'.[52]

Shaffer was clearly drawn to this historical subject because of the opportunity it provided for marvel and romance. The play represents, he says, the sort of theatre he had 'long dreamed of creating, involving not only words, but also mimes, masks and magics'. The use of these elements helped to realize 'the fantastic apparition of the pre-Columbian world, and the terrible magnificence of the Conquistadors'.[53] Shaffer shows no serious interest in history as such, stumbling across his source almost by accident. During an interview in October 1964, he says:

> You see, I first came on the subject some years back when I had to while away the time reading some big heavy Victorian book. The book I chose was Prescott's *Conquest of Peru* and I was absolutely riveted by it. The whole drama of the confrontation of two totally different ways of life: the Catholic individualism of the invaders, and the complete communistic society of the Incas . . . I started out with a history play; I hope I have ended up with a contemporary story which uses history only as a groundwork in the expression of its theme. What is its theme? Briefly it is a play about two men one of whom is an atheist, and the other is a god.[54]

This casual turning to history because he had to 'while away the time reading some big heavy Victorian book' is highly revealing of Shaffer's mentality and the superficiality of his concern with history. W. H. Prescott's *The Conquest of Peru*, first published in 1847, is a classic of history. It was the first comprehensive account in English of the civilization of the Incas. Prescott based his work on all the original documents available to him. They included records and manuscripts of contemporary chroniclers on Peru, and private and official correspondence of the period, drawn mainly from the archives of the Royal Academy of History at Madrid.

Since Prescott's time vast stores of material have come to light forming the basis for more modern accounts. These Shaffer does not seem to have been interested to read. Subsequent authorities in the field include Sir Clement Markham, the British historian who translated many Spanish chronicles into English and wrote *A History of Peru* (1910), and the American Peruvianist, Philip Ainsworth Means, who published *The Ancient Civilisations of the Andes* (1931) and *Fall of the Inca Empire and the Spanish Rule in Peru: 1530–1780* (1932). Other later studies include G. H. S. Bushnell's *Peru* (1956), Victor Wolfgang Von Hagen's *The Realm of the Incas* (1957) and *The Ancient Sun Kingdoms of the Americas: Aztec, Maya, Inca* [1962], J. Alden Mason's *The Ancient Civilisations of Peru* (1957),

Sally Falk Moore's *Power and Property in Inca Peru* (1958), and Edward and George Ordish's *The Last of the Incas* (1963).

Though Prescott's work is highly regarded by modern historians as an 'immortal narrative of the Conquest', its information in many respects has been superceded. John Hemming in his book *The Conquest of the Incas* (1970), states that:

> Since Prescott's time the archives have yielded their treasures. The Spaniards had a passion for keeping records and notarizing every aspect of their lives. Countless thousands of documents have been published in modern collections that sometimes run to over a hundred volumes but have no sequence or index. Historical journals have also proliferated, and there have been many fine specialised studies by professional historians. Almost none of these sources was available to Prescott.[55]

Prescott's account of the conquest was also further limited since it was largely based on contemporary Spanish chroniclers such as Pedro Pizarro, Miguel de Estete, Francisco de Xerez and Pedro Sancho (official secretaries of the Expedition), who describe events from the Spanish point of view. He also drew on the writings of sixteenth-century observers and historians such as Juan de Sarmiento, the Licentiate Polo de Ondegardo, and Pedro de Cieza Léon, Agustín de Zárate, the jingoistic Francisco López de Gómara and Antonio de Herrera Tordesillas (Phillip II's official historian of the Conquest). Indian sources are few and later in time because the Incas had no knowledge of the written word before the Spanish arrived.

Prescott did draw substantially on the famous works of Garcilaso de la Vega (1539–1619), son of an Inca princess, whose works, *Commentarios reales* and *Historia general del Peru*, dominated knowledge about the Indians for a considerable time, but their credibility has since been seriously questioned. J. Alden Mason indicates that 'Garcilaso wrote his "Royal Commentaries" long after he had returned to Spain, and based much of his historical accounts on the writings of the now discredited Jesuit Blas Valera.'[56] Garcilaso forfeits J. Hemming's confidence as a historian because he 'meanders, forgets, romanticizes or blatantly distorts too often to remain authoritative'.[57]

The importance of other Indian sources has been emphasized

during this century, such as the narrative of Titu Cusi Yapanqui, who reigned over the dissident State of Vilcabamba from 1557 to 1570, and dictated his report of the Conquest to the Spanish missionary, Diego de Castro, for the benefit of the Spanish King; Juan Santa Cruz Pachacuti's chronicle which dates from the early seventeenth century, and the chronicle of Guamán Poma de Ayala. Another form in which this historic confrontation was recorded by the Indian people, was through the oral tradition of poems and of plays which re-enact the events of the Conquest in dialogue, song and dance. These plays still exist and are performed annually in some regions, but are extremely difficult to date. Nathan Wachtel asserts that 'in some cases they seem to be very old, possibly even going as far back as the sixteenth century; they are evidence of the preservation of the past in the collective memory of the Indian people'. A very complete text, of *The Tragedy of the death of Atahuallpa*, transcribed in Chayanta in 1871, was published by Jesús Lara in 1957. Another version was collated at Oruro in 1942 and published by C. H. Balmori in 1955.[58] This would have been a fascinating source for a dramatist to consider, but Shaffer does not seem to have gone much beyond the outdated account he found in Prescott.

Prescott narrates events in a highly romantic manner. He also adopts a moralizing tone and brings a distinctly Victorian perspective to bear. Francisco Pizarro, he writes:

> was an illegitimate child, and that his parents should not have taken pains to perpetuate the date of his birth is not surprising. Few care to make a particular record of their transgressions.

'But little is told of Francisco's early years, and that little not always deserving credit. According to some, he was deserted by both his parents, and left as a foundling at the door of one of the principal churches of the city. It is even said that he would have perished, had he not been nursed by a sow . . .'.[59]

This is a good illustration of the old-fashioned romantic style of history and shows that this dated account is not in the same category as some of the historical sources used by other playwrights discussed in this book. Prescott weaves into his narrative, without pinning it down as such, the legend that Pizarro was a foundling brought up among pigs. A modern historian indicates that this 'legend was started by Francisco López de Gómara, a personal enemy of the Pizarros', and it has been 'entirely dis-proved by various documents that have come to light in recent years'. 'Although he was illegitimate and poorly educated, there was nothing otherwise discreditable about Pizarro's upbringing.' Porras Barrenechea did much to explode these myths by his publications in the 1940s.[60]

The use of myth, as argued in the introduction, is quite legitimate in a history play, since myth has its own variety of truth and an essential contribution to make to the understanding of the ultimate significance of a character or event in history. But Shaffer is obviously not concerned to penetrate to the deep innermost truth of history so much as to broadly exploit myth for the sake of gaudy sensation. Our first introduction to Pizarro is to a man in late middle age, 'commanding, harsh, wasted, secret', who makes contact at gut level: 'I was suckled by a sow. My house is the oldest in Spain – the pig-sty.' He received nothing on being born, so now he has nothing to give. Once the world could have had him for a song, but now it is going to know him as a name to be sung in ballads 'out there under the cork trees' where he sat as a boy 'with bandages for shoes'. He describes himself bitterly as 'the old pigherd lumbering after fame'. Where others inherited their honour, he had 'to root for [his] like the pigs' (Act 1, Sc. 1, pp. 1–7).

Prescott sees Pizarro as totally unscrupulous in his dealings with his fellow Spaniards, as well as the Peruvian Indians. His name 'became a byword for perfidy'. In mitigation he cites the deprivation of Pizarro's childhood and early youth.[61] Shaffer uses this as the mainspring for his interpretation of the adult psychology of the man. He is presented as totally disillusioned. 'Time cheats us all the way,' he says, 'I've been cheated from the moment I was born because there's death in everything' (Act 1, Sc. 10, pp. 30–2). He pours scorn on Young Martin's glowing idealism:

> You belong to hope. To faith. To priests and pretences. To dipping flags and ducking heads; to laying hands and licking rings; to powers and parchments, and the whole vast stupid congregation of crowners and cross-kissers.
>
> (Act 1, Sc. 5. pp, 17–18)

Pizarro is a solitary, emotionally maimed individual, beset by a sense of social and cosmic homelessness and resultant dread of the universe. Yet for all his professed cynicism, he is a frustrated

romantic at heart. When first he began to think of Peru there was a
longing in him 'for a new place like a country after rain, washed
clean of all badges and barriers'. On learning about Atahuallpa, he
is fascinated by the notion of a man like himself, illegitimate,
illiterate, and a warrior, arrogating to himself godhead: 'It's silly –
but tremendous. . . . A black king with glowing eyes, sporting the
sun for a crown. What does it mean?' Pizarro is driven on by a
sense of personal destiny, convinced that 'of all meetings [he has]
made in [his] life, this is the one [he has] to make . . . all [his] days
have been a path to this one morning' (Act 1, Sc. 10, p. 33).

Shaffer stresses Pizarro's contempt for the Church in order to
highlight this romantic fascination with the Inca. Here he diverges
from his source. Pizarro was much more conventionally religious-
minded, according to Prescott. He continually inflamed the religious zeal of his men, putting forward the propagation of Catholicism as the prime goal of the expedition. Before the hazardous
crossing of the Andes, he urged his company:

> Let every one of you, take heart and go forward like a good
> soldier, nothing daunted by the smallness of your numbers. For
> in the greatest extremity God ever fights for his own; and doubt
> not he will humble the pride of the heathen, and bring him to
> the knowledge of the true faith, the great end and object of the
> Conquest.[62]

Prescott's source for this quote is the chronicle of Gonzalo Fernan-
des de Oviedo who wrote a general history during the decades
after the Conquest. This history is highly accredited by a modern
historian because Oviedo was an 'important official in the West
Indies and interrogated travellers returning to Spain, so that much
of his material came from eyewitnesses'.[63]

Shaffer makes Pizarro a self-professed agnostic with no time for
pretences of any sort so that he contrasts sharply with the rank
hypocrisy of the salvation-mongering ecclesiastics who extol the
lofty nature of the mission: 'We are going to take from them what
they don't value, and give them instead the priceless mercy of
heaven. He who helps me lift this dark man into light I absolve of
all crimes he ever committed' (Act 1, Sc. 1, p. 5). The play is a
critique of the propaganda of ideological systems. It satirizes the
human propensity towards partisanship, and its exploitation by
religious and political institutions for their own acquisitive ends.

Shaffer has said that 'the neurotic allegiances of Europe, the Churches and flags, the armies and parties are the villains of *The Royal Hunt of the Sun*'.[64]

On another level the play attempts to probe beneath institutionalized forms of deification, to explore the latent subliminal forces in man that respond to party, cult, worship, ritual. Their expression often involves a combination of freedom and discipline, adventure and tradition. Even where men are led to repudiate and destroy, this is rarely done without some form of obedience, some solidarity, some hanging on to elusive values. These are religious forces that go far deeper than law or morality, springing from inner experience and even more primitive layers of being. Instinct with creative and destructive possibilities, they may be exploited for progressive or regressive alternatives.

Initially the play creates the impression of the Peruvian expedition as a journey into the interior where no sanctions exist. 'Do you know where you're going?' Pizarro asks Young Martin. 'Into the forest. A hundred miles of dark and screaming. . . . Take your noble reasons there, Martin. Pitch your silk flags in that black and wave your crosses at the wild cats. See what awe they command' (Act 1, Sc. 2, p. 11). Our introduction to the Inca world is to an alien unearthly realm where all familiar footholds are removed yet we are ultimately confronted with a world of teeming plenty and gentle hospitality, rigidly bound however by its own legal and religious codes.

Atahuallpa is a masked, stylized, ubiquitous presence in the play. When he speaks, his voice, like the voices of all the Incas is strangely formalized:

Villac Umu: Your people groan.
Atahuallpa: They groan with my voice.
Challcuchima: Your people weep.
Atahuallpa: They weep with my tears.

(Act 1, Sc. 4, p. 15)

The high degree of ritualism in the speech, walk and posture of the Incas emphasizes the over-organization of their lives. In the original production, Robert Stephen's Atahuallpa was described as a 'momentous piece of stylized acting', that singlehandedly conjured up the spirit of the Incas.[65] This is fitting since he concentrates within himself the spiritual and physical life of the community.

He is the State and the moving principle behind a strictly defined, intensely structured society.

The Peruvian world is thus not presented without its limitations and here Shaffer can be found weaving in many details of Prescott's account of the Inca civilization. Under Inca rule an individual's public and private needs were provided by law. Everyone was married at a certain age, presented with a dwelling, and assigned a plot of land sufficient for his own maintenance and that of his wife, and an additional portion was granted on the birth of each child. After the age of fifty no one was allowed to work, but was looked after by the State and treated with honour. A 'benevolent forecast watched carefully' over the people's 'necessities, and provided for their relief in seasons of infirmity and for their sustenance in health'. The Peruvians appeared happy and contented, going about the labours of the day with much singing and dancing.[66]

However Prescott concludes that the Peruvian government was the 'most oppressive though the mildest of despotisms' because it denied a human being the power of free agency:

> Where there is no free agency there can be no morality. Where there is no temptation there can be little claim to virtue. Where the routine is rigorously prescribed by law, the law, and not the man must have the credit of the conduct. If the government is the best which is felt the least, which encroaches on the natural liberty of the subject only so far as it is essential to civil subordination, then of all governments devised the Peruvian has the least claim to our admiration.[67]

This curious Victorian view is a historical phenomenon in itself. Shaffer reacts against it by attributing it in the play to De Nizza, the rabid ecclesiastic who sees Peru as a 'sepulchre of the soul' (Act 2, Sc. 10, p. 72), and the Inca system of government as a particularly insidious form of tyranny since it denies man the right to freedom and hunger, necessary spurs to self-improvement:

> All men are born unequal: this is the divine gift. And want is their birthright. Where you deny this and there is no hope of any new love; where tomorrow is abolished, and no man ever thinks 'I can change myself', there you have the rule of Anti-Christ.
>
> (Act 2, Sc. 4, p. 52)

What comes across is the bigotry and intransigence of the indoctrinated individual. We are prone to see the oppression which operates in another system, and find it difficult to believe that the indoctrinated individual of that system may feel as free and productive in his ideological captivity as we may feel in ours. Wider social contact reveals a world of disquieting cultural relativities. Our own ideological system tends to deter a fundamental questioning of its structure in order to maintain the fiction that we are free to believe what we choose to believe and have chosen to believe what we do. Basically, Shaffer says, that he 'saw the active iron of Spain against the passive feathers of Peru' as the 'conflict of two immense and joyless powers'.[68]

But he handles his huge themes without much subtlety or depth. His emphasis throughout is on flashy kaleidoscopic effects. The desecration of Peru is symbolized by the plundering of the giant sun emblem on the back wall of the stage. The sun gives out terrible groans, 'like the sound of a great animal being wounded', as the Spaniards with their daggers greedily dismantle it. They 'tear out the gold inlays and fling them on the ground'. 'In a moment only the great gold frame remains; a broken blackened sun' (Act 2, Sc. 6, p. 56). Of the 'Rape of the Sun', one reviewer writes, that 'to watch the gold of the Inca Empire being torn loose from its majestic moorings' is 'to be faintly sickened'.[69] The heinous treachery of the Spaniards earns Atahuallpa's lasting outrage and contempt. Even when he softens towards Pizarro, Atahuallpa's reading of him is that he is a man who has no word to pledge (Act 2, Sc. 2, p. 42). Atahuallpa's bearing, even in captivity, displays the most 'entire dignity and grace. Even when he moves or speaks, it is with the consciousness of his divine origin, his sacred function and his absolute power' (Act 2, Sc. 3, p. 45). Pizarro is drawn irresistibly to him: 'Yes. He has some meaning for me, this Man-God. An immortal man in whom all his people live completely. He has an answer for time' (Act 2, Sc. 3, p. 45).

Shaffer departs radically from his source in his depiction of the relationship between Pizarro and Atahuallpa. According to Prescott, it was Pizarro's half-brother, Hernando Pizarro, who established a certain rapport with the Inca. The 'haughty spirit of this cavalier had been touched by the condition of the royal prisoner, and he had treated him with a deference which won for him the peculiar regard and confidence of the Indian'.[70] Shaffer builds on the relationship between Pizarro and Atahuallpa to enhance the momentous nature of their encounter, adding an exotic religious and romantic interest to the play for the instinctive bond between the two men leads to the strange conversion of Pizarro into a disciple of Atahuallpa. There is no historical evidence that anything of this nature occurred.

Atahuallpa is shown momentarily reuniting Pizarro with the world. He dances for Pizarro. It is the 'ferocious mime of a warrior killing his foes' and is 'very difficult to execute, demanding great litheness and physical stamina' (Act 2, Sc. 5, p. 55). The dance of Atahuallpa is pristine, vulpine and has a powerful elemental appeal. One reviewer of the play in production describes it as the 'physical high spot of the evening', and the point when Pizarro's 'resistance to the Inca's fascinating magnetism begins to soften'. He is openly affected by this display of 'flowing grace and muscular athleticism', and 'the audience, too, bursts into spontaneous applause'.[71] The scene closes with Pizarro extending his hand to Atahuallpa, who takes it; and the two of them then go off quietly together (Act 2, Sc. 5, p. 55).

The relationship between Pizarro and Atahuallpa is curiously compelling. One reviewer describes Colin Blakely in the original production as a 'grizzled limping veteran who bodies out the figure of Pizarro as a desperate man risking everything on the last throw', and says that Robert Stephens, 'facially impassive as a carved idol, gives the sun-ruler a hieratic androgynous dignity'. The coming together of this oddly related pair is at times extraordinarily touching'.[72] Another reviewer finds it artificial and reductive:

> What has been a clash of cultures and a conflict of temperaments becomes, through over-concentration, a kind of homosexual, Genet-like, master-servant imbroglio, and suddenly epic drama dwindles into closet drama and loses in the exchange.[73]

Shaffer himself sees the play as centred around:

> the relationship, intense, involved and obscure, between these two men, one of whom is the other's prisoner: they are so different, and yet in many ways – they are both bastards, both usurpers, both unscrupulous men of action – they are mirror images of each other.

The theme behind their relationship is 'the search for God,' for the play is 'an attempt to define the concept of God'.[74]

Though the play falls far short of this immensely ambitious aim, the rough-hewn relationship between Pizarro and Atahuallpa has a strange charm. Atahuallpa makes a spontaneous unreasoned choice of Pizarro and Pizarro finds himself drawn out from the destitution of his non-involvement through this act of being singled out, accepted, affirmed. He experiences an inner joy and meaning that arises only in relation, an expansion of the self from its contraction and paralysis. Atahuallpa helps him to relocate a part of himself violently excised by the trauma of his early childhood, which has resulted in the dessication of the spirit. The transference from one to the other of a vital portion of his nature, whether one calls it love or sympathy, holds out the possibility of grace and communion, reconciliation and harmony in the universe.

It makes Pizarro's dilemma all the more excruciating when, after Atahuallpa has paid the ransom demanded for his freedom, the Spanish commander is pressured on one side for the Inca's release, and on the other for his execution. Atahuallpa finally saves Pizarro from making a decision when he asserts that as the son of God, he cannot be killed before his time. He promises Pizarro that he will return from the dead at daybreak, at the first touch of the sun: 'Believe in me. I will give you a word and fill you with joy. For you I will do a great thing. I will swallow death and spit it out of me' (Act 2, Sc. 2, p. 76). The crude analogy with Christ is obvious. Pizarro is now faced with a crisis of faith, asked to make the leap between the rational and the non-rational.

Shaffer uses myth as the basis for steeping Atahuallpa in an illusion of his own immortality. Prescott relates the Peruvian belief in the divine ancestry of the Inca, one of the many traditions which grew up to explain the origin of the Peruvian monarchy. Legend had it that 'the Sun, the great luminary and parent of mankind', in compassion sent two of his children, Manco Capac and Mama Oello Huaco, to rescue the people from the barbarism in which they were immersed and teach them the arts of civilised life. The elaborate obsequies that were celebrated on the death of the Inca, and the careful preservation of his body by skilful embalming, were the result of the popular belief that the soul of the departed monarch would return after a time to re-animate his body on earth.[75]

The Inca was the incarnation of the life-principle for the Peruvians, and Atahuallpa's death had enormous implications for them. John Hemming writes that:

> Atahuallpa's immediate followers were stunned by his death. 'When he was taken out to be killed, all the native populace who were in the square, of which there were many, prostrated themselves on the ground, letting themselves fall to the earth like drunken men.'

One of the conquistadors, Pedro Pizarro, relates how, after the Inca's death, two of his sisters remained and:

> went about making great lamentations, with drums and singing, recording the deeds of their husband. Atahuallpa had told his sisters and wives that if he were not burned he would return to this world. They waited until the Governor (Francisco Pizarro) had gone out of his room, came to where Atahuallpa used to live, and asked me to let them enter. Once inside they began to call for Atahuallpa, searching very softly for him in all the corners . . . I disabused them and told them that dead men do not return.[76]

Nathan Wachtel points out that a future Messianic hope exists in Indian folklore:

> A myth spread secretly among the Indians of Peru and Bolivia says that after Atahuallpa's death his head was cut off, carried to Cuzco and buried. But under the ground the head is alive and a body is growing on to it. When it is wholly reconstituted, the Inca will rise out of the earth, the Spaniards will be driven out, the ancient Empire will be restored.

The message of the Indian play, *The Tragedy of Atahuallpa*, also carries this Messianic hope. 'The return of the Inca is confidently expected; an Indian victory at some future date is forecast as a real possibility.' 'It is significant that at Oruro, after the Inca's death, the chorus prays for his resurrection. At La Paz, according to the evidence of Dr Vellard, the performance used, indeed, to end with the resurrection and triumph of Atahuallpa.'[77]

Thus Shaffer's emphasis on Atahuallpa's death and expected resurrection is in keeping with these mythic-historic traditions. In the original production, the final scene of the play was 'hauntingly staged'.

> A ring of celebrants converge chanting over the dead king, wearing fantastic golden masks fixed in expressions of expectation that miraculously grow to bewilderment, as the sun comes up and the body remains inertly supine on the floor.[78]

The masked Indians finally melt away in grief and despair. Pizarro is left alone, cradling the dead Inca, singing to it, weeping. 'The sun glares at the audience' before it is extinguished by the final black-out (Act 2, Sc. 12, pp. 79–81).

The Royal Hunt of the Sun is clearly a romantic play, providing another example of a popular treatment of history. It is not seriously concerned with history as such, and has no great intellectual depth. Shaffer's approach to history is casual and exploitative. Discovering a tale of epic adventure in Prescott's romantic historical narrative, he uses it in a shallow opportunistic way for its sensational theatrical possibilities. He shows no interest in going beyond this outdated account by reading more modern historical studies. There is no historical evidence for what Shaffer calls the 'emotional heart' of the play: 'the strange adoptive relationship between a dying Spanish general and a young Indian king', 'a relationship between an atheist and a self-acknowledged God',[79] which leads to the mysterious religious conversion of one by the other. The definition of a history play established in the introduction, postulates a serious regard for historical truth or historical issues, as the essential requirement for a history play. *The Royal Hunt of the Sun* is therefore not a history play, evaluated by this criterion.

John Osborne's *Luther* presents another instance of a playwright being drawn to a historical subject for its religious interest. Yet Osborne's approach and achievement vary significantly from Bolt's and Shaffer's. His play, an arresting psychological study of a turbulent individual, at odds with himself and the social and religious institutions of his time, is one of considerably greater force and depth. Like Bolt, Osborne incorporates many of his central historical figure's recorded sayings into the dialogue of his play, but, unlike Bolt, he is able to match them with an urgent vital language of his own. This often results in impressive flights of rhetorical virtuosity or sequences of balanced arguments. Like Shaffer, he uses striking physical images, flamboyant spectacle and theatrical posture to create telling dramatic moments, but, where Shaffer indulges in these for their own sake, Osborne uses them with purpose, to reflect inner meaning or make a broad public point.

Luther is not the only time we find Osborne going to documentary sources for material and inspiration. His television play, *A Subject of Scandal and Concern* (1960) is based on events in the life of George Holyoake, who in 1842 was the last person in England to be imprisoned in England for blasphemy. Another play, *A Patriot for Me* (1964) is about Colonel Redl, the homosexual Austrian intelligence officer, who was blackmailed by Russian agents into betraying secrets to them in the period before the First World War. *Luther* has been selected for consideration because of its greater historical weight and dramatic impact, and because its concern with religious motivation links it with the other two plays dealt with in this chapter. It also illustrates the kind of history play, discussed in the introduction, which explores the relationship between the exceptional individual and his environment.

Luther at first was severely censored by the Lord Chamberlain's office – eighteen passages, including whole speeches, were blue-pencilled. Osborne refused to concede the excisions required, in an indignant letter to George Devine:

> I don't write plays to have them rewritten by someone else. I intend to make a clear unequivocal stand on this because (a) it is high time that someone did so, and (b) . . . the suggested cuts or alternatives would result in such damage to the psychological structure, meaning and depth of the play that the result would be a travesty.[80]

The Lord Chamberlain's office finally gave in, and apart from a few small verbal changes, *Luther* was presented intact.

The play was first produced by the English Stage Company on 26 June 1961 at the Theatre Royal, Nottingham, and it was published in the same year. It was acclaimed as an 'excellent play which combined strength and clarity',[81] 'the most solid guarantee yet given of Mr John Osborne's dramatic stamina'.[82] It transferred to London to the Royal Court Theatre in July 1961, and then to the Phoenix Theatre in September for a fairly long spell, continuing to run in London till the end of March 1962. Opening in Paris in 1961 at the Théâtre Des Nations, the play was described by Kenneth Tynan 'as the most eloquent piece of dramatic writing to have dignified our theatre since *Look Back in Anger*'. The language of the play did cause a stir but, ironically 'the lines by which a presumably sophisticated audience was most shocked were nearly all direct translations from the hero's own works'.[83]

The production was also a great success in New York, opening on 25 September 1963 at St James Theatre, where it ran for 211 performances. New York theatre critics hailed it as a 'brilliantly acted historical drama',[84] 'a work of power and integrity',[85] 'an overpowering massive play of ringing authority – bold, insolent and challenging'.[86] The play offered a splendid opportunity to Albert Finney, who gave an explosive performance in the title role, establishing himself as an actor of international repute. 'He makes it clear by this one performance that he is an actor of extraordinary skill and endless potentialities.'[87] The role of Luther is extremely exacting, stretching an actor both physically and emotionally. Finney proved himself equal to its demands, as Walter Kerr indicates:

> We meet a spiritual epileptic. . . . Out of the sweetest plainsong, in a small forest of cowls, comes a strangled sound that can neither be released nor repressed. This swallowed howl rises as Mr Finney breaks towards us, severing the neat little pattern of religious life around him, until he has been hurled to the floor in a tongue-locked seizure, gasping to let the genius out of him. . . . Something beyond his own intelligence drives, shatters, and then pacifies this hero. Mr Finney elaborates it for us with magnetizing energy.[88]

John Osborne was drawn to the subject of Luther, not for its historical but for its religious interest:

> I wanted to write a play about religious experience and various other things, and this happened to be the vehicle for it. Historical plays are usually anathema to me, but this isn't costume drama. I hope it won't make any difference if you don't know

anything about Luther himself, and I suspect that most people don't. In fact the historical character is almost incidental. The method is Shakespeare's or almost anyone else's you can think of.[89]

It is ironical and oddly amusing that one of the plays that fits my definition of a history play is written by a dramatist who detests history plays! But in spite of what Osborne says, historical truth obviously does make a difference to him since he is careful to base his play on the facts and is quick to defend his play on historical grounds. John Russell Taylor recalls that 'Osborne and his supporters rapidly pointed out to the tender-minded, who quailed at the dramatist's obsession with constipation and defecation', that the playwright had used Luther's own words whenever possible.[90] This line of defence is one which Shakespeare would have felt no inward or outward pressure to assume, again revealing the much greater demand in our time for documentary evidence to support a view.

Critics were obviously unsettled by Osborne's portrayal of a Luther struggling with a private area of neurosis, and tended to attack the play as history. Simon Trussler calls it 'an exercise in scatology', and writes of its 'failure to realize Martin's society – and more particularly the causes and effects of his impact upon it'.[91] Laurence Kitchin asserts that 'the historical Luther became a public figure and Osborne's Luther doesn't'.[92] Alan Carter's complaint is that 'Luther's real problem – the nature of faith – is hardly even discussed, and surely the Reformation was essentially an intellectual movement.'[93] Ronald Hayman goes so far as to say that compared with Brecht's *Galileo* or John Whiting's *The Devil*, *Luther* is not a history play at all because of Osborne's exclusion of this social aspect.[94]

But what if Osborne does extricate Luther from his social background. Osborne claims that Shakespeare adopted a similar approach and professes to write along Shakespearean rather than Brechtian lines. Critics have understandably considered the play in Brechtian terms; it was fashionable to make the comparison with Brecht, and Osborne was aware of Brechtian stage techniques and undoubtedly influenced by them. There are features in the play that reflect this such as the episodic structure, and the use of the medieval Knight figure to announce the time and place of the action. But these are superficial outward resemblances, and the play is not essentially Brechtian in character nor is there any reason why it should be. Osborne's focus is much narrower, more personal and concentrated than Brecht's. Unlike Brecht who works for a degree of critical detachment in his spectators, Osborne is interested primarily in engaging their feelings:

I want to make people feel, to give them lessons in feeling. They can think afterwards.[95]

As for the nature of the Luther he presents, the use of Luther's Christian name throughout suggests an emphasis on the personal inward dimension of the man rather than the social public figure.

Many names could be given to Luther – great religious leader, rebel, scholar, preacher, iconoclast, publicist, poet. In his play, Osborne draws attention to all these facets of the man, but, focuses mainly on an aspect many people might be inclined to resist – Luther as victim or patient. Osborne was obviously influenced by E. H. Erikson's book, *Young Man Luther*, a psychoanalytical study of Luther, first published in England in 1959, just two years before the play was staged. In it Erikson quotes a statement of Søren Kierkegaard's – 'Luther is a patient of exceeding import for Christendom' – and comments that Kierkegaard saw in Luther 'a religious attitude (patienthood) exemplified in an archetypal and immensely influential way'.[96] The full text of Kierkegaard's statement is that Luther:

confuses what it means to be the patient with what it means to be the doctor. He is an extremely important patient for Christianity, but he is not the doctor; he has the patient's passion for expressing and describing his suffering, and what he feels the need of as an alleviation. But he has not got the doctor's breadth of view.[97]

What Kierkegaard seems to mean by this is that Luther expressed in himself the symptoms or consequences of what was wrong in the Church. His was the subjective response to the problem, but, not possessing the doctor's objective overall view, he was not in a position to prescribe the cure.

Osborne might have come across the portion of Kierkegaard's statement quoted in Erikson, or even been familiar with the original passage itself, because he did read Kierkegaard, Jaspers, and

Sartre in the 1940s, when he says 'existentialism was the macro-
biotic food of the day'.[98] At any rate in his play, Luther embodies
this subjective, 'patient' side of life. The intellectual impact of
Luther's achievement is not dealt with so much as the felt experience, the crisis of belief and identity.

Luther is presented equivocally, which is fitting, considering the
continuing controversy over this complex towering figure, enigmatic to admirers and detractors alike. He can be seen as the hyper-
conscious individual, the artist, the prophet, the Christlike figure
who takes on the tensions and torments of his age because he feels
more acutely than others – 'Am I the only one to see all this and
suffer?' The sense of being singled out and hounded is prevalent:

> Somewhere, in the body of a child, Satan foresaw in me what
> I'm suffering now. That's why he prepares open pits for me, and
> all kinds of tricks to bring me down, so that I keep wondering if
> I'm the only man living who's baited and surrounded by dreams,
> and afraid to move.
>
> (Act 1, Sc. 2, p. 30)

His condition can thus be seen as an aberration from the norm,
or indicative of 'an overstimulated conscience', as it is dismissed by
some fellow monks. Luther is also accused of megalomania by
Cajetan, the papal legate: 'Why, some deluded creature might
even come to you as leader of their revolution, but you don't want
to break rules, you want to make them' (Act 2, Sc. 4, p. 73). Even
Staupitz, Vicar General of the Augustinian Order, who immediately recognizes a greatness of mind and spirit, discerns a definite
leaning towards the theatrical: 'One thing I promise you, Martin.
You'll never be a spectator. You'll always take part' (Act 2, Sc. 2,
p. 56). Then again, Martin's predicament could reflect the inner
tumult of the man of creative intensity who wrestles with experience, and sees in his own imaginative terms. The Knight, who
bitterly confronts Luther at the end, regards him as out of touch
with reality in his exaltation of "the Word":

> Word? What Word? Word? That word, whatever that means, is
> probably just another old relic or indulgence, and you know
> what you did to those! Why, none of it might be any more than
> poetry, have you thought of that, Martin. Poetry! Martin, you're
> a poet, there's no doubt about that in anybody's mind, you're a

poet, but do you know what most men believe in their hearts –
because they don't see in images like you do – they believe in
their hearts that Christ was a man as we are, and that He was a
prophet and a teacher, and they also believe in their hearts that
His supper is a plain meal like their own – if they're lucky to get
it – a plain meal of bread and wine! A plain meal with no garnish
and no word. And *you* helped them to believe it.

(Act 3, Sc. 2, pp. 90–1)

Osborne presents all these alternate perspectives of the man and
leaves the questions open-ended.

The play opens on a compelling note, with Martin being received into the Augustinian Order of the Eremites at Erfurt. In the
original production the 'setting is dominated by an agonized Christ
hanging from a crucifix bent as if by the burden of humanity's
crime'. An 'atmosphere of reverence that amounts to awe'[99] is
created by prayer, music, ritual, as Martin proceeds to take his
vows. In the presence of the assembled convent, Martin is un-
dressed to represent the divestment of the former man, and re-
robed in the habit of the order, to signify investment of the new
man in Christ. Martin kneels, and swears the oath of obedience.
Then he prostrates himself, while the prior prays over him. A
newly lighted taper is put in his hands, and he is led up the altar
steps to be welcomed by the monks. Indistinguishable in their
midst, he marches with them slowly in procession and is lost to
sight (Act 1, Sc. 1, pp. 13–14). The powerful symbolism in the
ceremony strongly conveys the idea of the absorption of the
individual into the communal.

Martin's experience in the monastery is presented as a tremendous struggle for self-denial and subjugation. He is overscrupulous
in his attempts to conform to the rigours of a highly disciplined
life. Yet an exaggerated sense of being bound down and closed in
gets the better of all his efforts at self-abnegation. This again is
communicated in striking visual physical terms, in the form of a
violent fit which suddenly grips Martin during mass. When at first
the office commences he is lost to sight in the ranks of the monks.
Presently there is a quiet moaning, just distinguishable among the
voices. It becomes louder and wilder, until finally Martin appears
staggering between the stalls. Outstretched hands fail to restrain
him as he is seized in a raging fit. Two brothers go to him, but
Martin jerks with such ferocity, that they can scarcely hold him

down. He tries to speak, the effort is frantic, and eventually, is able to roar out a word at a time, 'Not! Me! I am not!' He finally collapses, and is dragged off. 'The office continues as if nothing had taken place' (Act 1, Sc. 1, pp. 22–3). The idea of the suppression of the individual by the institutional is put across vividly. The all-unifying world of the 'participation mystique' is set against the self-aware and self-imposing. The loss of uniqueness or identity takes on magnified proportions for Martin, who experiences it as abysmal self-loss.

The trammels of his environment – home, monastery, Church – all contribute to the sense of being fractured, dispersed and separated from himself. Hans Luther is an oppressive father-figure, affronting the dignity of the child, undermining his self-concept and presiding as a dominant factor in Martin's adult psyche. Hans who feels no less threatened than his son, is continually asserting himself to cover up his own feelings of inadequacy and insecurity. There is great strain and aggression in the relationship. In a Pinter-like situation, both can be found playing for the upper hand, manoeuvring to keep the advantage, shrinking from direct contact, yet striving to make connection. Here Osborne dramatizes the archetypal father and son conflict. Martin has to fight free of the identity of being Hans's son in order to discover his own personhood. At the very close of the play, we hear Martin telling his son, Hans:

> You know, my father had a son, and he'd to learn a hard lesson, which is a human being is a helpless little animal, but he is not created by his father, but by God. . . . You should have seen me at Worms. I was almost like you that day, as if I'd learned to play again, to play, to play out in the world, like a naked child.
>
> (Act 3, Sc. 3, p. 102)

Martin here recalls his experience at Worms as a rare moment of contact with his spontaneous untouched self.

The child is used as a powerful leitmotif in the play to suggest Martin's sense of wrested childhood, of having lost something that at root he is, underneath the demands and distortions of his environment. This feeling of self-loss is symbolized in the poetic image of the lost body of a child. Dredged out of Martin's tormented subconscious, this image haunts him continually. Martin's troubled interior state is forcefully realized in Act 2, Scene 1, partly by the expressionistic setting. A huge knife is suspended above the acting area of the stage with the torso of a naked man hanging over its cutting edge. Below this is 'an enormous round cone, like the inside of a vast barrel, surrounded by darkness' which suggests the deep corridors of the subconscious. 'From the upstage entrance seemingly far, far away, a dark figure appears against the blinding light' inside the cone, approaching slowly until it reaches the downstage entrance. 'It is Martin, haggard and streaming with sweat.' He cries out from some deep dimension of himself:

> I lost the body of a child, a child's body, the eyes of a child; and at the first sound of my own childish voice. I lost the body of a child; and I was afraid, and I went back to find it . . . I'm afraid of the darkness, and the hole in it; and I see it sometime of every day! . . . The lost body of a child, hanging on a mother's tit, and close to the warm, big body of a man, and I can't find it.
>
> (Act 1, Sc. 2, p. 24)

Osborne must have come across this image of 'the lost body of a child, hanging on a mother's tit and close to the warm big body of a man' in Erikson, who relates how the historical Luther once said that he did not know the Christchild any more; 'in characterizing the sadness of his youth, he had lost his childhood.' But later he could say that 'Christ was defined by two images: one of an infant lying in a manger, "hanging on a virgin's tits"' and 'one of a man sitting at his Father's right hand.'[100] Erikson talks of man as being bound in the loves and rages of childhood – the child is in the midst – and asserts that

> man's adulthood contains a persistent childishness: that vistas of the future always reflect the mirages of a missed past, that apparent progression can harbour partial regression and firm accomplishment hidden childish fulfilment.[101]

Osborne uses these ideas in his dramatization of Luther's interior state and thus can be found keeping close to history even in his depiction of the kind of image that could mentally possess Luther.

Martin's tortured self-consciousness brings home the idea that man is the centre of his own experience and subject to an inescapable narcissism of outlook. Man relates with others, but only from within a consciousness of which he is the focus. Society might

present a picture of selves together, but essentially it is each alone
in his own tragedy. This is brought out strikingly when the monks
are shown at communal confession. The stage directions indicate
that the scene throughout should be 'urgent, muted, almost whispered, confidential, secret like a prayer'. They are all prostrated
beneath flaming candles, and the formal confession of trifles by the
other monks is punctuated by Martin's wrenched outcries: 'I am
alone. I am alone, and against myself.' 'I am a worm and no man, a
byword and a laughing stock. Crush out the worminess in me,
stamp on me' (Act 1, Sc. 1, pp. 19–20). The close physical presence
of the other monks going through the motions of the office,
oblivious of Martin's anguish, emphasizes his essential isolation.

Martin suffers from an excessive emotional sensibility, and the
fact that his condition is partly of his own making, contributes to
his dilemma. He confesses to an oppressive dream:

> I was fighting a bear in a garden without flowers, leading into a
> desert. His claws kept making my arms bleed as I tried to open a
> gate which would take me out. But the gate was no gate at all. It
> was simply an open frame, and I could have walked through it,
> but I was covered in my own blood, and I saw a naked woman
> riding on a goat, and the goat began to drink my blood, and I
> thought I should faint with the pain and I awoke in my cell, all
> soaking in the devil's bath.
>
>   (Act 1, Sc. 2, pp. 19–20)

The nightmare conveys the experience of being incarcerated in a
self-imposed prison and assaulted by feelings of overwhelming
fear and guilt, related to sex.

Luther's frightening sensation of being encased, closed in, dominates his personal sense of dilemma in the play. Osborne again
probably derives this idea from Erikson, who describes Luther's
traumatic experience of this sensation during a thunderstorm
which occurred just before he became a monk:

> In the thunderstorm, he had felt immense anxiety. Anxiety
> comes from *angustus*, meaning to feel hemmed in and choked
> up; Martin's use of *circumvallatus* – all walled in – to describe his
> experience in the thunderstorm indicates he felt a sudden con-
> striction of his whole life space, and could see only one way out:
> the abandonment of all his previous life and of the earthly future

it implied, for the sake of total dedication to a new life. This new life, however, was one which made an institution of the very configuration of being walled in.[102]

Osborne seems to have taken up this idea and built on it. The whole play dramatizes the agonized thrust to break free. Luther is man making a bid for independent judgement, and experiencing a guilt which is very closely associated with freedom. It is the sense of being accused by some enclosing whole or order – family, Church, or more radically, the psychic womb – from which the independent self seeks to break out. This guilt grows with self-consciousness, and inheres in any free as opposed to 'being part of' action. Its gravamen is not merely non-conformity but independence, and it is inseparable from loneliness – 'Am I the only one to see all this and suffer?' (Act 1, Sc. 2, p. 30).

Tormented by thoughts of judgement and hell, Luther finally breaks through to some sort of release, in the sudden revelation he receives of the profound implications of St Paul's affirmation that 'The just shall live by faith.' Throughout the play, Luther's sensation of being hemmed in by spiritual fear and tension is linked to his physical struggles with constipation – 'I am blocked up like an old crypt.' (Act 1, Sc. 2, p. 29). Consistently, Luther's great moment of spiritual inspiration occurs at a time of relief from acute physical and emotional stress caused by this chronic disability:

> It came to me while I was in my tower, what they call the monk's sweathouse, the jakes, the john or whatever you're pleased to call it. I was struggling with the text I've given you 'For therein is the righteousness of God revealed, from faith to faith.'' And seated there, my head down, on that privy just as when I was a little boy, I couldn't reach down to my breath for the sickness in my bowels, as I seemed to sense a large rat, a heavy, wet, plague rat, slashing at my privates with its death teeth. I thought of the righteousness of God, and wished his gospel had never been put to paper for men to read; who demanded my love and made it impossible to return it. And I sat in my heap of pain until the words emerged and opened up. "The just shall live by faith." My pain vanished, my bowels flushed and I could get up. I could see the life I'd lost.
>
> (Act 2, Sc. 3, p. 63)

Luther is driven to this spiritual discovery by his pervasive anguish at the unbearable destiny of being human and hence totally vulnerable and susceptible. Throughout the play there is great emphasis on the physical as well as the spiritual. The reek and weight of the body are continually registered. Martin often appears pouring with sweat, as if suffused with the sense of his own mortality. He continually feels betrayed by his body:

> If my flesh would leak and dissolve, and I could live as bone, if I were forged bone, plucked bone, warm hair and a bony heart, if I were all bone, I could brandish myself without terror, without any terror at all – I could be indestructible.
>
> (Act 1, Sc. 1, p. 21)

His father tells him:

> You can't ever, however you try, you can't ever get away from your body because that's what you live in, and it's all you've got to die in, and you can't get away from the body of your father and your mother!
>
> (Act 1, Sc. 2, p. 41)

It is as if Martin is terrified of his own animality, and this relates to his emerging conviction that all men fall inescapably short of God's law, because God requires assent from the heart and concupiscent man cannot give obedience with total spontaneity of mind and body.

The first Act of the play concentrates on the interior dimension and for this Osborne is heavily indebted to Erikson. Osborne's treatment of history has been criticized in relation to his use of this source. Trussler claims that Osborne 'fails to assimilate all his available source material – mainly garnered from the psycho-analytical study *Young Man Luther*, by Erik H. Erikson'.[103] Hayman states that Osborne 'seems to have done hardly any reading outside this one book'.[104] But this is not the case because he also appears to have drawn substantially upon another source which critics do not seem to have noticed – Roland Bainton's concise but authoritative biography, *Here I Stand: the Life of Martin Luther* (New York: Mentor, 1950). I shall be turning to this later to illustrate Osborne's interesting use of Bainton. But even if Erikson's study had been Osborne's only source, it is a well documented work, based on a sound reading of collated evidence and the most significant modern scholarship on the subject.

E. Gordon Rupp, a well-known modern Luther scholar, acknowledges this in an article, 'John Osborne and the Historical Luther,' first published in *The Expository Times*, volume 73 (February 1962).[105] This article is the substance of a lecture delivered at the University of Aberdeen on 31 October 1961, after the play had aroused much public discussion. Rupp cites Erikson's *Young Man Luther* as the book of the play and comments:

> Erikson brings to his highly intelligent study not only his clinical experience but a wide reading which includes all the more notable modern books of Luther study. His work is a pyscho-analytical commentary on Martin Luther's development. It is not the first such study, but is perhaps the most effective . . . in 1941 a Danish medical man and a Catholic, Paul J. Reiter, wrote two volumes on *Luther's World, his character and psychosis*. His picture of Luther as a tipsy manic-depressive is not very convincing, but his second volume puts together almost all the available evidence about Luther's physical and spiritual troubles and is very useful. On this and the valuable collection of historical documents by Otto Scheel, Erikson has drawn, so that this study of first-hand evidence has been to Mr Osborne's advantage.[106]

Rupp points out the vastness of the material on Luther – the great spate of Luther's own writings, and the immense international field of Luther study, which has caused attention to be turned to 'histories of the histories of Luther' – and admits that:

> one of the refreshing and valuable points of Osborne's play is that he does pry Luther loose, so to speak, from his orthodox framework – from theology and piety as Protestants have conceived it, and gives us a kind of "existential" Luther who is really disturbingly and excitingly alive.

However he maintains that 'we have very little really reliable evidence about Luther's home and childhood', and ultimately sees the play as a 'highly complicated psychological interpretation read into or out of chancy little bits of historical evidence which have haphazardly survived'.[107]

But, as has been emphasized in the introduction, it is the historian's and not the playwright's function to weigh the evidence. What the historian sees as 'evidence' the dramatist sees more as 'material'. Historical truth however is more than the available evidence. We cannot be sure we have the whole truth no matter how solid the evidence. Our knowledge of historical truth will always be fragmentary and the attempt to discover it will always involve the certain, the plausible and the purely speculative. The historian's contribution towards the recovery of the truth is specialized knowledge and systematic controlled inquiry. The dramatist's is imaginative sympathy and insight which must be given full play over his material, as long as no violence is done to history, and there are reasonable grounds for his portrayal. Of course Osborne did not set out to write a history play and might not even regard *Luther* as one. But I am calling it a history play because it fulfils the requirements of my definition for no matter how controversial a portrait of Luther Osborne presents, there is a firm historical basis for the vision presented.

Rupp finds the story that Luther had some kind of fit during Mass, 'more than suspect', asserting that it comes from four Catholic writers who were Luther's enemies. Erikson accepts the story, he says, because 'it fits with his pre-fabricated psychological pattern – the interpretation of Luther's troubles as a persistent identity crisis.' Rupp insists this is important 'since it is in fact the only evidence that Luther had any attacks of this kind', there is no trace of epilepsy before or after. But, as he amazingly goes on to admit, Luther had 'psychosomatic attacks' which first occurred in his forties and were 'connected with his heart, dizziness, palpitations, and fainting fits. That as a monk he had desperate moments and occasional anxiety states is beyond doubt'.[108] Here we see a fine example of the historian's concern with accuracy of a precise narrow type which a playwright would not be bothered with. Osborne naturally pounced on the wonderful dramatic possibilities of the story of the fit during Mass, which vividly epitomizes the kind of intense psychological ordeal Luther was so prone to suffer. Luther's conflict with his father on entering the monastery, the emotional trauma of his first Mass, his prodigious imagination, his force of rhetoric and often bitter scatological invective, his physical maladies and the periods of intense religious doubt and anguish which hounded him all his life, are firmly attested facts. If Osborne includes incidents that are historically suspect – the fit in the choir, the nailing of the 95 theses on the door of the Castle Church at Wittenberg, the celebrated statement at the Diet of Worms: 'Here I stand, I cannot do otherwise' – it is because the fascination of these is immense. This is so even for historians who deny their authenticity; irresistibly these stories have been repeated and are now an inextricable part of the legend surrounding the man.

Rupp however is impressed when Osborne keeps 'marvellously close to the details' of actual dialogue and incident, and dubious when he does not. His criticism of the play as history is on rather narrow, selective and inconsistent lines:

> Now it is a valid point of Erikson that "nobody who has read Luther's private remarks can doubt that his whole being always included his bowels." But since so much is made of this in the play, in the end to a comic and rather nauseating degree, and since it seems to me to damage the play as an historical chronicle, let it be firmly said that there is no evidence whatever that Luther had troubles like this as a monk, or indeed before the autumn of 1521 . . . To harp on this and show it as a constant factor in Luther's career from beginning to end, is quite unhistorical . . .

Yet he acknowledges nonetheless that:

> Luther's illnesses are important and from 1521 onwards, there is a long list of them, deafness, noises in the head, dizziness, fainting, ophthalmia, hardening of the arteries, stone, bladder trouble, angina, so that when he died perhaps of a coronary thrombosis at the age of 63 he had been for some years a really old man.[109]

Osborne has solid grounds for emphasizing Luther's physical disabilities and suggesting a correlation between his physical and spiritual condition since he did suffer acutely from such ailments and from states of neurotic anxiety. As another historian, Roland Bainton, asserts, the recurrence of Luther's severe depressions 'raises for us again and again the question whether they had a physical basis and the question really cannot be answered'.[110] Osborne's 'harping' on this surely is in keeping with the new psychological perspective of our age, which sees the mind and body as inseparable, and stresses the indivisibility of the human personality.

Osborne's view of Luther is by no means limited to the purely personal. The play portrays a state of spiritual crisis that reflects the climate of Luther's age as it does ours. In some periods of history, Erikson writes, 'man needs a new ideological orientation as surely and sorely as he must have air and food', and Luther, 'a young man (by no means lovable all the time) faced the problems of human existence in the foremost terms of his era'.[111] It is this fiery young Luther that not surprizingly caught the imagination of John Osborne.

As indicated earlier, although Osborne draws considerably on Erikson for his vision of Luther, this is not his only major historical source as critics have claimed. He also appears to have used Roland Bainton's biography of Luther, *Here I Stand* – the internal evidence is overwhelming. One of the strongest features that points to this is the inspiration Osborne derived from drawings and woodcuts of the period for there are numerous illustrations of these in Bainton's book. In the play Osborne states in a note on décor:

> After the intense private interior of Act One, with its outer darkness and rich, personal objects, the physical effect from now on should be more intricate, general, less personal; sweeping, concerned with men in time rather than particular man in the unconscious; caricature not portraiture, like the popular wood-cuts of the period, like DÜRER.

As a backdrop for Act 2, Scene 4, which dramatizes Luther's interview with Cajetan, Osborne specifies as a backcloth:

> a satirical contemporary woodcut, showing for example, the Pope portrayed as an ass playing the bagpipes, or a cardinal dressed up as a court fool. Or perhaps Holbein's cartoon of Luther with the Pope suspended from his nose.
>
> (*Luther*, pp. 46, 64)

Illustrations of all these woodcuts are reproduced in Bainton's biography, and it seems obvious that Osborne found a ready source in Bainton.

Bainton writes of Dürer's profound disquiet at the futility of all human endeavour, and provides a graphic description of his engraving, *Melancholia*:

There sits a winged woman of high intelligence in torpid idleness amid all the tools and symbols of man's highest skills. . . . The bell above is ready to toll. Yet in sable gloom she broods, because the issues of destiny strive in the celestial sphere. In the sky the rainbow arches, sign of the covenant sworn by Noah, never to bring again the waters upon the earth; but within the rainbow glimmers a comet, portent of impending disaster. Beside Melancholia, perched upon a millstone, sits a scribbling cherub alone active because insouciant of the forces at play. Is the point again, as with Erasmus, that wisdom lies with the simplicity of childhood, and man might better lay aside his skills until the gods have decided the issues of the day? What a parallel have we here in quite other terms to Luther's agonizing quest for the ultimate meaning of life![112]

Osborne must have been struck by the interesting parallel Bainton draws between Dürer's engraving and Martin's predicament for this passage brings inescapably to mind a similar idea and picture in the play. Martin encounters a child, dirty, half-naked, and playing intently by himself, on the steps of the Castle Church at Wittenberg. It is the year 1517 and Martin is just about to nail up his 95 theses on the Castle Church door, that legendary action that was to propel him into the vortex of international conflict and ultimately bring about overwhelming repercussions for the whole of the western world. Martin 'puts out his hand to the child, who looks at it gravely and deliberately, then slowly, not rudely, but naturally, gets up and skips away sadly out of sight' (Act 2, Sc. 3, p. 61).

Bainton also prints a reproduction of a drawing of Christ the Judge sitting upon a rainbow with a lily protruding from one ear and a sword piercing the other. Beneath him on one side there are figures being lifted up to heaven, and on the opposite side there are others being dragged down to hell. Bainton comments that the:

Christ upon the rainbow with the lily and the sword was a most familiar figure in illustrated books of the period. Luther had seen pictures such as these and testified that he was utterly terror-stricken at the sight of Christ the Judge.[113]

In the play Luther is haunted by this particular image of Christ on a rainbow judging the world. Just before he is about to celebrate his first Mass, he falls to his knees crying out in desperation:

> Oh Mary, dear Mary, all I can see of Christ is a flame and raging on a rainbow. Pray to your Son, and ask Him to still His anger for I can't raise my eyes to look at Him.

(Act 1, Sc. 2, p. 30)

This strongly suggests that Osborne used Bainton, since he picks on the very drawing that Bainton chooses to illustrate exactly the same point.

Then again, Osborne's representation of Pope Leo X relates directly to Bainton's delineation of him·

> The pontiff at the moment was Leo X, of the house of the Medici, as elegant and as indolent as a Persian cat. His chief pre-eminence lay in his ability to squander the resources of the Holy See on carnivals, war, gambling and the chase. The duties of his Holy Office were seldom suffered to interfere with the sport. He wore hunting boots which impeded the kissing of his toe.[114]

This figure springs to life in Osborne's play. He enters 'with a HUNTSMAN, dogs and DOMINICANS'. He is indolent, cultured, intelligent, extremely restless, and well able to assimilate the essence of anything before anyone else. As Miltitz kneels to kiss his toe, he dismisses him impatiently, 'I should forget it. I've got my boots on. Well? get on with it. We're missing the good weather.' On receiving Martin's final appeal to the Church, he reads the young monk's plea for judgement and correction of his views as mere attitudinizing, and lets loose the full weight of his secular and ecclesiastical powers. His attitude is cold and unequivocal: 'There's a wild pig in our vineyard, and it must be hunted down and shot' (Act 2, Sc. 5, pp. 75–8).

The episodes in the play involving the Pope and Tetzel, the notorious seller of indulgences, come over as caricature with their broad but incisive lines of depiction. For these public figures, Osborne creates the effect of a caught attitude or impression, very much in the style of satirical cartoons of the period of which Bainton provides many examples.[115] It is intriguing to find Osborne making rich dramatic use of the source material supplied by this whole tradition of popular criticism in the form of polemical woodcuts, drawings, engravings and cartoons that flourished in the period.

There are other indications that Osborne drew inspiration from Bainton's account. In the early half of the play, Luther's conversations with Staupitz show the older man coping with the young man's importunate questionings, and gently reproving him for his obsession with various mortifications: 'All these trials and temptations you go through, they're meat and drink to you' (Act 2, Sc. 2, p. 53). There is a distinct parallel in Bainton who gives accounts of such theological discussions, with Luther beside himself when Staupitz failed to understand his torment:

> Was then, Luther the only one in the world who had been so plagued? Had Staupitz himself never experienced such trials? 'No,' said he, 'but I think they are your meat and drink.' Evidently he suspected Luther of thriving on his disturbances. The only word of reassurance he could give was a reminder that the blood of Christ was shed for the remission of sins. But Luther was too obsessed with the picture of Christ the avenger to be consoled with the picture of Christ the redeemer.[116]

Osborne similarly uses Staupitz as the voice of sanity and reason in the play. His balance and moderation serve as a foil to Martin's inordinacy and obsession.

Bainton emphasizes the fact that Luther was assailed by doubt all his life. 'This man who so undergirded others with faith had for himself a perpetual battle for faith.' The content of his 'depressions was always the same, the loss of faith that God is good and that he is good to *me*. After the frightful *Anfechtung* of 1527 Luther wrote, "For more than a week I was close to the gates of death and hell. I trembled in all my members. Christ was wholly lost. I was shaken by desperation and blasphemy of God." His agony in the later years was all the more intense because he was a physician of souls, and if the medicine which he had prescribed for himself and for them was actually poison, how frightful was his responsibility.'

Luther held that the way of man with God cannot be tranquil: 'David must have been plagued by a very fearful devil. He could not have had such profound insights if he had not experienced great assaults.' Bainton comments that:

> Luther verged on saying that an excessive emotional sensibility

is a mode of revelation . . . Luther felt that his depressions were necessary. At the same time they were dreadful and by all means and in every way to be avoided and overcome. His whole life was a struggle against them, a fight for faith.[117]

Osborne takes precisely this angle in the play, presenting Luther equivocally as a man of extraordinary spiritual vision yet a man who is also continually 'struggling for certainty, struggling insanely like a man in a fit, an animal trapped to the bone with doubt' (Act 2, Scene 4, p. 73).

In the second half of the play the accent is on the public figure rather than the private individual. The fast-moving episodic scenes provide sweeping cinematic flashes, a telescopic view of the personalities involved. John Tetzel cuts a flamboyant figure. The actor is required to have a commanding voice and presence for he has to hold the stage in a scene that is pure monologue. Tetzel's arrival is a spectacle in itself. To the accompaniment of loud music, bells, singing, and the smoke of incense from lighted tapers, a slow-moving procession makes its way to the centre of the market-place at Juterbög. Behind the Pontiff's bull of grace carried on a cushion and cloth of gold, and the arms of the Pope and the Medici, comes the focus of the procession, John Tetzel, Dominican, inquisitor and the most famous indulgence vendor of his day. With the rhetorical flourish and histrionic flair of the born salesman, he comes into his own as lord of the market-place:

. . . won't you for as little as one quarter of a florin, my friend, buy yourself one of these letters, so that in the hour of death, the gate through which sinners can enter the world of torment shall be closed against you, and the gate leading to the joy of paradise be flung open for you? And, remember this, these letters aren't just for the living but for the dead too. . . . It isn't even necessary to repent. So don't hold back, come forward, think of your dear ones, think of yourselves! . . . For remember: As soon as your money rattles in the box and the cash bell rings, the soul flies out of purgatory and sings!

The speech ends with Tetzel flinging a large coin into the open strong box, where it rattles furiously. There follows the sound of coins clattering like rain into a great coffer as the light fades (Act 2, Sc. 1, pp. 47–50). In production this was one of the most arresting scenes of the play. Tetzel was played by Peter Bull who turned this speech into 'a juicy theatrical turn'.[118] 'Corpulent under his mitre and hawking indulgences to a rattle of tambourine and drums', he spoke with a 'jolly, sleazy mission-week intimacy' that was 'lovely caricature'.[119] This meretricious display of pomp and rhetoric provoked a spontaneous round of applause. Gaudy spectacle and sensation are used with a serious purpose here to convey the prostitution of the Church – the corruption of the truth for cheap commercial ends. The vulgar bigotry of Tetzel is contrasted with the vision and sophistication of Cajetan, 'Cardinal of San Sisto, General of the Dominican Order, as well as its most distinguished theologian, papal legate, Rome's highest representative in Germany.' Urbane, subtle, the practised diplomat, Cajetan puts forward the strongest arguments for the Church. In an interview with Martin he makes an eloquent plea for its authority and unity. If these are destroyed he predicts a time of great social disquiet when there will be 'frontiers, frontiers of all kinds – between men – and there'll be no end to them'. 'How will men find God if they are left to themselves each man abandoned and only known to himself?' (Act 2, Sc. 4, p. 74).

Cajetan's anticipation of what will ensue from the kicking away of traditional supports prefigures the state of things to come – the disintegration of the Church and the gradual dissolution of all real order and cohesion in Western society with the lack of an all-embracing structure to provide anchorage and direction. The Church and the world rent by schism is precisely the opposite of what the historical Luther intended, and Osborne's inclusion of a forward perspective here adds dramatic weight and edge to the discussion. As Katharine Worth points out, the trial scene in Shaw's *Saint Joan* 'must surely have been in Osborne's mind when he constructed the argument between Luther and Cajetan'. 'Like Cauchon, Cajetan argues with moderation, civilized wit and understanding', warning Luther of the 'far-reaching consequences of his "heresy," consequences which Luther himself, like Saint Joan in her play, has not envisaged'.[120]

At the Diet of Worms, Martin finally takes an irrevocable stand which is also a personal expression of identity and freedom:

Unless I am shown by the testimony of the Scriptures – for I don't believe in popes or councils – unless I am refuted by Scripture and my conscience is captured by God's own word, I cannot and will not recant, since to act against one's conscience is neither safe nor honest. Here I stand; God help me; I can do no more.

(Act 3, Sc. 1, p. 85)

Like Bolt, Osborne places stress on the self as the ultimate point of reference. Thus Martin admits later, with reference to this critical moment: 'I listened for God's voice but all I could hear was my own' (Act 3, Sc. 3, p. 101). This harmonizes with the fact that the historical Luther made the subjective element overt and central in the question of faith, taking religion away from the monopoly of Church or institution.

From this bold heroic moment at Worms, there is a sudden dismaying shift of mood and perspective as we are confronted with the uprising of the peasants in 1525 and its ruthless suppression. The shock of this transition came through with ironic impact through its staging in the original production:

Mr Finney stands there in the foreground against a rich tapestry, proudly holding aloft one of the books he has refused to disown as a glowing light irradiates him. Then a light comes up in the background making the tapestry transparent and showing the peasants with their tattered banners marching to the fray. It is as if hero and anti-hero were revealed in a flash to be one, like Luther's strength and weakness.[121]

A Knight steps out from among the carnage. He fiercely upbraids Luther for his failure to support the peasants he roused to rebellion by letting loose the floodwaters of change, that now threaten to sweep everything away, including what Luther upholds himself. He stands accused from all sides:

Martin: The princes blame me, you blame me and the peasants
       blame me –
Knight: *You* put the water in the wine didn't you?

The Knight places his hand deliberately, ritually, on the lifeless body of a peasant and smears Martin with the blood. 'You're all ready now,' he says, 'You even look like a butcher – ' Martin cries out in despair, 'God is the butcher – ' (Act 3, Sc. 3, pp. 88–9).

Martin attempts to reconcile his faith with the reality of the catastrophic suffering around him. Preaching a sermon with enormous effort, he relates the story of Abraham's obedience in the face of God's command to sacrifice Isaac, his son, another spiritual dilemma which involves a morally dubious decision:

> Never, save in Christ, was there such obedience as in that moment, and, if God had blinked, the boy would have died then, but the Angel intervened, and the boy was released, and Abraham took him up in his arms again. In the teeth of life we seem to die, but God says no – in the teeth of death we live. If He butchers us, He makes us live.
>
> (Act 3, Sc. 2, p. 92)

Martin can only suggest blind faith in God's ultimate redeeming purpose, in the face of the horrific violence and suffering that follow as part of the consequence of his actions.

In depicting Luther as clinging to the Bible for strength and solace, Osborne was almost certainly influenced by Bainton who asserts that:

> The Scriptures assumed for Luther an overwhelming import-ance, not primarily as a source book for antipapal polemic, but as the one ground of certainty. He had rejected the authority of popes and councils, and could not make a beginning from within as did the prophets of the inward word. The core of his quarrel with them was that in moments of despondency he could find nothing within but utter blackness. He was com-pletely lost unless he could find something without on which to lay hold. And this he found in the Scriptures. He approached them uncritically, from our point of view, but not with credulity. Nothing so amazed him as the faith of the participants: that Mary credited the annunciation of the angel Gabriel; that Joseph gave credence to the dream which allays his misgivings . . . that the Wise Men were ready to go to Bethlehem at the word of the prophet.

To illustrate Luther's feelings of wonder at such faith, Bainton quotes from one of Luther's sermons in which he narrates the sacrifice of Isaac by Abraham:

The father raised his knife. The boy bared his throat. If God had slept an instant, the lad would have been dead. I could not have watched. I am not able in my thoughts to follow. The lad was as a sheep for the slaughter. Never in history was there such obedience, save in Christ. But God was watching and all the angels. The father raised his knife; the boy did not wince. The angel cried, "Abraham, Abraham!" See how divine majesty is at hand in the hour of death. We say, "In the midst of life we die." God answers, "Nay in the midst of death we live."[122]

Osborne uses precisely the portion of this particular sermon of Luther's which Bainton quotes. He modifies the language a little to blend in with his own modern prose style, but keeps close to the essential spirit and simple vigour of the original.

The final scene of the play again clearly derives its tone and shape from Bainton, who relates how Luther, grown famous and rather imperious in later years (having angered Henry VIII, infuriated Duke George and estranged Erasmus) was concerned that perhaps he had also hurt Staupitz who had not written for some time. Bainton quotes Staupitz's reply to Luther's letter of inquiry:

> My love for you is unchanged, passing the love of women . . . but you seem to me to condemn many external things which do not affect justification. Why is the cowl a stench in your nostrils when many in it have lived holy lives? There is nothing without abuse. My dear friend, I beseech you to remember the weak. Do not denounce points of indifference which can be held in sincerity, though in matters of faith be never silent. We owe much to you, Martin. You have taken us from the pigsty to the pasture of life . . . I hope you will have good fruit at Wittenberg. My prayers are with you.

Shortly after he had received this letter news reached Luther that Staupitz was dead.[123] Staupitz's fatherly attachment to Luther, his wise advice, and the note of nostalgia, sadness and gentle reproach struck in this letter, characterizes his role in the final scene of the play. Osborne resurrects Staupitz (who actually had died many years before this time) and has him return in 1530 to the monastery which is now Martin's household. He is the same benevolent spirit, but grown tired and old. As Martin begins to dogmatize in his usual strident fashion, Staupitz gets up to retire:

Staupitz: I'd better get off to bed.

Martin: They're trying to turn me into a fixed star, Father, but I'm a shifting planet. You're leaving me.

Staupitz: I'm not leaving you, Martin. I love you. I love you as much as any man has ever loved most women. But we're not two protected monks under a pear tree in a garden any longer. The world's changed. . . . You've taken Christ away from the low mumblings and soft voices and jewelled gowns and the tiaras and put Him back where He belongs. In each man's soul. We owe so much to you. All I beg of you is not to be too violent. In spite of everything you've said and shown us, there *were* men, *some* men who did live holy lives here once. Don't – don't believe you, only you are right.

(Act 3, Sc. 3, p. 100)

Staupitz does not deny Luther's crucial contribution to a vital reformulation of faith, but his warning is against Luther's setting himself up as an infallible authority, against the dangers of intransigence.

Staupitz in a way puts forward the Christian's only viable position in a new world perspective. His world deprived of firm lineaments, man walks uneasily with a sense of shifting footholds; thus God is groped for through a nightmare of uncertainty. The contemporary wisdom now lies in openness, toleration, flexibility. In the play, doubt and deep questioning are ultimately affirmed as a means to truth. The play ends quietly. Martin is shown speaking to his sleeping child: 'A little while, and you *shall* see me. Christ said that, my son. I hope that'll be the way of it again. I hope so. Let's just hope so, eh?' With the child asleep in his arms, Martin walks off slowly (Act 3, Sc. 3, p. 102). We are left on this pregnant note of mixed hope and doubt.

Thus, like Bolt and Shaffer, Osborne is drawn to a historical subject for its religious interest, but treats it with far greater depth and force of imagination. He firmly grounds his play on documentary evidence, but at the same time he is experimental in a vital individual way, combining his gift for rhetoric with vivid aural, visual and physical elements to convey both an inner state of tension and unrest, and an outer state of public conflict and debate. Music was richly employed to define the mood in the original production, becoming monastic or primitive by turn in the first half of the play, and public and strident in the second. The historical Luther's grand hymn, 'A Mighty Fortress', was movingly introduced at key points, at first 'whispered to a lone drum beat', then sung out triumphantly.[124]

The bold use of dialogue, ritual, expressionistic settings, striking visual and physical effects, all point to a more poetic dynamic form of theatre. Running through the play is a chain of subconscious images drawn from memories, dreams, nightmares such as the lost body of a child, the monstrous rat assailant, the goat drinking blood, and the people reduced to their clothes all 'neatly pressed and folded on the ground'. This is in keeping with the play's emphasis on a condition of spiritual anxiety, fracture and uncertainty. These images are rationally placed to fit in with a picture of a personal and collective neurosis.

From *Luther*, with its roots in psychoanalysis, Edward Bond's *Early Morning* seems an almost inevitable next step. It is a powerful surrealistic drama where rationality in artistic form is denied, and dreams intrude fantastically into waking life to depict a world of political madness.

6

Edward Bond: *Early Morning*

In this chapter Edward Bond's *Early Morning* is singled out for
attention because it is an extraordinary achievement. Revolutionary in approach and intention, it opens up new possibilities for the
treatment of history. Bond, who emerged as a new major playwright in the 1960s, is the most compelling dramatist to have
appeared on the contemporary English theatrical scene. His genius
is for a poetic theatre where language, staging, dramatic tempo
and brilliantly realized visual images are skilfully balanced. Ideas
are transformed into potent stage metaphors, a serious political
concern into theatrical action which is electrifying on both an
emotional and intellectual plane, for an audience is brought up
short against a vision of the mind and character of whole societies.

Bond's attitude to drama lends itself to the treatment of history.
He sees the need for a new theatre in keeping with the urgent
concerns of our time, a theatre of change related to history and
politics:

> The bourgeois theatre set most of its scenes in small domestic
> rooms, with an occasional picnic or a visit to the law courts. . . .
> But we need to set our scenes in public places, where history is
> formed, classes clash and whole societies move. Otherwise
> we're not writing about the events that most affect us and shape
> our future.[1]

Bond makes a distinction between the plays of Chekhov and the
sort of play he writes, which he calls, 'the story play' or the 'theatre
of history'. Chekhov's characters, he says:

> exist between the important events of history, and so they have
> very little else apart from their emotional life. *We* must be caught
> up in the events of history. But we must also be in control. We
> must analyze these events, not merely reproduce them.[2]

213

He claims that some form of epic theatre is the historically correct theatre for us. Epic theatre is the theatre of destroyed illusion and wide-awake audiences. It narrates events and compels an audience to examine and understand them. Human beings are creatures of culture, of history. The function of history is to put reason into the world. He does not believe that golden ages are all in the past for he sees in history the increasing autonomy of the individual. History can develop an awareness of implications; thus it has the potential to free men. Epic theatre, which provides a particular analysis of the world, demonstrates the connection between events, how problems are created as well as how you solve them.[3] 'Chekhov's plays,' he says, 'have no beginning and no ending, all they have is a middle. But we have to do that highly subversive thing: tell a story with a beginning, a middle and an end.' Telling such a story, describing history, demands a new sort of acting:

> broad unfidgety acting that moves from image to image, each image graphically analysing the story. When the audience's attention has been won in this way it's possible to do very small, subtle things. This combination of large and small, far and near, is a visual language of politics.[4]

This technique of presenting both the broad view and the detailed close-up to show that they are inextricably connected provides Bond's plays with their peculiar cutting edge. Large and all-embracing as the issues loom, the personal and domestic is never lost. The audience is allowed no safety-valve. What is projected is immediately related to the sphere of their own everyday lives. The scene in *Saved* (1965) which raised such a storm, where a baby is stoned to death, is so shocking partly because of the ordinary familiar context in which it is placed: a group of youths in a park on a Sunday evening indulge in a mindless act of violence. Bond drives home physically and metaphorically what the weight of aggression in a society can do through man's making his environment a hostile unnatural one. Men are shown to have no real economic and political control of their lives, and Bond's plays demonstrate the destructive and dehumanizing effect of unjust repressive social structures on all facets of human behaviour and experience.

Bond refers all troubles back to a social and economic basis. In *Bingo* (1973) Shakespeare's strained relations with his wife and daughter are shown bound up with the non-human values of a cruel, acquisitive society. John Clare's madness in *The Fool* (1975) owes much to the bitter class conflict and oppression of his time. Unlike Bolt and Osborne who concentrate on the individual as a private spiritual entity, Bond does not see man as existing in any way separate from the society of which he is a part. His plays are about 'the quest for freedom of one man',[5] but the individual's plight, however personal, is always shown in relation to the social and political context which has given rise to it. For Bond believes that our 'most private experiences are intermingled with our social life – and in the end an individual can only resolve his own conflicts by helping to solve those of society'.[6] Bond thinks and feels in political terms and this is because he 'grew up in a political situation where everything was seen in terms of politics. . . . You were always involved in questions of necessity'.[7]

His plays at first caused an uproar because of the violent elements in them, but it is being increasingly recognized that a deep moral concern lies behind this preoccupation with violence. Bond states bluntly:

I write about violence as naturally as Jane Austen wrote about manners. Violence shapes and obsesses our society, and if we do not stop being violent we have no future. . . . It would be immoral not to write about violence.[8]

Bond's art is his response to the world around him. His work reveals the urgent need to express the violent surge of the times through a vital and symbolic vocabulary. The destructive impulses unleashed in the war, the increasing fascism of a depressed Europe, and the disruptive shock of revolutionary political situations, impelled artists to answer social violence with a violence internalized in technique and imagery. In his response to the horrors of the times, Picasso said that painting is an 'instrument of war' to be 'waged against brutality and darkness'.[9] Bond is motivated by a similar moral passion. Oppression must be made apparent: 'You must tread on its toes and make it declare itself.'[10]

Bond sees violence as the dominant problem of our age. 'People,' he says, 'could always be cruel to each other; but now there exists the possibility of a total cruelty. Because of our technical advance, we are confronted with something which really does demand an answer.'[11] Modern historians can be found expressing a similar view. David Thomson, editor of the twelfth volume of the *New Cambridge Modern History* entitles the period it covers, 1898–1945, 'The Era of Violence', and explains:

> To label it thus is not to minimise the important role of violence in all earlier periods of history, nor to neglect the persistence of men and peoples in this half-century in seeking safeguards against the use of violence in human affairs. It is merely to emphasise that the capacity of modern nations and governments to generate power, to accumulate resources of power in more mighty agglomerations than ever before, has in these years far exceeded their ability to harness such power for creative and constructive ends alone.[12]

It is this acquired potential of modern societies to destroy each other and even annihilate the human race which gives rise to the scope of Bond's plays. The subjects he deals with are 'full scale. They are about the future of our society, the survival of the human species'.[13] Bond uses theatre as 'a way of judging society and helping to change it'.[14] Katharine Worth has indicated how very close Bond is 'in some ways to the moralist playwrights in the Shavian tradition, to Osborne and even to Shaw himself.' For both Bond and Shaw 'unjust social arrangements are a root cause of the evils we suffer from'. They both use prefaces and pamphlets 'to drive home prophetic warnings' and continually point to the social optimism of their plays.[15] There are other ways in which these two playwrights are closely linked. Both see politics and economics as the basis of all social and individual life, and their stance is not that of detached critic and observer, but of passionate reformer and participant. They seek to jolt an audience awake to the evils they may be helping to perpetuate as unquestioning members of a system.

Both approach history with respect for their plays reveal deep insight and wide reading, and a familiarity with primary documents. But in Bond we observe a great leap of the imagination, and his fidelity to history is often obscured by the extraordinary nature of his treatment. They each work from a whole vision of life, but their ideas of history and evolution are markedly different. Bond is, essentially, a materialist in his view of the development of man and society. He rejects the notion of God or a creative consciousness behind the scheme of things. Shaw is implacably antimaterialist and conceives of an aspiring Life Force at the heart of being, striving towards self-development and fulfilment through its creatures. Then again, Shaw is a Victorian in origin, and thus his idea of history demands strong heroic figures. His plays reveal an admiration for supermen, exceptional individuals who he believes stand at the forefront of the evolutionary process and prefigure the superhumanity of the future. Thus though Saint Joan is shown rejected by her own society, which can only see in the limited terms of its own age, she is presented as a forerunner of future movements in history. She points the way of historical progress. Bond, on the other hand, a product of the twentieth century, with bitter memories of the human and social disasters caused by such soulless ironhand dictators as Hitler and Stalin, is highly suspicious of supermen. He sees too much power and authority in the hands of a single individual as all too frequently leading to an inhuman despotism. Victoria in *Early Morning* is presented as a superwoman indeed, but a terrible figure presiding over a world which has regressed into savagery.

Shaw and Bond are both masters of humour, and their humour is motivated by deeply serious moral concerns. Their plays blend the grave and the jocular, and they can often be found bringing a situation to the verge of farce. Bond's comedy, however, is much more violent. The humour in *Saint Joan* is toned down, and in a much softer, gentler vein than the brutal, relentless drive of the humour in *Early Morning* which, even where it leads into slapstick, provides a biting comment on the world portrayed. Bond's theatre, as a whole, is much more aggressive and unsettling, and is centred in action rather than in words.

His achievement marks a definite movement away from a theatre of discussion or analysis through rhetorical argument. With Bond the play *is* the analysis. It is the sub-text rather than the text that is dramatized, the interpretation of the story rather than the story itself. Explanations are replaced by incidents fraught with implications, and his plays present us with a new and enigmatic system of poetic metaphor. Bond works through images so that one finds continually a poetic dimension taking form, and meaning is registered at a deep imaginative level. Yet Bond's images are startling because they have their origin in the real world. There is a dualism in his work between a highly realistic style and a highly charged abstraction. Bond's plays negotiate a particularly difficult area between the political and the spiritual, evoking both exterior and interior landscapes, and demonstrating in compelling theatrical terms, his interpretation of the modern condition.

Like Shaw, Bond's interest in history, though deep and searching, relates essentially to the probing of modern questions. He can be found turning to history again and again because he sees the present as bound up with the past.[16] Reaction, he says, 'likes to keep its hand on the past because it throws too much light on the present'.[17] The essential concerns of his history plays have direct implications for our time. The nineteenth century, focused in both *Early Morning* (1969) and *The Fool* (1975), is an era Bond seems particularly interested in, for he sees it as the source of many of the tensions and aggressions of modern society. *The Fool* has for its background the radical overturning of England's rural world by an emerging commercial, industrial culture, and the destruction done to its art and traditions is embodied in the predicament of rural poet John Clare, driven mad and institutionalized. For Bond art is the expression of moral sanity and robbing a people of this renders a society stagnant and inhuman.[18]

Bond is not interested in historical accuracy in a narrow way. The play is written in a Suffolk dialect, though Clare was a Northamptonshire poet. Three Irishmen are brought into a scene with Clare, not because of any known confrontation, but because the play is about the pauperization and displacement of the peasantry and the Irish suffered acutely in this respect. Typically, Bond can be found crossing boundaries of time and space, by integrating the story of John Clare, who was born in 1793 in Northamptonshire, and witnessed during his lifetime numerous injustices precipitated by early nineteenth-century Enclosure Acts, with the nineteenth-century Littleport food and enclosure riots in Cambridgeshire, which resulted in the hanging of several rioters at Ely and the deportation of numerous others. Clearly therefore, despite the surface manipulation of facts and events, the play is based on genuine historical experience. The Industrial Revolution brought about one of the most radical changes in English culture, for until as late as 1850 most Englishmen still lived rural lives. In dealing with these changes, Bond is concerned to examine the severe divisions created by the Industrial Revolution which set the origin for our own times. For Bond emphasizes that he is not concerned with the story of Clare for its own sake: 'I'm only interested in it in that it's a paradigm for our own age, in the way it reflects our own problems.'[19]

A similar motivation lies behind his play, *Bingo* (1973), which dramatizes the last days of Shakespeare. It evokes the impression of a haunted genius, deeply alive to the horrors of an inhuman society, but unable to act in accordance with the values he upholds in his works. Bond has said, 'I wrote *Bingo* because I think the contradictions in Shakespeare's life are similar to the contradictions in us. He was a "corrupt seer" and we are a "barbarous civilization".'[20] The play speaks as a public parable rather than a personal drama. Shakespeare, as England's national monument, is representative of the society of his time and of ours. Through him, Bond focuses a modern dilemma – the contradictions of progress and affluence in an age of cruelty and poverty. In *Bingo* Bond mixes fact and legend, but, paradoxically, when he is being the most disconcerting, he can be found going to the known facts, such as they are. Shakespeare is portrayed as having betrayed his art, for a contradiction emerges between his writings and his actions when his own financial interests are at stake. Bond bases this conception on the surviving material evidence, meagre though it is. Shakespeare's involvement with fellow landowners who were intent on enclosing Welcombe, is suggested by an agreement drawn up between him and William Replingham, to safeguard himself against any pecuniary loss that might result from the venture. An entry recorded in the diary of Thomas Greene, clerk of the Town Council, indicates that Shakespeare was petitioned by the town's citizens to aid them in the fight against the enclosing of Welcombe. It is not known if Shakespeare took any action with regard to this appeal.[21]

Bond sees Shakespeare as acting, when it came to his own business transactions, quite contrary to the moral priorities he asserts in plays like *King Lear*. Before a production of *Bingo* in 1976, Bond commented, 'Of course there's a lot of curfuffle about "you have no evidence to prove this" – but that is my whole point: *if* he had behaved as he should have done, as Lear told him he should have done, you would have known.'[22] Bond takes considerable pains to make it clear that his vision is backed up by a responsible examination of the facts. When the play was first staged at the Northcott Theatre, Exeter, in November 1973, the surviving contract between Shakespeare and William Replingham was quoted in the programme.[23] In his introduction to the published text Bond indicates where he has made changes to the facts – altered dates, telescoped characters and events – for the sake of dramatic concentration or convenience. He even cites his source for the supportive documentary evidence and asserts:

> I mention all this to protect the play from petty criticism. It is based on the material historical facts so far as they're known, and on psychological truth so far as I know it. The consequences that follow in the play follow from the facts, they're not polemical inventions.[24]

Once again we see the concern of modern historical playwrights to show that their accounts are not arbitrary, but based on available documentary evidence, an indication of the much greater demand in our time for historical accuracy.

In *Lear* (1971) and *The Woman* (1978), Bond can be found using historical myth as a vehicle through which he explores ideas about the nature of power politics in human society. Bond's writing of *Lear* was influenced by the colossal impact of Shakespeare's *King Lear* on the western mind. He sees Shakespeare's Lear as 'a sort of archetypal culture figure which lays down certain standards for civilized perception – the way civilized people ought to think and feel'. He felt that this should be criticized. Shakespeare's Lear is part of the 'dead hand of the past' which should be removed.[25]

Bond is iconoclastic in his approach to history, in the sense that he is aware how easily the past is mythologized and how images can dominate a whole society. History creates myth, and myth in turn can create history. Historical ages, events, figures are often simplified and idealized. Their effective role becomes symbolic and they can shape subsequent events with far-reaching implications. Bond is concerned to explode such images which simplify and distort reality. It is only by critically analysing the past that 'we can escape the mythology of the past which often lives on as the culture of the present'.[26] In plays like *Lear* and *Early Morning*, what comes across powerfully is this sense of a world dominated by myth, in which societies are condemned to live out the grotesque fantasies they have created. Through a surrealistic treatment of history in *Early Morning*, Bond demolishes pious legends about the influence of law and order, morality and religion, in the nineteenth century, and lays bare the operating principles of a society that thrives on strident competitiveness and aggressive acquisition.

First privately performed on 31 March 1968 at the Royal Court Theatre, London, and published by Calder and Boyars in the same year, *Early Morning* was one of the most controversial plays of the 1960s. Prevented from having even a second Sunday-night private club performance by the threat of police action, it was the last play to be banned in its entirety by the Lord Chamberlain, before his office was stripped of its powers of theatrical censorship. Bond openly invites controversy by prefacing his play with the statement – 'The events of this play are true.' And yet we are introduced to a Victorian England where Queen Victoria has two sons, Arthur and George, who are Siamese twins; Prince Albert continually conspires to overthrow his wife; Florence Nightingale is Victoria's lover; and Gladstone and Disraeli connive at each other's destruction and their own advancement like political hoodlums. Since the play so obviously distorts external historical facts, it might seem astonishing that it was seriously accused of slandering respected figures in history. The conducting of a ludicrous trial on a charge of cannibalism, the seemingly endless sequence of bizarre intrigues, the mass murder of nearly every character in the play, and their subsequent resurrection in a heaven where people devour each other interminably are integral parts of the play's action.

Yet despite all this fantasy, the play was taken seriously by the Lord Chamberlain's Office, so seriously that it was banned. W. A. Darlington in the *Daily Telegraph* reports that the shocks Bond administers in the play:

> drove the Censor up the wall. He considered that Mr Bond had offered "gross insults" to highly respected characters of recent history – Queen Victoria, Prince Albert, Gladstone, Disraeli, Florence Nightingale – and, as that was the kind of thing his office had been empowered to stop, he stopped it.[27]

Other newspaper reports offer no fuller idea of the official reasons for the play being banned, and Richard Findlater in his book, *Banned!* (1967), a review of British theatrical censorship, provides a very sketchy account of the event. On writing to the Lord Chamberlain's Office to obtain the full reasons for the banning of the play, I received a courteous reply, saying that a further letter would be sent when the writer had been able to ascertain what information they had available.[28] Six weeks later I received another letter, notifying me that they could not give the reason why this play was not licensed for public production.[29] It seems strange that there should be such secrecy over the matter; and it leaves us free to surmise that they saw the play as subversive, and even as posing some kind of threat to the establishment. However, though we may consider that they overreacted, it is a tribute to their understanding if they consciously or unconsciously recognized that the play was making a very serious attack on the nineteenth century.

Ever since its first reception, the play has excited both high praise and virtual dismissal. When it was first produced, Irving Wardle of the London *Times* regretted that 'the Royal Court's just and necessary fight for theatrical free speech should be conducted on behalf of a piece as muddled and untalented as this'.[30] On the opposite side Ronald Bryden declared vehemently that it was 'a serious and passionately moral play' and that a country which forbade its performance was 'unfree to an extent we should not countenance a day longer'.[31] Those unhappy about the play fasten on its oddity and quirkiness, its obscurity and inconsistency, its apparent lack of organization or formal development, its repetitiously long and needlessly complicated plot. One critic complains of its utter lack of "artistic probability' and describes it as a 'demonstration of total anarchy'.[32] Another finds it notable merely for being 'bizarre and repulsive'.[33] Those who affirm the play commend it for its deep and powerful imaginative vision. It has been described as a 'gargantuan Swiftian metaphor of universal consumption'.[34] Another critic likens 'this horrific, funny and upsetting world in which "angry gleeful ghosts" chase each other for their next meal' to 'a world of Blake's crossed with Lewis Carroll's, a child's view of a baffling terrifying grown-up life'.[35]

There is no doubt that *Early Morning* is a difficult play which makes enormous demands on directors, actors and audiences. Directors have found it hard to give it shape and focus, in terms of a story-line, or a thesis indicated, or values underwritten.[36] Elements of grotesque fantasy combine with commonplace details of everyday experience, and the text requires great technical expertise from actors, who are under constant pressure to maintain the fluidity of the multiple-plot action and yet retain clarity. The play's first director was William Gaskill whose feeling about it finally was that 'you just have to live with it. It's one of the strangest experiences in the theatre'.[37] After the 1969 production Bond conceded some understanding of those who could not follow what was happening all the time, but said, 'It goes through all I know about life and it was very difficult to get all that in one play.'[38]

Early Morning is a challenge to our powers of assimilation – with its proliferating events, its bizarre distortions, its strange opposites of plausibility and farce, its continually shifting emotional climate caused by its serio-comic extremes. Yet, despite the harlequinade of events and emotions we are taken through, the play is not just a context-less nightmare. If we accept it on its own terms, and attend to its sardonic tone and form, we find that the play does carry conviction as an artistic unity, that a deep moral purpose and a certain consistency of temper do bind it into a single imaginative experience. We are presented with a vision both terrifying and absurd, but it is not so grotesque a distortion of reality as, for the sake of humanity, we might wish.

'The events of this play are true', states Bond categorically, challenging us to consider the question of historical truth. Is *Early Morning* a serious exposé of the past or is it a purely arbitrary invention of the mind? Critics and reviewers generally have dismissed the idea (supported by the Lord Chamberlain's allegations) that the play has any direct relation to actual historical persons and events. Martin Esslin asserts that 'the characters so named had no relation to their historical models beyond the fact that they bore their name, and that, in reality, they were archetypal figures that haunt the subconscious of our society'.[39] Michael Anderson claims that the 'unhistorical comic-strip extravagance of this fantasy was never likely to endanger or even offend the institution of the monarchy'.[40] In *Early Morning*, Irving Wardle comments, 'Bond proceeds logically from a hatred of social order to a fully anarchic action, mixing up past and present and treating historical figures with a complete indifference to recorded fact'.[41] And Benedict Nightingale talks of Bond in *Bingo*, consistently aiming 'at an authenticity he never contemplates in that mad fantasy, *Early Morning*'.[42]

Yet Bond claims unequivocally that 'the events of this play are true'. There is a tremendous paradox here. The play is a mad fantasy, and yet it is in some way true. It is the nature of this truth and its basis in history that I intend to explore. Again in this play, Bond can be found to be irreverent and iconoclastic in his approach to history. And yet, typically, in the areas where he strains the limits of probability, he can be found dealing with historical truth of a very serious nature. An examination of possible historical sources reveals how close Bond keeps to history in many respects. For, though Bond uses his own amazing theatrical form, he is treating central features of Victorian society, and is continually bringing in facets of character, social ideas and concerns, popular sentiments and attitudes, prevalent in the nineteenth century. It is all dealt with fantastically, taken to an outlandish extreme as a form of satirical comment. But despite the remorseless distortions, the blowing-up out of all proportion, as in bizarre lampoons or caricatures, there is a pith of truth that underlies the absurdity, and it is this that is driven home with fierce intensity.

We are plunged into a restless vehement world of furiously competing entities. It is a world, wholly indifferent to the claims of morality, that has in fact created its own primitive morality out of strength, cunning and self-preferment. Albert and Disraeli scheme at Victoria's overthrow with unabashed zeal. They strive for Prince Arthur's involvement to give their coup 'the appearance of legality'. They 'must strike now' because Victoria is going to announce the Prince of Wales' engagement. 'Victoria's not popular. She's frightened and she knows a royal wedding will pacify the people'[43] (Sc. 1, p. 7). Gladstone, with a mob of unruly disciples at his heels, is out to make his own bid for power and advancement.

Victoria stalks the stage like some monstrous predator. With George as her stooge, she fights to preserve the supremacy of her position. Bent on Albert's destruction, she is determined that her line begun at Stonehenge 'shall not fall till Stonehenge falls'. At her throne-room in Windsor she formally announces that she has arranged a 'normal marriage' for her son, George. His bride is to be Florence Nightingale – 'Miss Nightingale is an expert sanitarian. We believe that to be a branch of Eugenics.' As her name is announced Florence Nightingale comes into the room. She curtsies to Victoria and then to George. George reads his note – 'Dear Miss Nightingale, I welcome you to Windsor and hope you will be happy here.' Florence reads hers – 'Thank you' (Sec. 3, pp. 14–15). It is all treated in a highly farcical vein. The characters have an intense life of their own, but less as personages than as vigorous plastic forms. They are like brilliantly animated puppets. In the first production Peter Eyre's performance as Prince Arthur was described as a beautiful blend of 'caricature and pathos', and Moira

Redmond's Victoria as a remarkable achievement of a 'fairy-tale queen'.[44] Reviewers saw the characters coming across as 'grotesque caricatures' or 'bizarre lampoons'.[45]

Energy and exuberance are there in plenty, and the play is riotously funny, but the humour keeps turning black. The court's presiding over the trial of Len and Joyce provides a vivid example. Len and Joyce explain how the crime took place while they were queuing up to see a film:

> Len: We'd bin stood there 'ours, and me guts starts to rumble. 'Owever, I don't let on. But then she 'as to say 'I ain arf pecky'.
>
> Joyce: Thass yer sense a consideration, ain it! I'd 'eard your gut.
>
> Len: I 'as an empty gut many times, girl. That don't mean I'm on the danger list. But when you starts rabbitin' about bein' pecky I –
>
> Joyce: Now don't blame me, love.
>
> Len: Truth ain' blame, love.
>
>   . . .
>
> Look, we're stood outside the State for Buried Alive on 'Ampstead 'Eath' – right? – me gut rumbles and there's this sly bleeder stood up front with 'is 'ead in 'is paper – right? so I grabs 'is ears, jerks 'im back by the 'ead, she karatichops 'im cross the front of 'is throat with the use of 'er handbag, and down 'e goes like a sack with a 'ole both ends – right? – an she starts stabbin' 'im with 'er stilletos, in twist out . . . an 'e says 'Ere, thass my place', an then 'e don't say no more, juss bubbles like a nipper, and I take this 'andy man-'ole cover out the gutter an drops it on 'is 'ead – right? – an the queue moves up one.
>
> (Sc. 4, pp. 21–2)

Despite the sickening ghoulish turn, the spirit in which it is discussed is very natural and matter of fact, as if it is all quite the norm. Everyone in the queue and about joined in to lend a hand in overcoming the poor 'bleeder,' so that when the couple decided to make a meal of him they naturally had to share it with the others – 'Yer can't nosh an' not offer round, can yer?'

The trial presided over by Victoria is conducted in an equally ludicrous fashion, and it is only Arthur who is consternated:

Arthur: Why did you kill him?

Len: 'E pushed in the queue.
Arthur: Why?
Len: It's 'is 'obby.
          . . .
Arthur: Why did you kill him –
Len: I said it ain' I? 'Is shirt! 'Is shoes! 'Is vest! (He kicks the
          exhibits at Arthur) I done it! Get, mate, get! They're 'is!
          'Is! I got a right a be guilty same as you! . . .

                                              (Sc. 4, pp. 24–6)

An everyday situation is suddenly transformed into a bizarre
one that speaks of underlying guilt, anxiety, fear, suspicion erupt-
ing into violence. One reviewer comments: 'Mr Bond offers us
moral affront after moral affront, but without enough expertise to
get us fuming. However he does keep us laughing for the first
two-thirds of a long afternoon.'[46] Yet surely the humour provides
an entry into the horror, but also helps to control and contain it.

This scene leads into a maze of events in the political arena
treated in a vein of grisly slapstick. Disraeli and Albert launch their
offensive during a royal picnic at Windsor Park. Their man, Len,
disguised as a rustic, turns on Victoria with a pistol after Albert has
proposed and drunk a toast of loyalty to her. But Victoria has had
Albert's drink poisoned and when he starts to feel the effects – 'I'm
not well.' – she finishes him off herself, strangling him with his
own garter sash, murmuring, 'I don't like to see them linger – I'm a
patron of the RSPCA.' Disraeli enters but, discovering Victoria
very much alive and in possession of Albert's rifle, which she has
trained on him, exclaims, 'A counter-attack. I'll fetch reinforce-
ments', and dashes out. In terms of graphic pictures we are made
to see that the aggression committed by Len and Joyce, condemned as a criminal act of homicide, is perpetrated on a far
greater scale by the state. The law of the jungle prevails, and
justice and legality are merely an expedient façade.

At one point we are confronted by Gladstone leading a lynching
mob comprising Joyce, Jones and Griss. Len is in their midst,
hobbling along with his feet shackled and arms tied behind him.
The mob clamours to hang him instantly, but Gladstone insists
that 'Yer 'ave t' 'ave yer trial t' make it legal. Yer don't wan' a act
like common criminals. Trial first death after: yer got a copy a the
book.' To 'explain the legal situation' to Len they all start kicking

him, but are again stopped by Gladstone, who proceeds to demonstrate how to kick with maximum efficiency, inflicting the greatest amount of injury, yet expending the least energy. It involves some degree of technical expertise:

> The secret is: move from the thigh an' let the weight a the tool do the work. That economizes yer effort so yer can keep it up longer. (He demonstrates without touching Len) Watch that toe. Keep a good right angles t' the target. The other way looks good but it's all on the surface. Yer don't do your internal damage. Study yer breathin': in when yer go in, out when yer come out. Got it? (He swings his boot back) Out – thigh – toe – in! (He kicks Len once) Child's play.
>
> (Sc. 7, p. 46)

In physical metaphorical terms, Bond drives home the fact of violence legalized in the form of officialdom, and torture developed to a science under the auspices of the state. People institutionalize their violence, and people are institutionalized to express their pent-up frustrations and aggressions in the service of the establishment.

The play hurtles on its grisly larkish course in a seemingly endless turn-over of events, in which leaders continually ambush each other, and firing-squads keep turning around on their commanders with strenuous glee. Through this insane and ignoble spectacle, what comes across most strongly is the sense of a people with no commitments except to self. Bond conveys meaning through theatrical incidents which become provocative symbols of the cruel reality of an age of aggressive competition.

Situations are treated in the mode of highly extravagant farce, and political leaders romp the stage as monstrous images of authority and repression. On one level it is clear, as Ronald Bryden points out, that Bond's:

> Victoria is no more the historical queen than his Disraeli, a darting-eyed Balkan conspirator, is the genuine Disraeli, or his Gladstone, a bluff TUC veteran who calls everyone 'Brother,' is the real people's William.[47]

These are obviously not fully-rounded, humanized portraits of the actual historical figures, and yet the gross distortions should not blind us to the fact that they mirror a certain truth about these historical characters and their positions.

For instance, we might be tempted to reject out of hand, Bond's setting Victoria and Albert against each other, as totally absurd in the light of her adoration of her husband, which is now legendary. And yet there were times when Queen Victoria could be absolutely unyielding even with Prince Albert, as he soon discovered. Their first clash of wills occurred just before their marriage, over the formation of his household, which Prince Albert desired to be non-political, but he found the Queen intractable. A biographer comments:

> In the midst of affection and longing the iron hand appeared within the velvet glove, as already had been the experience of Lord Melbourne. As Lady Lyttelton, when governess to the royal children, remarked, "a vein of iron runs through her most extraordinary character" and Prince Albert had no choice but to submit.[48]

Early Morning satirizes both the velvet glove and the vein of iron underneath:

Victoria: Albert, dearest, where have you been since breakfast?
Albert: (Kisses her cheek) My love.
Victoria: Thank you. You've cured my headache. (She makes a formal address). Our kingdom is degenerating. Our people cannot walk on our highways in peace. They cannot count their money in safety, even though our head is on it. We cannot understand most of what is called our English. Our prisons are full. Instead of fighting our enemies our armies are putting down strikers and guarding our judges. Our peace is broken. You know that the Prince of Wales poses certain constitutional questions. Because of this the anarchists and immoralists say that the monarchy must end with our death, and so they shoot at us. They are wrong. Our son will follow in our footsteps, with his brother at his side, and in time, his son will follow him. . . . We shall not abandon this kingdom to anarchy . . .

(Sc. 3, p. 14)

A vein of truth informs this speech. The country was restless, and often rent by industrial and agricultural uprisings during her reign. Chartism was the expression of revolutionary democratic agitation among the masses of the population clamouring for extension of the franchise. In his book, *The Political Influence of Queen Victoria*, published in 1935, Frank Hardie writes that the Queen 'never learnt to distinguish between the people and the mob', that she:

> never had any conception of the real meaning of the word "Socialism" and apparently confused it with rioting: "The Queen cannot sufficiently express her *indignation* at the monstrous riot which took place the other day in London, and which risked people's lives and was a *momentary* triumph of socialism and disgrace to the capital."

To 'keep her position was one of the ruling passions of her life.' She mistook the main trend of the constitutional changes of her time, and felt that any threat to the House of Lords was in fact a threat to the Monarchy itself. She could not and would not be the 'Sovereign of a Democratic Monarchy', she asserted on more than one occasion:

> She was determined to hand on to her successors, unimpaired and undiminished, all the rights and privileges which she had acquired at her accession. . . . So she seems always to have seen herself as fighting a rearguard action in defence of the institution of monarchy.[49]

Though treated in a highly exaggerated ludicrous manner, this is what is reflected in the broad action of the play, which suggests that Bond might have been familiar with Hardie's account.

The other work that appears to have been a historical source for Bond's play due to definite links throughout is Elizabeth Longford's biography of Queen Victoria, *Victoria R.I.*, published in 1964, a few years before the play was first produced. It is significant that Elizabeth Longford asserts that Victoria, like her ancestress, Elizabeth I, 'thought prison the best place for public enemies'.[50] Such a remark could only arouse the satirist in Bond. In the play Albert tells Arthur, 'Your mother's the first danger.' 'We must stop her before she causes the wrong revolution. She should have been a prison governess. She's afraid of people. She thinks they're evil, she doesn't understand their energy. She suppresses it.' It is highly probable that Bond was influenced by both these historical accounts because of the strong internal evidence that points to this.

In the play Prince Albert is shown vying for the dominance of his own position. At Arthur's scathing denunciation of this he protests:

No, you don't understand. I'm not doing this because I hate your mother. Hate destroys, I want to build. The people are strong. They want to be *used* – to build empires and railways and factories, to trade and convert and establish law and order. I know there'll be crimes, but we can punish them.

(Sc. 2, p. 11)

Again a substratum of truth can be seen to underlie this speech. According to Hardie, the Prince Consort's 'main constitutional work had been that of establishing his own position' and his influence had not really begun to be felt when he died prematurely in 1861.[51] (Albert is the first one to be killed off in the play). And, though she claims there is nothing in it, Elizabeth Longford recalls Disraeli's gibe that 'had the Prince lived he would have given England the benefits of absolute government'. She also relates how:

sinister in the eyes of the Conservatives was Prince Albert's appearance in the House of Commons, showing royal bias in favour of Free Trade. Such was the outcry among Protectionists that the Prince was forced to make his first his last appearance at a Parliamentary debate.

Of the mid-Victorian creed of self-help, she states, that if Samuel Smiles was its publicist, Prince Albert was its impresario. 'To work is to pacify and to do both these things is to pray – this was Prince Albert's message to a world barely recovered from the fury and war of revolution. It was his own deepest religion.'[52]

The prevailing view of the England of that time was basically individualistic and moralistic. It rested on the notion of personal autonomy through self-help. It was a world view that derived from emergent industrialization. The gospel of work and deference to authority was preached. The working man should be hard-working, thrifty and virtuous. Thus we find Bond embodying in his characters notable stances or attitudes that existed in history. His characters are not fleshed out to come through as the actual persons in their full humanity. They are cartoon-like figures which project salient views or aspects of personality, that Bond is concerned to satirize.

The nineteenth century was a new era of the big stick, and, in discussing *Early Morning*, Bond has talked of Arthur becoming so desperate under the pressures that everybody lives under, that:

> he becomes schizophrenic, he really goes mad, and he swallows the Victoria line, the law and order bit, completely, and he says, "So we are violent, so what we must do is we must have law and more law enforcement and more and more pressure just to keep the animal in control . . ."[53]

Bond's attributing an obsession with law and order to Victoria is well founded. In her letters, she often expressed an urgent desire for sterner measures of control in reaction to public disturbances. To quote just one instance:

> What is the use of trying to stop these outrages without strong means to enable us to punish these horrible people? And is it right to wait till fresh outrages take place, and more innocent lives are sacrificed, before we resort to such measures?
> (Letter to Mr Gathorne Hardy, 19 Dec. 1867)[54]

In numerous sequences, the play can be seen reproducing, with distortions, actual views of the time, and it is probably because Bond keeps very close to history, that his play was taken so seriously by the Lord Chamberlain. Realizing the fantastic element in the play, therefore, should not blind us to the fact that Bond was familiar with the style of various kinds of criticism current in the nineteenth century.

We find Bond turning to history of a very different nature in the Victoria/Florence Nightingale/John Brown episodes. Florence Nightingale is portrayed as Victoria's lover, which we are bound spontaneously to reject. Then we see her later coming on as John Brown. When she protests at having to wear a kilt, complaining that she 'can't do the accent', Victoria implores:

Try. If they knew you were a woman there'd be a scandal, but if
they believe you're a man they'll think I'm just a normal lonely
widow.

(Sc. 12, p. 71)

We are brought back to history with a jolt, because the scandal
caused by Queen Victoria's growing dependence on her Highland
servant, John Brown, after her husband's death is well known. She
made him her constant personal attendant, and he became a new
and formidable influence in her life. Elizabeth Longford states that
by the year 1867 it was widely believed that another 'King John'
ruled. Rumours arose that the Queen had married, and in elegant
drawing-rooms jokes were made about 'Mrs John Brown' and
scurrilous cartoons and pamphlets went round.[55] Thus underlying
the grotesque satirical distortion in Bond's depiction of the
Victoria/Florence Nightingale/John Brown affair, is the marriage
myth that continually surrounded the Queen, because of her
strong tendency towards forming extreme attachments. Elizabeth
Longford talks of the Sovereign's 'infatuation with Lord Melbourne' and of Disraeli coming to her like a 'second bridegroom'.
Florence Nightingale, the Queen so greatly admired, that the
biographer refers to Victoria's 'Florence Nightingale cult'.

The Queen required intense undivided affection, yet this often
led her into strong biases and intemperate opinions, which sometimes resulted in political indiscretions. Victoria herself confessed
to this quality to Prince Albert. When they discussed what had
caused her 'unbounded admiration and affection' for Melbourne,
she said that 'she scarcely knew; she could only suggest that it was
her having "very warm feelings" and needing to cling to someone'.[56] Bond satirizes this trait of Victoria in the play. We are
confronted with her thoughtfully contemplating – 'I wonder if we
can make John Brown archbishop' – or wildly running after her
lover, protesting:

I need you, Florrie! You'll be killed! You're all I live for. Again,
again! Things seem to get better, and then suddenly I lose
everything. Freddie don't leave me! I'll let you do all the amputa-
tions. Don't! Don't!

(Sc. 12, p. 74)

Indeed this is not much of an exaggeration, when compared to similar expressions of impassioned feeling recorded in Victoria's journal, from which Bond obviously derived his style and tone:

> All ALL my happiness gone! that happy peaceful life destroyed, that dearest kind Lord Melbourne no more my Minster!

> Poor dear Albert, how cruelly are they ill-using that dearest Angel! Monsters! You Tories shall be punished. Revenge, revenge![57]

These passages in Victoria's journal, so clearly echoed by Bond, are also quoted by Elizabeth Longford. This suggests that Bond might have come across them in her account, rather than the actual journal. It is evident, at any rate, that a serious truth lies behind even the most bizarre distortions in the play.

Bond can be seen bringing in history of a different dimension, when he weaves into the play this element of biographical gossip, which reveals something about the nature of popular criticism of the time, and the kind of social attitudes that were held. The following exchange between Queen Victoria and the Lord Chamberlain, with Florence Nightingale present, dressed as John Brown, is a lively illustration:

Victoria:	John keeps an eye on me. (Florence and Lord Chamberlain exchange nods. Victoria nods.) Lady Flora Hastings says you got her with child.
Chamberlain:	Accidentally, Madam. It was dark. My wife and I don't converse during intimacy, apart from the odd remark about the weather. It was only afterwards that I discovered she was not my wife . . .
Victoria:	(Knits) I won't have a divorce.
Chamberlain:	O no, ma'am! We're a respectable couple. (Aside to Florence) What's up that kilt?

(Sc. 9, p. 55)

In a winning comical way Bond satirizes the sanctimonious hypocrisy of the time. Yet behind the humour lies a snippet of painful truth. The reference to Lady Flora Hastings directs us back to history yet again. The furore which broke out over Flora Hastings, who was falsely accused of being 'with child' when she was actually dying of a terminal cancer condition, caused the first major problem of Victoria's reign. It arose from the unkind gossip in the Royal Court which Victoria herself was party to. This sort of libelling and malicious small talk was a dominant feature of Victorian life for scandal was revelled in and played a significant part in public affairs.

There are numerous ways in which the play's dialogue reveals Bond's close adherence to historical material. Disraeli sympathizing with Victoria – 'Ma'am, you wear a crown of thorns' – points directly to a letter which Queen Victoria wrote to Disraeli, expressing her deep humiliation at the government's abandonment of a particular standpoint that she favoured. Her one first impulse, she writes, is 'to throw everything up and lay down her thorny crown which she feels little satisfaction in retaining if the position of this country is to remain as it is now'.[58] It was an expression she had used on a previous occasion when she had felt herself equally thwarted.[59] In the play Disraeli's feint of compliance with royal wishes and his flattery of Victoria are sharply satirized – 'Ah, ma'am. Having no teeth suits you.' The historical Disraeli's urbane charm and deliberate flattery of Victoria are well known. His famous remark to Matthew Arnold at the end of his life is often quoted by historians and biographers:

> You have heard me called a flatterer, and it is true. Everyone likes flattery and when you come to royalty, you should lay it on with a trowel.[60]

Thus we find Bond attributing to the persons concerned attitudes and sentiments which are matters of historical record.

Despite a certain repetitiveness in the play's action, there are continually shifting moods. The horror takes on different shades; we are confronted with a psychologically gripping complex of images and profiles, each more spectral than the last. Arthur and George are confronted by their father's ghost beside his open grave and begged by him to 'listen to it.' 'That's the pit,' he says, 'I lie there and you tramp round and round on top of me. There's no peace. The living haunt the dead. You will learn that.' He lifts his arms and heavy chains are seen to run down from them into the grave – 'I dragged these with me. Help me.' (Sc. 8, p. 49). Enslavement is a dominant image in the play. It forcefully puts over the idea that people are slaves of their social and political environment. Again this is conveyed in concrete visual terms. Characters continually appear physically shackled in some way or other. Ropes, chains, pulleys, abound on the stage. In the most wrenching image of the play, Arthur and George as Siamese twins are seen painfully yoked together, and we are forced to feel the emotional and physical weight of this enslavement. Even after George dies he remains attached to Arthur in the form of a skeleton, which continues to haunt Arthur.

Extraordinarily, in spite of the grotesquerie, there are moments of almost unbearable poignancy, as when Arthur, weary and half demented, talks to the skeleton at his side:

> . . . I know I gave your clothes away! They were beggars! They were cold . . . I'm a limited person. I can't face another hungry child, a man with one leg, a running woman, an empty house . . . I don't like maimed cows, dead horses, and wounded sheep. I'm limited.
>
> (Sc. 11, pp. 67–8)

Arthur's anguish and despair at the violence, the deformity, the poverty and waste in human life is profound. He decides that not many people rise to the heights of Hitler. Most of them nurse little hates. They kill under licence. But Hitler had the vision to know that men hated themselves and each other, and so he let them kill and be killed. 'Heil Hilter! Heil Einstein!' he cries, 'Hitler gets a bad name, and Einstein's good. But it doesn't matter, the good still kill. And the civilized kill more than the savage.' (Sc. 11, p. 69)

The anachronisms force us to relate events, recognizing in the process that history creates history and that myths can bring about their own reality. The violence that man attributes to himself and seeks to control by even greater violence is brought about so that men who are not motivated by a personal desire to be violent, become the makers of H-bombs and the authors of holocaust. Anachronisms like this keep intruding in the play. They intensify an audience's involvement, driving home the sense of historical consequence and continuity as past, present and sometimes, future, are brought together in one burning point in time.

Arthur's conclusion that violence is a product of human nature leads him to the logical deduction that since the end of society seems to be mutual destruction, what is needed is the great traitor who will kill both sides, not just one. He approaches Victoria and Florence and finds them surrounded by corpses hanging on gallowposts. 'They were all called Albert,' Victoria explains, 'I can't take chances.' Florence chimes in with the proud declaration: 'I'm the first hangwoman in history – public hangwoman that is. It's part of our war effort' (Sc. 12, pp. 71–2). Historically, Florence Nightingale, the archetypal nurse, is the nineteenth-century ideal of womanhood. Queen Victoria in a letter to Miss Nightingale refers to her as 'one who has set so bright an example to our sex'.[61]

In the play Florence epitomizes complete submission to authority. She is married to the establishment. She accepts Victoria's arrangement of a marriage to George, the heir apparent. She is Victoria's ready tool in the poisoning of Albert. Again, she assents to an affair with Victoria against her own desires. In a scene that is a parody of the Lady with a Lamp legend we see Florence literally prostituting herself in the service of the war effort. She adds that 'little touch of feminine sensibility' that is 'very precious in war' (Sc. 12, p. 72). Tony Coult suggests that she is the 'establishment's archetype of correct femininity, a gentle nurse symbolically mopping the fevered brow of an Empire'.[62] Another critic, Richard Scharine, points out that 'the image of the historical Florence, lovingly caring for wounded soldiers by the soft glow of lamplight, has been used for a hundred years to sentimentalize and glamorize warfare'.[63] Bond treats this popular image in striking contrast to Berkeley in *The Lady with a Lamp* where it is registered not satirically, but with some lapse into sentiment. Berkeley's concern, however, is to present the person behind the myth. Bond's interest, on the other hand, is to present the myth rather than the person, and demonstrate its power to shape future events, creating history in its image.

It is interesting to note that Bond sees the first World War as 'the myth of the nineteenth century'.[64] Arthur lives out this myth of man's essential violence. He engineers his great betrayal to end all betrayals. The two sides are lined up in a massive tug-of-war near the edge of a precipice. When they are pulling full stretch, Victoria's side lets go of the rope and their opponents rush backwards over the cliff. As foreseen by Arthur, the victors do the 'natural thing, the normal thing, the human thing'. They rush over to the edge of the cliff to look down, cheer, laugh, wave. The cliff roars and gives way, and they all go crashing to their deaths. Bond drives home the monumental irony of warfare, for it all takes place to such cries as 'Freedom! Justice!' 'Culture! Democracy!' 'Science!

Civilization!' 'Fraternity! Brotherhood! Love! Mankind!' and the crowning irony of all – 'Peace!' (Sc. 14, p. 80)

This tremendous tug-of-war is a mordant comment on the standard of international morality of the time. The last cry of 'Peace!' is uttered by Victoria herself. In history we can find Victoria advocating war in the name of peace. During the Eastern Crisis of 1876–8, the Queen wrote to Disraeli:

> The Queen thinks great progress is being made with respect to a Congress, though she must own to disbelieving any *permanent* settlement of Peace until we have fought and beaten the Russians. . . .[65]

In her letters, Queen Victoria can often be found enunciating Palmerstonion sentiments:

> If *we are* to *maintain* our position as a first-rate Power . . . we must, with our Indian Empire and large Colonies, be *prepared* for *attacks* and *wars*, somewhere or other, CONTINUALLY.[66]
>
> (28 July 1879)

> If only we had a really good large Army properly supported by Parlt., not in the miserable way it is at present . . . we could carry everything before us, all over the world![67]
>
> (3 April 1857)

It is this spirit of Victorian imperialism that is attacked in the play. Through the spectacular stage picture of a great gleeful tug-of-war resulting in horror and catastrophe for both sides, Bond satirizes the tragic ignorance of an age of aggression and absurd self-certainty.

Arthur takes this sort of political madness to its logical conclusion. We must definitely feel with him a sense of overwhelming relief that the insanity is over. All that is left is for him to shoot himself, and he can now die in peace, he thinks. But before he can finish congratulating himself for setting everybody free, the nightmare lurches back in a form even more ghastly than before. A line of ghosts rises up from among the broken bodies. They stand close together in black cowls. They move apart, and we see that they are joined together, like a row of paper cut-out men. George detaches himself from the line, and starts to fasten himself onto Arthur. We enter into Arthur's thrashing despair as he shudders from the renewed enslavement, and groans: 'No. No. No. No. No' (Sc. 15, pp. 81–2).

We are continually drawn in to identify with Arthur's experience. Arthur carrying George around, and struggling to get free of him, is meant to be our dilemma too. Through the image Bond dissects a mental and emotional state. One is reminded of the schizophrenia of the split characters of Brecht's plays summed up by Mr Peachum in *The Threepenny Opera*:

> Who would not like to be a good and kindly person. . . . But circumstance won't have it so!

In Brecht's plays, the natural instinct of man to be good, kind, generous and loving is shown to be constantly thwarted by the harsh necessities of survival in a competitive world. Bond takes this dilemma of inner division, of being separated from one's natural self, a step further, projecting it in startling visual terms in the form of George and Arthur as Siamese twins, and the other characters as one-dimensional, cartoonlike, strangely dehumanized creatures. By distorting, even demonizing the human figure – using the spontaneity and irresponsibility of a dream as dramatic licence – Bond shows how people can cease to be human under certain conditions.

From a gruesome earth of wild and nervous excess, we are plunged into a heaven of rampant cannibalism. It is the philosophy of Victoria's world – eat or be eaten – taken to its literal conclusion. 'Nothing has any consequences here – so there's no pain,' rejoices Victoria. 'Think of it – no pain! Bon appétit' (Sc. 16, p. 88). The world celebrated here is literally a world of unrestricted appetite. People fight like sparrows over torn-off human limbs which are voraciously devoured only to sprout again. A sense of men's lives being fed into machines must emerge from the sight of men being strung up on a pulley and then deposited in hampers on trolleys to be wheeled around for corporate consumption – quite a supermarket. At one point a one-legged man starts to hop out from under the pulley while the others are fighting over his torn-off leg. The rope hangs from his neck and dances along behind him. The others suddenly catch sight of him escaping and tear after him. Arthur is left alone on the stage, with the leg which has been thrust into his hands.

In stunning theatrical terms Bond creates the horror of what has been called 'an age of political materialism that aspires only to wealth'. In his novel, *Sybil*, Disraeli writes, 'If a spirit of rapacious covetousness . . . has been the besetting sin of England for the past century and a half, since the passing of the Reform Act the altar of Mammon has blazed with triple worship.'[68] Shaw also saw the British Empire as standing for sheer Mammonism. Stephen Winsten, recalling personal conversations with Shaw, says that:

> Shaw was not in the least deceived by the peace and prosperity of Victorian days. The peace was the peace of a lunatic living in the world of fantasy, and the prosperity was the prosperity of the vulture.[69]

It is interesting indeed that Shaw, a Victorian, sees nineteenth-century peace and prosperity in the same terms as Bond – as a kind of mad political fantasy.

Early Morning is the materialization of a nightmare vision. It projects a hideous truth about the nature of social relations with all the disquieting force of a dream. Everything is seen in terms of some anxious nightmare with its sense of dream and disparate realities. Like a dream what is so disturbing is that elements of the real, features of our everyday experience, keep intruding to mingle with the more obviously fantastic. Conflicts often revolve around a commonplace incident before there is a sudden lurch into the macabre. Bond subverts common sense, yet remains faithful to the condensed, vividly heightened and portentous symbolism of dreams, with their charge of anxiety. The play works through extravagant image elaboration. The picture is constantly enlarged until it becomes a gigantic tapestry of horror. We enter into a world of jostling competing entities and the horrors are incalculably compounded until we find ourselves in a heaven where men pursue and devour each other interminably. The play dramatizes the dilemma of individuals in a society which has ceased to be compelled by human values. The barely mitigated moral chaos the play embodies, projects the kind of living a moral universe such as that implies. Through a surrealistic treatment of history, Bond registers his vision of the underlying nature of human relations in Victorian society, and its enduring effect on the present. The play is a vivid ironic comment on a rampant reckless consumer society.

It is a protest against the insane spectacle of collective homicide, against the furious folly of our times.

In the play Victoria towers over the other characters as a monstrous figure of demonic energy, which one might find hard to reconcile with her diminutive physical size as portrayed in all contemporary documents. Yet historians and biographers refer to her tremendous force of will and personality. Frank Hardie talks of her 'volcanic energy'.[70] Cecil Woodham-Smith claims that it 'was impossible for anyone even remotely acquainted with the Queen's character not to recognize it as formidable'.[71] Gladstone is reported to have stated, 'The Queen alone is enough to kill anyone.' And Bismarck, the Iron Chancellor, is said to have retired from an interview with the Iron Queen, 'mopping his brow: "That was a woman! one could do business with her!"'[72]

She was the living symbol of an Empire and embodied the character and spirit of her age, as Kingsley Martin, writing in 1926, comments:

> If . . . it is the duty of the English monarch to be passive and impartial, the Queen was the least constitutional of sovereigns. That she retained the reputation of a model monarch was due to the fact that, though she strained the constitution almost to breaking point, her prejudices and her convictions were so exactly those dominant in her age that she seemed to embody its very nature within herself.[73]

Early Morning explodes the notion of Victoria as a 'model monarch,' and any sentimental nostalgia one might be tempted to have about the nineteenth century, which was an age of European power and thrust. The certainty and self-confidence generated by its titanic material achievements, contrasts sharply with the anxiety and uncertainty of a crisis-ridden world a century later. Macaulay talks of belonging to 'the most enlightened generation that ever existed'.[74] *The Wonderful Century* is the title of a book by A. R. Wallace, the biologist, published in 1898 in which he sees the nineteenth century as 'superior to any that have gone before it'. It must be 'held to constitute the beginning of a new era of human progress'.[75] When Queen Victoria died at Osborne on 22 January 1901, her funeral was described as marking the end of a splendid epoch, 'the most glorious one of British history'. Orators and leader-writers indulged in wild outpourings of praise for the past, and anxious forebodings about the future.[76]

Yet past and present were indissolubly connected, for the nineteenth century was an age of revolution, which set in motion changes which can be said, without exaggeration, to have affected the whole human condition. Bond sees the nineteenth century as having bequeathed us many of the most pressing problems that confront us today. In reply to my letter to him regarding his treatment of history in *Early Morning*, Bond writes, 'Obviously I knew about the history of Victorian England and its Iconography – both congratulatory and critical.' But the imagery of the play came from 'a consideration of the disasters of my own time – which seemed to reflect the horrors of Victorian imperialism'. 'By the calendar, we have passed that epoch – culturally we have not. If I were writing the play now I might include imagery from the Falklands fighting.'[77]

In an interview Bond states:

I'm not saying that before the nineteenth century, society was moral, kind, generous. It wasn't, because the economic grounds for these things weren't there. But I am saying that it broke up communities on which culture was founded, pushed these people off into factory ghettoes, and therefore destroyed the artistic consciousness of the people. And in that way, I think, it destroyed their self-integrity, which they had to set about the long business of finding again.[78]

This search for self-integrity can be seen embodied in the Arthur/ George (as the product of Victoria) predicament in *Early Morning*. Arthur has to struggle against George, who personifies the limits and constraints imposed on human personality and behaviour by society, represented by Victoria. In another note to me, Bond explains, 'I wanted to show an individual divided into two selves – a "socialized" self and a self that was trying to create its own freedom.' The danger of a society which exists through the subordination of some of its members to others is 'cultural and intellectual – and this means, also, emotional'. The distortions and perversions of ideas and culture needed to maintain an unjust society 'debase human personality and lead to violence and cultural waste'.[79] Through the play's imagery, exploitation and slavery are intended to come across as oppressive features of Victorian life.

Early Morning presents a radical uncompromising view of the operating principles of Victorian society. It is a mordant comment on an insane world of suicidal competition. Arthur's nightmare about 'the mill' focuses the illusion and reality behind its economic aspirations:

> There are men and women and children and cattle and birds and horses pushing a mill. They're grinding other cattle and people and children: they push each other in. Some fall in. It grinds their bones you see. The ones pushing the wheel, even the animals, look up at their horizon. They stumble. . . . They shout. Half of them run in their sleep. Some are trampled on. They're sure they're reaching the horizon. . . . Later I come back. There's white powder everywhere. I find the mill, and it's stopped. The last man died half in.
>
> (Sc. 11, p. 68)

This picture of the mill grinding all humanity to dust, with each person pushing and treading the other underfoot, eyes on a distant horizon which continually recedes before them, brings home the horror and futility of dreams of universal abundance, of social milennium through increased production by autonomous individual effort. An image, extremely close to this one, of people trampling each other down in the effort to get ahead, is conveyed in an admission by John Stuart Mill[80]:

> I confess I am not charmed with the ideal of life held out by those who think that the normal state of human beings is that of struggling to get on; that the trampling, crushing, elbowing, and treading on each other's heels, which form the existing type of social life, are the most desirable lot of human kind . . .[81]

Thus again and again we find the play reproducing in a remarkably close way, types of social commentary which actually were made in the nineteenth century.

In *Early Morning* individuals are seen quite literally to devour one another. They are disparate, calculating, competing entities in a society which operates on the principle of eat or be eaten, or survival of the fittest. Bond is satirizing the philosophy of a mercantilist empire of which Queen Victoria is the supreme symbol.

The nineteenth century brought in an age of competition and economic rivalry, and the operation of the laws of capitalism. It was the century of great trade profits, and had immense repercussions for the twentieth century in the attitudes it fostered, with its emphasis on aggressive individualism and untrammelled enterprise. England, as the world's greatest commercial power, its main exporter, customer and financier, held sway as an autocrat of trade. It was seen by some as the citadel of *laissez-faire* or the free play of economic forces. Commercial monopoly was the theoretical foundation of its mercantilist empire. Nineteenth-century philosophical ideas, derived from Darwin's theory of evolution, reinforced the acceptance of the principle of the survival of the fittest as an unalterable law of nature.[82] *Laissez-faire* was in accordance with the immutable laws which regulate human existence. We see this notion parodied in the play. 'You were first in the womb,' Albert informs Arthur, 'Your mother screamed and struggled and your brother thrashed his way out in front' (Sc. 8, p. 50). In striking disconcerting terms Bond weaves into the play ideas and attitudes that exerted a dominant influence in the nineteenth century.

Political life in England was affected by this climate of unbridled competition. In *Early Morning* Disraeli and Gladstone are depicted as virtually indistinguishable power-hungry gangsters, vying for supremacy of position. Through them Bond registers the spirit of narrow class interest and fierce party warfare representative of the time. In its leading editorial of the 1 January 1888 the London *Times* states, ' . . . party spirit in politics has displayed a bitterness which the most experienced politicians confess to exceed anything within their remembrance'. The Whigs and the Tories in Parliament seemed to be motivated by the same passions. William Morris, writing in 1888, comments:

> This, therefore, is what Parliament looks to me; a solid central party, with mere nebulous opposition on the right hand and on the left. The people governed; that is to say, fair play amongst themselves for the money-privileged classes to make the most of their privilege, and to fight sturdily with each other in doing so . . .[83]

Thus behind what Bond depicts in an extraordinary way are views which were held in the nineteenth century, and these views can be found to be shared by some twentieth-century historians as well.

Writing in 1945, H. M. Lynd talks of two parties in competition at that time and comments that 'the habit of English politics was a choice between two sensible versions of the same thing' for they both represented property interest and defended the 'same principles of inequality and privilege in English life, conceding to the People whatever concessions were unavoidable in order to maintain the existing social order'.[84] L. C. B. Seaman writing in 1973 describes Disraeli and Gladstone in terms dramatic enough to come close to the picture of the scheming, fiendish rivals in *Early Morning*. He talks of the 'histrionic character of their political behaviour'. Disraeli was England's Louis Napoleon, 'a man who came in from the outside and who, by an ingenious combination of intuition, charlatinism and courage, climbed to the top of a greasy pole'. The passing of the 1867 Reform Act manoeuvred by Disraeli was the work of a 'consummate political conspirator'. On returning to office in 1880, Gladstone's mind 'was so clouded with a messianic desire to purge the land of the evils of "Beaconsfieldism" that he had few clear ideas about anything'.[85]

In Bond's view the cause of human ill is not 'an irredeemable natural fault but the class nature of society'. This class nature distorts consciousness and is responsible for the myths that pervert culture.[86] In *Early Morning* what comes across powerfully is a sense of mutually hostile layers of leaders and followers, dominators and dominated, presided over by the imperious sovereign lady herself. Nobody has any real loyalty to the other, within ranks or without. The royal family is seen divided against itself and followers are continually turning on their own leaders. This reflects the authoritarian structure of Victorian society, which was a class society divided into mutually antagonistic layers, each united by a common source of income. The interdependence of the British social hierarchy is demonstrated in an etching by George Cruikshank in 1867, called 'The British Beehive' and intended as propaganda against those demanding further reforms of the franchise.[87] The Queen, the Constitution, the Law, and the Church, are shown resting on hard-working but happy labourers and tradesmen, and the whole structure is seen standing on the Bank and the Army. *Early Morning* dramatizes this hierarchical authoritarian class structure, with Victoria reigning as Queen Bee, fighting to preserve her precarious position in the face of continual harassment and designs upon her supremacy.

A drawing like Cruikshank's could only rouse the satirist in Bond. When I wrote to inquire whether he had come across it while he was writing *Early Morning*, Bond replied that he knew the etching, but thought he had only come across it after he had written the play.[88] The nineteenth century was particularly rich in violently satirical, often grostesque, social and political cartoons and caricatures by James Gillray, Thomas Rowlandson, George Cruikshank, Robert Seymour, Sir John Tenniel and many others. These might have been a stimulus for a playwright like Bond with his strong visual imagination, and might account for the cartoon-like nature of his characters in *Early Morning*.[89]

The play also explores the role of the family as a form of social control, a transmitter of accepted values. The image of the ideal family – happy, disciplined, moral – is a force of considerable social influence, and the royal family must present a model to the nation. 'I will not permit family bickering in public!' Victoria admonishes her contentious brood (Sc. 3, p. 15). We see Arthur struggling against the enormous pressures imposed on him by mother, father, and brother before he finally achieves his own freedom and truth. Again, in focusing on the tutelary role of the head of the family, Bond is highlighting a significant feature of Victorian life. 'Family tradition and family life meant more to the Victorians than they do to the present generation', Hardie comments, and in most Victorian families there was 'some one person, usually a matriarch, exercising a kind of planetary influence'. Such a person, it was claimed, was the Queen-Empress.[90] Elizabeth Longford notes that Victoria felt that her happy family life would keep the country morally safe. When she opened the Royal Exchange in October 1844, her press had been so good that she writes in a letter:

> They say no Sovereign was ever more loved than I am (I am bold enough to say), and *this* because of our domestic home, the good example it presents.[91]

The Victorians were almost obsessively interested in discovering the bases of social order because of what Bond describes as the:

> explosive atmosphere of the nineteenth century where there was a great deal of economic injustice and a working class that really could have risen up and cut the landlords' throats.[92]

Thus the cannibalistic heaven of *Early Morning* is an allegorical denunciation of the exploitation that prevails on earth:

> You don't eat anybody physically but you eat their mental suffering, you eat their despair, you eat the waste of their lives. . . . Our economic relationship to the earth is through eating and destroying each other.[93]

The nineteenth century brought about the massive advance of industrial capitalism. E. J. Hobsbawm in his book, *The Age of Capitalism 1848–1875* (1945), asserts that the:

> global triumph of capitalism is the major theme of history in the decades after 1848. It was the triumph of a society which believed that economic growth rested on competitive private enterprise, on success in buying everything in the cheapest market (including labour) and selling in the dearest.[94]

According to Bond, 'capitalism creates a schizophrenic society of tension and aggression'. 'Our economy depends on exploitation and aggression. . . . At the same time we expect people to be generous and socially considerate.' Advertising incites the worker as consumer to be master without responsibility to anyone but himself. He must know his place in the factory and be a placid worker, but be an insatiable egotist, a rampaging selfish consumer outside it. We need anti-social behaviour to keep society running, but this behaviour destroys society. 'The good citizen must be schizophrenic.'[95] In *Early Morning* this schizophrenia is depicted in the physical form of Arthur and George as Siamese twins. A reckless rampaging consumer society takes the haunting shape of a cannibalistic earth and heaven. The play conveys in unsettling metaphorical terms the racking problems created by the divisive nature of Victorian society.

There is no doubt that marvellous strides in many spheres were made in the nineteenth century. But one was also confronted with the contradictions of progress – the paradox of poverty in midst of plenty. In 1884 it was stated on the basis of government reports that:

> in the wealthiest nation in the world, almost every twentieth inhabitant is a pauper, that according to poor-law reports, one-fifth of the community is insufficiently clad; that according to

medical reports to the Privy Council, the agricultural labourers and large classes of working people in towns are too poorly fed to save them from what are known as starvation diseases.[96]

Slums were a characteristic feature of nineteenth-century industrial life. Child labour persisted into the last decades of the century. Of England of the 1880s it was written, 'What a satire upon our boasted civilization that plenty should bring misery to many and that people should starve because of the very abundance.'[97]

In Bond's view capitalism creates such deep destructive ironies. Affluence 'impoverishes and produces the social conditions of scarcity'. The richer the organization becomes, the more impoverished the schools, hospitals and welfare and social services. 'Affluence isn't well-being, but a form of aggression. It makes the greedy hungry and the warm cold.'[98] 'I'm hungry! They're hungry! You're hungry! We're all dead and hungry!' exclaims Florence to Arthur in the play (Sc. 19, p. 103). Arthur's answer to that persistent cry of hers is: 'The dead are always hungry' (Sc. 20, p. 110). Bond sees us as now living in a 'scientific barbarism, the most irrational society that ever existed'.[99] Rather than having brought enlightenment, the nineteenth century is viewed by him as having returned man to an uncultured savage state, his desires shrunk to the psychology of the market place. Thus cannibalism is the dominant image in the play.

Modern historians can be found holding a similar view of the effects of nineteenth-century capitalism in Victorian England. E. J. Hobsbawm, a Marxist, states:

There is, of course, no dispute about the fact that *relatively*, the poor grew poorer, simply because the country, and its rich and middle class, so obviously grew wealthier. The very moment when the poor were at the end of their tether – in the early and middle forties – was the moment when the middle class invested in railways and spent on bulging, opulent household furnishings displayed at the Great Exhibition of 1851, and on the palatial municipal constructions which prepared to rise in the smoky northern cities.[100]

L. C. B. Seaman talks of the continuous expansion of traditional industries, and the export of surplus capital abroad in order to maximize profit for the investor. 'The effect of this was to starve the nation of social improvements (in relation to the scale of the need for it) and to reinforce the Victorians' obstinate resistance to investment in public health, housing and education.' He comments acidly that:

> it might have been better for the late Victorians and their descendants, if, for instance, John Chamberlain had sought to instruct his generation, not that the Empire was 'an undeveloped estate'; but that much of the United Kingdom had been turned into a slum.[101]

It therefore becomes patently clear that there is a substantial basis in history for the vision of the nineteenth century which Bond presents in *Early Morning*. In fact an amazing paradox consistently emerges, for where the play is most fantastic and outlandish, Bond can be found dealing with history of a very serious nature. The play is a severe indictment of Victorian society, and the legacy it has left to the present. The events of this play are true in a deep sense, for though it assumes the form of a bizarre dream-fantasy, it deals with dominant features of Victorian social and political life. They are treated in the manner of some hideous cartoon which magnifies the subject to absurdity, but within the grotesque distortion is a point of truth that is driven home with bitter potency.

Bond creates an uncompromising imagery of human violence and affliction, which comments bleakly on the possibility of resisting a cruel universe of economic rapaciousness, and exploding political evil. And yet hope lies in a persistent humanity which keeps reasserting itself. Arthur thought, to quote a phrase from Webster's play, *The White Devil*, that he would 'cease to die by dying', but finds there is something in him that dies hard. In fact I am often reminded of that play of Webster's, where goodness too has scant chance of surviving, and yet even in the most unsympathetic characters, a humanity persists which much of their behaviour denies. Thus, says Flamineo, the least attractive of them all:

> I have a strange thing in me, to the which
> I cannot give a name, without it be
> Compassion . . .

(Act 5, Sc. 4, ll. 110–12)

Arthur too finds that, in spite of joining the living dead, and participating in the eating of others out of sheer desperation and futility, there is something in himself he cannot quite kill:

> I've tried but I can't die!
> Even eating didn't kill me. There's something I can't kill – and they can't kill it for me.

(Sc. 19, p. 102)

Webster's play dramatizes a similar dilemma of individuals in a society which has ceased to be constrained by moral values. Bond, perhaps, was influenced by that play because he goes on to write an adaptation of *The White Devil* which was first performed in 1976 at the Old Vic theatre.

Arthur, in finally refusing to eat, becomes a catalyst in this world of mutual cannibalism. He soon starts to attract a ragged following, and is seen to have a humanizing effect on others. Even Florence, who is sent by Victoria to decoy Arthur into her hands, because he is a threat to the establishment, is affected. Where the norm in this world is a total disintegration of relationship, we see, incredibly, a genuine bond beginning to form between Arthur and Florence. Arthur tries to persuade Florence to run away with him:

Florence: What good is that? You still won't eat.
. . .
Arthur: You keep me alive.
Florence: You're not alive! This is heaven! You can't live or laugh
          or cry or be in pain! You can't torture people! Let me
          alone! You're a ghost. Ghost! Ghost! You're haunting
          me – O stop it.
Arthur: You're crying.
Florence: No, no, no, no.
Arthur: My hand's wet.
Florence: Nothing to cry for. Too late. Why didn't you tell me
          this before? What d'you think I did while I waited? I'm
          not crying. Perhaps I'm alive, perhaps we needn't be
          like this . . .

(Sc. 19, pp. 102–3)

Against all odds, in spite of the play's outlandish material, Bond is able to render it human and immediate at many points, as at a moment like this when the emotion is felt to be very real.

We see a change taking place in Florence, who had not been able to conceive the possibility of an alternative to what seemed the inevitable nature of things. Florence is afraid of society and her own impotence in it. Victoria is the controller and Florence is the controlled, both almost, as it were, trained to their roles. When Arthur is finally captured and eaten by Victoria and her party, Florence joins in the eating because 'Victoria was watching' (Sc. 20, p. 109). Arthur is an embarrassment to Victoria. His actions ought to be guided by his status as a member of the ruling order. He is expected to fulfil his role as the visible embodiment of authority, by his support of the social system. Only when he joined in the killing, and engineered all their deaths, could Victoria say: 'for the first time I was able to call him son' (Sc. 16, p. 86).

But Arthur now finds that in not eating, even if they eat him for it, he is 'alive' or 'beginning to live'. 'I'm like a fire in the sea or the sun underground', he tells Florence after having been reduced to nothing but a head which she has hidden from the rest. When they discover his head and begin eating it too, Arthur laughs as they do. It is an extraordinary image of the triumph of life over the forces of death and destruction. In another of Bond's plays, *The Sea* (1973), a character expresses the belief that 'all destruction is finally petty and in the end life laughs at death' (Sc. 8, p. 64). We see in *Early Morning* this verbal idea translated into startling physical form. It is in such ways that Bond's plays make for compelling theatre. He is a poet not just of words, but of words transformed into vivid action, potent stage metaphors that haunt the mind.

The play concludes with a parody of the Last Supper. Victoria, 'head of the church', distorts what Arthur dies for, and uses it to support the world she symbolizes. 'He told you not to eat each other', she tells his followers. 'But he knew he was asking something unnatural and impossible. Something quite, quite impossible. . . . So he died, to let you eat each other in peace.' 'His last words were "Feed them."' She signals Albert to come on in with the hamper and it is a gruesome supper indeed (Sc. 21, p. 117). Through this grotesque picture Bond drives home the bizarre fusion of politics and religion that took place in Victorian England.

The Church was frequently used as a tool to reinforce the social order. Clergymen often explained and justified the existence of poverty and inequality in society, preaching the merits of due subordination to authority and acceptance of the status quo. The social system derived from God, who willed different grades and orders in society, and a disparity in rank, wealth and power.[102] A modern historian points out that one of the principal reasons the Established Church failed to embrace the 'dark, uninstructed masses' was recognized by Charles Kingsley, who said, 'It is our fault. We have used the Bible as if it was a mere constable's handbook – an opium dose for keeping beasts of burden patient while they were being overloaded.'[103] Elizabeth Longford quotes Victoria on what she calls 'the Victorian version of the divine right of kings':

> Obedience to the laws of the Sovereign, is obedience to a higher Power, divinely instituted for the good of the *people* . . . [104]

Religion and politics were interlinked more closely in England during the latter half of the nineteenth century than they have been at any time since. Bond satirizes the Victorian manipulation of religion to support and preserve the state.

The play ends with everyone sitting around Arthur's coffin, all cheerfully tucking into the food laid on top of it, except for Florence who sits a little to one side, crying silently, while Arthur, a Christlike figure in a white shroud, hands half-raised, rises silently into the air above them in obvious contradiction of Victoria's self-satisfied pronouncement – 'There's no dirt in heaven. There's only peace and happiness, law and order, consent and co-operation. My life's work has borne fruit. It's settled' (Sc. 21, p. 120). Arthur resurrected over Victoria's world suggests powerfully that we *can* shake off the domination of the past that imposes itself on the present. In order to recognize and rediscover the social and moral sanctions that help create a sane world, we have to make an effort of memory and imagination.

Bond's choice of the play's title with its pun on 'mourning' reinforces this meaning. It was chosen partly, because he thought the play 'might be taken to suggest something catastrophic and final' when just the opposite was meant.[105] Bond's purpose, therefore, is ultimately optimistic. Arthur transcends Victoria's world and has planted the seeds of unrest and discontent. Florence's tears signal hope for the future. Bond has said that he is afraid of the past; he is not afraid of the future. In a 'rapidly-changing technocracy it is important to throw some light on the future, so that people can say, yes, the future is chooseable and it is malleable, we can form it'.[106]

Bond's history plays invite us to examine the past, so that the future is not created in its image. His view of history is not fatalistic or deterministic. He believes in the power, freedom and responsibility of individuals to choose, to break down inhuman repressive social structures, and to build what he calls a rational society which exists for the equal good of all its members. His plays, which expose fallacies, provoke inquiry and stimulate the individual and social conscience are intended as a contribution to this end. 'Art,' he says, 'has to be the equivalent of hooliganism on the streets.' It has to be 'disruptive and questioning' if society is to be changed rationally and not by force.'[107] Bond's plays certainly are extremely disquieting, and shock us out of any tendency to complacent thinking and emotional glibness. They compel attention not only because we are confronted by questions that really do demand an answer, but also because of the amazing force of Bond's imagination which realizes them in brilliant theatrical terms.

In *Early Morning* this tremendous creative power is revealed in its extraordinary treatment of history. What clearly emerges from this study is that Bond is not just taking perverse liberties with history. *Early Morning* is not an arbitrary invention of the mind, but a highly serious vision of the past. Bond's use of the fluidity, spontaneity and irresponsibility of a dream structure to approach history, is very freeing. Yet I think it is important to note that he does not attempt to create the *illusion* of a dream, such as we find, for example, in the dream plays of Strindberg. Bond wants his audiences wide awake and present, not blurred and transported into a different realm. The play confronts us like a *remembered* dream that haunts the waking consciousness with a macabre beauty and grandeur.

Early Morning opens up new possibilities for the treatment of history. In a way, looking back to the past is a sort of fantasy, with potent hints and associations of things remembered or discovered adding to the mystery of what is irrecoverable in any total sense. Through the creation of a disturbing dream imagery of great power and intensity, Bond has also managed to capture the spirit of our age, to convey its sense of irremediable anxiety and uncertainty. The dream form is an eloquent vehicle, particularly suited to the modern psyche and our troubled times, and to the fact that our understanding of the past is, to a large extent, clouded, fragmented, intuitive and inextricably bound up with our apprehension of the present.

7

Conclusion

The history play is a most popular genre among English playwrights of this century. This could be partly due to the distinctive power inherent in the form, arising from its tacit claim to be engaging directly with reality. An audience's involvement in what is presented on the stage is heightened and intensified by the sense of history, since they credit events enacted with a degree of factuality. The historical playwright thus has a responsibility not only to his subject but also to his audience, to be regardful of historical truth, since the audience is unable when emotionally strained to escape from distress by dismissing what is being presented as purely fictitious. This responsibility on the part of the playwright needs to be given due weight in any attempt to redefine the genre of the history play in terms of modern ideas of, and attitudes to, history.

In this study, plays of different concerns and different approaches have been closely examined in order to ascertain their particular use and treatment of history, and their regard for historical truth and historical issues, which I established in the introduction as the basis of my definition of a history play. This definition seems to be both workable and satisfying. It has proved comprehensive and flexible enough to encompass plays of widely varying treatments, including some which are extremely imaginative and daring, even revolutionary, in their approach to the past, like Edward Bond's *Early Morning*. Yet it has also posed its own controls and been sufficiently discriminating and limiting to exclude plays which reveal a superficial and peripheral concern with history. Thus it disqualifies plays like Clifford Bax's *The Rose without a Thorn*, which is sentimental and romantic in its approach to history, revealing an ignorance of or indifference to the facts, and plays like Peter Shaffer's *The Royal Hunt of the Sun* which has only faint pretensions to historical and political concerns, and exploits history for its sensational and theatrical possibilities.

In plays like these history is used in a shallow way. Their playwrights are content with superficial externals. They go for colour, atmosphere, pageantry, a mere veneer of history, in order to set their romantic stories of love and betrayal against a picturesque or marvellous backdrop. These were the dominating features of nineteenth-century historical drama, from which Shaw made such a radical break. He revolted against this outward semblance of historical reality in the form of false period atmosphere, artificial impassioned sentiments and exotic colouring. He led the way for a very different kind of theatre, stimulating a new tradition of history play that was dynamic and alive, in touch with real human motives and characters, and concerned both with vital historical events and issues, and with their relevance to urgent social needs and problems of contemporary life. Shaw was clearly pivotal in the field of twentieth-century historical drama, providing the 'germinal impulse' that awoke modern dramatists to the need to be researchers as well as playwrights.

This has resulted in a dominant feature of the twentieth century English history play. Modern playwrights feel a much greater sense of responsibility in putting history over on the stage. They can often be found making a vigorous scrutiny of the original sources, as in the case of T. S. Eliot. Most reveal a strong inner and outer compulsion to support the view of history their plays present, in prefaces, introductions and notes appended to the text by drawing attention to the data on which they are based. This owes something to the intellectual climate of our time, the great zeal for documentation and much greater demand for evidence to support a view. Looking at the English history play of the twentieth century, as distinct from the nineteenth and preceding centuries, what seems to have increased significantly is this attitude of intellectual awareness.

Modern playwrights attempt to be sharper and more searching in their approach to history. Most playwrights, even those who are comparatively minor and lightweight, like Robert Bolt, Reginald Berkeley and Gordon Daviot, reveal a reluctance to take over uncritically a received version of history. They strive for a distance from conventional and approved accounts, and attempt to shatter false historical myths or images. Where minor playwrights challenge but are unable to displace powerful historical images which dominate the human mind, as for instance those created by Shakespeare, major playwrights like Shaw and Edward Bond, great in their own right, are able to compete and impress vital historical images of their own upon the modern consciousness.

But, though the modern English historical playwright reveals a serious concern to examine historical sources and verify the facts, paradoxically, he is at the same time very free with history. Possessing a supportive basis for his vision, he then takes it as far as it will go. He is immensely audacious and challenging in his treatment of history. Thus we find Osborne's portrait of Luther stirring much inquiry and discussion and Bond's deeply unsettling vision of the nineteenth century, with its enormous scale and acute relevance to the present, arousing a storm of journalistic and governmental censure on its first production. Thus this tremendous paradox emerges – modern English playwrights are both extremely regardful of and extremely free with history.

Then again another distinctive feature is the overtly modern perspective registered by these playwrights, stemming once again from Shaw's influence. Modern historical playwrights continually draw upon the present, which enables us to see history as knit into the fabric of our own time. The present is carried into the past as the past is sometimes carried into the future. Startling anachronisms are very much a part of the style of modern playwrights in their effort to drive home the connections between past and present. They may appear to be departing violently from history by their apparent and deliberate inserting of the present into the past, but in fact they are reflecting a deep truth about the nature of history. All we can know of the past is largely a subjective interpretation, and each observer rewrites history according to the bias of his own age. This radical yoking of the past and present brings home the unity of human experience, though each successive generation may perceive some fresh aspect of the historical situation it alone can understand. We can see, for instance, the change that has taken place in the general attitude towards the exceptional individual or leader figure, from the various treatments of playwrights in this book. In *Saint Joan* Shaw, a Victorian, explores the impact of the extraordinary individual upon her environment though her immediate society is unable to accept or comprehend the progress and inspiration she embodies. In stark contrast, Edward Bond, in the light of his own time, sees leaders of nineteenth-century society as terrible figures, the embodiment of savage inhuman social and political forces that enslave and devour men beneath a respectable, civilized exterior. Again, Osborne in *Luther* sees the exceptional individual primarily as a victim of himself and the mental and spiritual fracture of his age, as it is equally of ours.

This brings us to another salient characteristic of twentieth-century English history plays. Playwrights tend to bring themselves and their consciousness right up to the threshold of history. In *Murder in the Cathedral* we can see the overflow of a personality that has made a particular appropriation of the past. Eliot appears to have found in history something of himself, a historical condition or dilemma which mirrored his own very private needs and experience at the time. Modern playwrights tend to emphasize the universe that lies within, the private man behind the public mask, the complexity and precariousness of personality. They register the great unfathomable depths of the subconscious that lie beneath the social political exterior. Thus we find T. S. Eliot's *Murder in the Cathedral* and John Osborne's *Luther* with their disturbing renditions of a tormented interior state. Edward Bond too in *Early Morning* registers a troubling spiritual/political landscape in his surrealistic vision of the past. This reflects the new psychological perspective of our age, a post-Freudian era, with its awareness of the tremendous impact and implications of psycho-analysis. In his exploration of history the playwright is able to probe beneath and beyond the shell of evidence, and register the deep hidden dimensions of the human psyche.

A playwright thus can strive for the innermost attainable truth, and in some respects can give a fuller vision of the past than the historian. He gains something by his greater degree of independence in the imaginative appropriation of the past. A sensitive artist may reveal more of the essential truth of history than a historian, who is more strictly limited by the facts and must subdue his imagination to the controls of scholarship and accept the primacy of his evidence. This accounts for the unique power of the history play arising from its dual character. It is a form of fiction as well as a form of history and its fictive nature is as vital a part of that power as its historical nature. It allows the playwright to go into large areas of imaginative conjecture closed to the historian, enabling him to engage with historical reality in a much more total sense. A play supplies what history cannot give. Infused with the spirit that quickens, it breathes life into the bare bones of history. A playwright is concerned with re-enactment, resurrection, of historical material in a vital, immediate way, because he has to deal ultimately, not with bloodless abstractions, but with people on a stage who are required to move and be. The actors bring their own reality and understanding to bear and can make or break a dramatic situation. This is part of a play's essential truth and strength. A playwright flashes light upon the past in unexpected ways. He brings to it an artist's power of imagination and insight, his intuitive grasp of character and situation, and his genius for synthesis. Thus, in relation to history, the English historical playwright of the twentieth century at his best, emerges as no mere borrower from the past, but a poet, a prophet and a visionary.

Notes

CHAPTER 1: INTRODUCTION

1. *The Tudor Drama: a History of English National Drama to the Retirement of Shakespeare* (London: Constable, 1912) p. 297.
2. For a review of various philosophical opinions on the subject, see William H. Dray, *Philosophy of History* (Englewood Cliffs, N. J. Prentice Hall, 1964) pp. 21–40.
3. Acton, *The Cambridge Modern History: an Account of its Origin, Authorship and Production* (Cambridge University Press, 1907) pp. 10–2. (N. B. This book is an independent publication and not part of the *Cambridge Modern History* series. There is no printed reference to it in the *British Museum General Catalogue of Printed Books* or the *National Union Catalogue*. A copy was eventually located in the Cambridge university library.)
4. See G. Clark in G. R. Potter (ed.), *The New Cambridge Modern History*, vol. 1 (Cambridge University Press, 1957) p. xxv.
5. *What is History?* (London: Macmillan, 1961) p. 21.
6. Ibid., pp. 4–7.
7. *The Practice of History* (Sidney University Press, 1967) pp. 55–7.
8. Ibid., pp. 51–3.
9. *The English History Play in the Age of Shakespeare* (Princeton University Press, 1957) pp. 3–32.
10. Op. cit., p. 59.
11. *Historical Drama: the Relation of Literature and Reality* (Chicago and London: University of Chicago Press, 1975) p. 3.
12. Op. cit., pp. xx–xxi.
13. Cecil Ferard Armstrong records this response of London audiences in *Shakespeare to Shaw: Studies in the Life's Work of Six Dramatists of the English Stage* (London: Mills & Boon, 1913) p. 277.
14. *An Actor and His Time* (London: Sidgwick & Jackson, 1979) pp. 104–5.
15. Cited in St. John Ervine, *Bernard Shaw, His Life, Work and Friends* (London: Constable, 1956) pp. 499–500.
16. *The Material of English History* (London: Thomas Nelson, 1938) pp. 128–9.
17. E. H. Erikson, *Young Man Luther* (London: Faber & Faber, 1959) p. 34.
18. Theodore Rozdak, *Where the Wasteland Ends: Politics and Transcendence in Post-industrial Society* (London: Faber & Faber, 1972) pp. 133–4.
19. *The Judgements of Joan: Joan of Arc: A Study in Cultural History* (London: Allen & Unwin, 1961) p. 33.
20. In *Major Critical Essays* (London: Constable, 1932) pp. 283–4.
21. B. Croce, *History as the Story of Liberty* (London: Allen & Unwin, 1938) p. 19.
22. 'Fifty Years of Change in Historical Teaching and Research' in *The Historical Association Jubilee Addresses 1956* (London: George Phillip, 1956) p. 34.

23. In James Walter McFarlane and Graham Orton (eds. and trans.), *The Oxford Ibsen* (London: Oxford University Press, 1963) p. 603.
24. See A. B. Harbage, *As They Liked It: An Essay on Shakespeare and Morality* (New York: Macmillan, 1947) pp. 123–4; L. Campbell, *Shakespeare's 'Histories': Mirrors of Elizabethan Policy* (San Marino: Huntingdon Library, 1947) p. 17.
25. 'History in the Twentieth Century' in *The Historical Association Jubilee Addresses 1956* (London: George Philip, 1956) pp. 20–2.
26. Op. cit., pp. 12–13.
27. *The New Cambridge Modern History*, vol. 12 (Cambridge University Press, 1960) p. 1.
28. *History in Special and in General* (Cambridge University Press, 1964) pp. 7–8.
29. *Historical Drama*, p. 25.
30. Ibid., p. x.
31. S. H. Butcher, *Aristotle's Theory of Poetry and Fine Art: With a Critical Text and Translation of 'The Poetics'* (New York: Dover Publications, 1894) pp. 35–7.
32. Albert Feuillerat (ed.), *The Prose Works of Sir Phillip Sidney*, vol. 3 (Cambridge University Press, 1962) pp. 5–17.
33. *The Historian and Character and Other Essays* (Cambridge University Press, 1963) p. 14.
34. *History and Human Relations* (London: Collins, 1951) pp. 232–49.
35. *English Dramatic Form: A History of its Development* (London: Chatto & Windus, 1965) p. 13.
36. Martin Meisel, *Shaw and the Nineteenth-Century Theater* (Princeton University Press, 1963) p. 353.
37. See E. Martin Browne, 'The Two Beckets', *Drama*, no. 60 (Spring 1961) p. 28.
38. Frederick Jackson Turner, 'An American Definition of History' in Fritz Stern (ed.), *The Varieties of History: from Voltaire to the Present* (Cleveland and New York: The World Publishing Co., 1956) p. 201.
39. See W. H. Prescott, *History of the Conquest of Peru: with a Preliminary View of the Civilisation of the Incas* (London: Allen & Unwin, 1847) p. ix.

CHAPTER 2: GEORGE BERNARD SHAW: *SAINT JOAN*

1. *Shaw and the Nineteenth-Century Theater* (Princeton University Press, 1963) p. 349.
2. Cited in M. Meisel, *Shaw and the Nineteenth-Century Theater*, p. 350.
3. See Cecil Ferard Armstrong, *Shakespeare to Shaw: Studies in the Life's Works of Six Dramatists of the English Stage* (London: Mills & Boon, 1913) p. 277.
4. Preface, '*In Good King Charles's Golden Days*': *a True History that never Happened* in *The Bodley Head Bernard Shaw: Collected Plays with their Prefaces*, vol. 7 (London: Max Reinhardt, 1898) p. 203.

5. 'The Theatre Today and Yesterday according to George Bernard Shaw', *The Manchester Evening News*, 6/12/38.
6. MS, Texas (17 Apr., 1894); Reprinted in Stanley Weintraub (ed.), *Shaw: An Autobiography 1856–1898* (London: Max Reinhardt, 1970) p. 288.
7. *Our Theatres in the Nineties*, vol. 3 (London: Constable, 1932) p. 110.
8. Ibid., vol. 1, p. 177.
9. *George Bernard Shaw's Historical Plays* (Delhi: Macmillan, 1976) p. 12.
10. *The Historian and Character and other Essays* (Cambridge University Press) p. 5.
11. *George Bernard Shaw's Historical Plays*, p. 93.
12. 'G. B. S. and Isaac Newton' in Max Beerhohm *et. al.*, *G. B. S. 90: Aspects of Bernard Shaw's Life and Work* (London: Hutchinson, 1946) p. 106.
13. *George Bernard Shaw: Man of the Century* (New York: Appleton-Century-Crofts, [1956]) p. 556.
14. 'Bernard Shaw and the Heroic Actor', *The Play Pictoria*, 10, no. 62 (Oct. 1907) p. 110.
15. 'Ovation for Shaw' in R. J. Kauffman (ed.), *G. B. Shaw: a Collection of Critical Essays* (Englewood Cliffs, N.J.: Prentice-Hall [1965]) p. 17. [Originally published in *Berliner Börsen-Courier*, 25/7/26]
16. See Hesketh Pearson, *Bernard Shaw: His Life and Personality* (London: Collins, 1942) p. 213.
17. 'Some Remarks on Shaw's History Plays', *English Studies*, 36 (Oct. 1955) pp. 239–46.
18. 'Shaw's Mommsenite Caesar,' in Philip Allison Shelley and Arthur O. Lewis (eds), *Anglo-German and American-German Crosscurrents*, vol. 2 (University of North Carolina Press, 1962) p. 271.
19. *Julius Caesar in Shakespeare, Shaw and the Ancients* (New York: Harcourt, [1960]) p. 5.
20. Dan H. Laurence (ed.), *Bernard Shaw: Collected Letters 1898–1910* (London: Max Reinhardt, 1972) pp. 180–1.
21. C. R. 'Mr Shaw's Future: a Conversation', *The Academy* (Apr. 1898) p. 476.
22. See Hesketh Pearson, *Bernard Shaw: His Life and Personality*, p. 476.
23. Theodor Mommsen, *The History of Rome*, translated by W. P. Dickson, vol. 5 (London: Macmillan, 1913) p. 314.
24. Preface, *Three Plays for Puritans* in *The Bodley Head Bernard Shaw*, vol. 2, 45–6.
25. Thomas Carlyle, 'On Heroes, Hero-Worship and the Heroic in History' in Fritz Stern (ed.), *The Varieties of History: From Voltaire to the Present* (New York: The World Publishing Co., [1956]) p. 103.
26. 'Caesar and Cleopatra: The Making of a History Play', *The Shavian Review*, 14, no. 2 (May 1971) p. 88.
27. Desmond MacCarthy, *Shaw* (London: MacGibbon & Kee, 1951) p. 99.
28. *Plutarch's Lives: the Dryden Plutarch*, rev. by A. H. Clough, vol. 3 (London: J. M. Dent, 1910) pp. 284–5.
29. Alternative to the prologue, p. 176.
30. 'Saint Joan in Paris' in Stanley Weintraub (ed.), *Saint Joan Fifty Years After: 1923/24–1973/74* (Louisana State University Press, [1973]) pp. 202–3.

31. James Graham, 'Shaw on Saint Joan' in Stanley Weintraub (ed.), *Saint Joan Fifty Years After*, pp. 15–18.
32. See Archibald Henderson, *Table-talk with G. B. S.: Conversations on Things in General between Bernard Shaw and his Biographer* (London: Chapman & Hall, 1925) p. 43.
33. Preface, *Saint Joan* in *The Bodley Head Bernard Shaw*, vol. 4, p. 40. All quotations from the text are from this edition.
34. Percy Mackaye, *Jeanne d'Arc* (London: Macmillan, 1906) p. 128.
35. See Archibald Henderson, *Table-talk with G. B. S.*, p. 40.
36. See Lawrence Langner, *G. B. S. and the Lunatic: Reminiscences of the long, lively and affectionate Friendship between George Bernard Shaw and the Author* (London: Hutchinson, 1964) pp. 63, 75.
37. See R. J. Minney, *The Bogus Image of Bernard Shaw* (London: Leslie Frewin, 1969) p. 129.
38. Lawrence Langner, *G. B. S. and the Lunatic*, p. 75.
39. Ernest Short, *Theatrical Cavalcade* (London: Eyre & Spottiswoode, 1942) p. 201.
40. *Mr Shaw and 'The Maid'* (London: Richard Cobden-Sanderson) pp. 17, 25, 38.
41. 'Rt Hon. J. M. Robertson: *Mr Shaw and "The Maid"'*, *The Criterion*, 4, no. 2 (Apr. 1926), pp. 389–90.
42. 'A Commentary', *The Criterion*, 3, no. 9 (Oct. 1924) pp. 4–5.
43. 'Bernard Shaw's *Saint Joan*: An Historical Point of View' in Stanley Weintraub (ed.), *Saint Joan Fifty Years After*, pp. 44–9.
44. 'Bernard Shaw's Saint' in Stanley Weintraub (ed.), *Saint Joan Fifty Years After*, pp. 54–63.
45. Ibid, p. 85.
46. See Bernard F. Dukore, *Bernard Shaw, Director* (London: Allen & Unwin, 1971) p. 94.
47. Preface, *Saint Joan*, pp. 45–6, 58.
48. Desmond MacCarthy, *Shaw*, p. 163.
49. *The Shavian Playground: an Exploration of the Art of George Bernard Shaw*, pp. 239–40.
50. *A Critical History of English Literature*, vol. 2 (London: Secker & Warburg, 1960) pp. 1106–7.
51. Edgar Wagerknecht, *A Guide to Bernard Shaw* (New York: D. Appleton, 1929) p. 35.
52. *Shaw the Dramatist: a Study of the Intellectual Background of the Major Plays* (London: Allen & Unwin, 1971) p. 202.
53. *What is Theatre?: Incorporating the Dramatic Event and other Reviews 1944–1967* (London: Methuen, 1969) p. 256.
54. Op. cit., pp. 56, 78–81.
55. *The Judgements of Joan: Joan of Arc, A Study in Cultural History* (London: Allen & Unwin, 1961) pp. 103, 107.
56. Preface, *Saint Joan*, p. 73.
57. *The Trial of Jeanne d'Arc* (London: George Routledge, 1931) pp. 2–3.
58. See Lawrence Langner, *G. B. S. and the Lunatic*, pp. 70–1.
59. Maurice Valency, *The Cart and the Trumpet: the Plays of Bernard Shaw* (New York: Oxford University Press, 1973) p. 386.
60. Ibid., p. 75.

61. Alan Dent (ed.), *Bernard Shaw and Mrs Campbell: Their Correspondence* (London: Victor Gollancz, 1952) p. 147.
62. See Dan H. Lawrence, *Shaw: An Exhibit* (Austin: University of Texas, 1977) column 450.
63. See Hesketh Pearson, *Bernard Shaw*, p. 357.
64. J. L. Wisenthal, *The Marriage of Contraries*, p. 173. Louis Crompton, *Shaw the Dramatist*, p. 213.
65. St John Ervine, *Bernard Shaw: His Life, Work and Friends* (London: Constable, 1956) p. 72.
66. *Shaw the Dramatist*, p. 211.
67. *The Judgements of Joan*, p. 170.
68. *The True History of Joan 'of Arc.'* translated by William Oxferry (London: Allen & Unwin, 1972) p. 205.
69. *Inquisition and Liberty* (London: William Heinemann, 1938) p. 335.
70. *Mr Shaw and 'The Maid,'* p. 89.
71. See B. Patch, *Thirty Years with G. B. S.* (London: Victor Gollancz, 1951) p. 53.
72. See Vincent Hall, *Bernard Shaw: a Pygmalion to Many Players* (University of Michigan Press [1973]) p. 145.
73. Ibid., p. 150.
74. Preface, 'The Sanity of Art' in *Major Critical Essays*, p. 296.
75. Quoted in Eric Bentley, *What is Theatre?*, p. 254.
76. T. D. Murray (ed.), *Jeanne d'Arc: Maid of Orleans: Deliverer of France* (London: William Heinemann, 1902) pp. 272, 269.
77. Ibid., p. 305.
78. Ibid., pp. 18, 299.
79. Ibid., p. 277.
80. Ibid., p. 306.
81. Ibid., p. 307.
82. Ibid., pp. vii–viii.
83. Ibid., p. xvii.
84. *The Judgements of Joan*, pp. 155–6.
85. 'The Shavianisation of Cauchon', *The Shaw Review*, 20, no. 2 (May 1977) p. 64.
86. T. D. Murray, *Jeanne d'Arc*, pp. 103–4.
87. 'Shaw and John Osborne', *The Shavian*, 2 (Oct. 1964) p. 31.
88. *Bernard Shaw*, p. 195.
89. Ibid., p. 195.
90. Wilfred Philip Barret (trans.), *The Trial of Jeanne d'Arc* . . . with an essay 'On the Trial of Jeanne d' Arc' by Pierre Champion, trans. from the French by Coley Taylor and Ruth H. Kerr (New York, 1932) p. 480, Cited in C. W. Lightbody, *The Judgement of Joan*, p. 139.
91. Murray, pp. 145–6.
92. Reprinted in T. F. Evans (ed.), *Shaw: the Critical Heritage* (London: Routledge & Kegan Paul, 1976) p. 289.
93. '*Saint Joan,' English Studies*, 7, no. 1 (1925) p. 18.
94. See L. Langner, *G. B. S. and the Lunatic*, p. 80.
95. 'Shaw's *Saint Joan* as Tragedy', *Twentieth Century Literature*, 3, no. 2 (July 1957) p. 66.

96. *George Bernard Shaw* (Boston: Twayne [1978]) p. 133.
97. See Archibald Henderson, *George Bernard Shaw: Man of the Century* (New York: Appleton-Century-Crofts [1956]) p. 600.

CHAPTER 3: THREE PLAYS OF THE 1930s

1. Preface, *Harold, the Last of the Saxon Kings* (London: Knebworth, 1874) pp. xi–xii.
2. Katharine Worth, *Revolutions in Modern English Drama* (London: G. Bell, 1973) p. 5.
3. See K. Robbins, *The Abolition of War: The Peace Movement in Britain. 1914–1919* (Cardiff: University of Wales Press, 1976) pp. 192–217.
4. See John Gielgud, *Early Stages* (London: Methuen, 1939) p. 234.
5. Preface, *Machines: a Symphony of Modern Life* (London: Robert Holden, 1927) pp. 5–6, 10–13.
6. All quotations from the text will be cited from the following edition: *Plays of a Half-Decade* (London: Victor Gollancz, 1933).
7. *The Life of Florence Nightingale*, vol. 1, p. 34.
8. Foreword, *The White Château* (London: Williams and Norgate, 1925) pp. v–vi.
9. *Dawn* (London: W. Collins, 1929) p. 138.
10. *The Daily Telegraph*, 7/1/29.
11. *Theatre World*, 9, no. 49 (Feb. 1929), p. 16.
12. *The Times*, 9/2/29.
13. *The Times*, 13/2/29.
14. Katharine Worth, *Revolutions in Modern English Drama*, p. 5.
15. *Eminent Victorians* (London: Chatto & Windus, 1918) pp. 115, 119.
16. Michael Holroyd, *Lytton Strachey: a Critical Biography*, vol. 2 (London: Heinnemann, 1968) p. 291.
17. *Eminent Victorians*, pp. 154, 148.
18. Ernest Short, *Theatrical Cavalcade* (London: Eyre & Spottiswoode, 1942) p. 114.
19. *The Times*, 7/1/29.
20. *Eminent Victorians*, p. 160.
21. *Lytton Strachey*, vol. 2, p. 295.
22. See Sir Edward Cook, *The Life of Florence Nightingale*, vol. 1 (London: Macmillan, 1913) pp. 405, 407.
23. *Eminent Victorians*, p. viii.
24. See Charles Richard Sanders, *Lytton Strachey: His Mind and Art* (New York: Yale University Press, 1957) pp. 202–3, Michael Holroyd, *Lytton Strachey*, vol. 2, pp. 287–8, 297.
25. See for example, the description of Florence Nightingale's personal appearance in early womanhood in a letter by Mrs Gaskell to Catherine Winkworth (quoted in Cook's *The Life of Florence Nightingale*, vol. 1, p. 39) which Berkeley has clearly been influenced by (Act 1, Sc. 1, pp. 207–8).
26. Ibid., pp. 97–102.

27. *Florence Nightingale: 1890–1910* (London: Constable, 1950) pp. 76–87.
28. *The Times*, 7/1/29.
29. *The Life of Florence Nightingale*, vol. 1, pp. 99–100.
30. See *The Times*, 7/1/29.
31. C. H. Lockitt, Introduction, *The Lady with a Lamp* (London: Longmans, Green, 1929) p. 7.
32. *The Lady with a Lamp* (London: Samuel French, 1929) p. 15.
33. Ibid., p. 96.
34. *The Daily Telegraph*, 7/1/29.
35. Clifford Bax, *Whither the Theatre . . .? a Letter to a Young Playwright* (London: Home & Van Thal, 1945) p. 27.
36. *Inland Far*, p. 187.
37. See *Inland Far*, p. 328; *Ideas and People* (London: Lovat Dickson, 1936) pp. 287–9.
38. *Bianca Cappello* (London: Gerald Howe, 1927) pp. 91–3.
39. *The Distaff Muse: an Anthology of Poetry written by Women* (London: Hollis & Carter, 1949) p. 202.
40. *Some I Knew Well* (London: Phoenix House, 1951) pp. 94–5.
41. *Ideas and People*, p. 226.
42. *Some I Knew Well*, p. 116.
43. *Whither the Theatre . . .?*, p. 27.
44. Ibid., p. 23.
45. Bax considered Stephen Phillips the greatest poetic dramatist since Elizabethan times. See *Some I Knew Well*, p. 18.
46. *The Times*, 22/11/62.
47. *Early Stages*, p. 260.
48. *Theatrical Cavalcade* (London: Eyre & Spottiswoode, 1942) p. 116.
49. *Dramatists of Today*, pp. 77–8.
50. (a) *The Reformation in England: the English Schism: Henry VIII (1309–1547)* (London: Sheed & Ward, 1934) p. 441; (b) ibid., p. 441.
51. *Henry the Eighth* (London: Jonathan Cape, 1929) p. 454.
52. Ibid., pp. 459–62.
53. All quotations from the text will be cited from the following edition: *Plays of a Half-Decade* (London: Victor Gollancz, 1933).
54. Op. cit., pp. 469, 471.
55. *Letters and Papers*, vol. 16, pp. 665–6, 646.
56. Henry Jenkyins (ed.), *The Remains of Thomas Cranmer, D. D., Archbishop of Canterbury* (Oxford University Press, 1833) pp. 308–10.
57. See review of the original production in *The Times*, 11/2/32.
58. Op. cit., pp. 478–9.
59. See J. Gairdner and R. H. Brodie (eds), *Letters and Papers, Foreign and Domestic, of the Reign of Henry VIII*, vol. 16 (London: Her Majesty's Stationery Office, 1898) pp. 618, 652.
60. See Historical Manuscripts Commission, *Calendar of Manuscripts of the Marquis of Bath preserved at Longleat, Wiltshire*, vol. 2 (Dublin: HMSO, 1907) pp. 9–10. *Letters and Papers, Foreign and Domestic, of the Reign of Henry VIII*, vol. 17 (London: HMSO, 1900), pp. 44, 45, 50.
61. Lacey Baldwin Smith, *A Tudor Tragedy: the Life and Times of Catherine Howard* (London: Jonathan Cape, 1961) p. 163.
62. See Martin A. Sharp Hume (trans.), *Chronicle of King Henry VIII of*

England: Being a Contemporary Record of Some of the Principal Events of the Reigns of Henry VIII and Edward VI (London: George Bell, 1889) pp. 75–87.

63. Lacey Baldwin Smith, *A Tudor Tragedy: the Life and Times of Catherine Howard*, pp. 9–10.
64. Preface, *Claverhouse* (London: Collins, 1937) pp. 9–10.
65. Historical Notes, *Plays*, p. 236.
66. Author's note, *The Privateer* (London: Peter Davies, 1952) p. 254.
67. W. A. Darlington, *The Daily Telegraph*, 3/2/33.
68. See John Gielgud, *Early Stages*, p. 239.
69. *Theatre World*, 19, no. 98 (Mar. 1933) pp. 123–8.
70. Ernest Short, *Theatrical Cavalcade*, p. 201.
71. John Gielgud, *Early Stages*, p. 225.
72. *An Actor and his Time* (London: Sidgwick & Jackson, 1979) pp. 104–5.
73. *Early Stages*, p. 242.
74. Foreword, in Gordon Daviot, *Plays*, p. xi.
75. *Early Stages*, p. 227.
76. Gielgud observes that the play's pacifist angle had a great appeal. See *An Actor and his Time*, pp. 104–5.
77. *Theatrical Cavalcade*, p. 200.
78. Ashley Dukes, 'The London Scene and Others', *Theatre Arts Monthly*, 17 (1933), p. 350. Desmond MacCarthy, *Drama* (London: Putnam, 1940) pp. 286–7.
79. John Gielgud, Foreword in Gordon Daviot, *Plays*, p. x.
80. Ibid., p. x.
81. Letter to Niloufer Harben, 4/10/80.
82. *The Daughter of Time*, pp. 125–6.
83. Thomas Johnes, trans., *Chronicles of England, France and Spain and the adjoining Countries from the latter Part of the Reign of Edward II to the Coronation of Henry IV by Sir John Froissart*, vol. 2 (London: William Smith, 1848) pp. 237–8.
84. All quotations from the text will be cited from the following edition: *Plays of the Thirties*, vol. 1 (London: Pan, 1966).
85. Op. cit., p. 318.
86. Op. cit., pp. 578–9.
87. Op. cit., p. 164.
88. *Richard II*, p. 7.
89. See David Hume, *The History of England from the Invasion of Julius Caesar to the Revolution in 1688*, vol. 1 (London: Routledge, 1894) pp. 375–97. H. Hallam, *The Constitutional History of England: Edward I to Henry VII* (London: Alex Murray, 1870) pp. 39–54.
90. *The Constitutional History of England*, vol. 2 (Oxford: Clarendon Press, 1880) pp. 555–6.
91. See B. Williams (ed.), *Chronique de la Traïson et Mort de Richart Deux Roy d'Angleterre* (London: English Historical Society, 1846) p. 134.
92. See Leslie Stephens (ed.) *Dictionary of National Biography*, vol. 1 (London: Smith, Elder, 1885) p. 420.
93. Op. cit., pp. 556–7.
94. *England in the Later Middle Ages* (London: Methuen) pp. 267, 287.
95. Op. cit., p. 269.

96. Op. cit., p. 292.
97. Another marked parallel lies in the portrait of Henry, the Earl of Derby, who becomes Henry IV after Richard's deposition. Vickers describes him as 'pre-eminently a man of business. Efficiency was his greatest virtue' (see *England in the Later Middle Ages*, p. 303.). In *Richard of Bordeaux* a cold business-like disposition is Henry's salient feature and this is satirized in the abdication scene (see Part 2, Sc. 7, p. 106).
98. Op. cit., pp. 299–300.
99. Sidney Armitage-Smith, *John of Gaunt* (London: Constable, 1904) pp. 338–9.
100. Op. cit., p. 263.
101. For further details see Kenneth H. Vickers, *England in the Later Middle Ages*, p. 267. W. Stubbs, *The Constitutional History of England*, p. 510.
102. *An Actor and his Time*, p. 104.
103. See A. R. Myers (ed.), *English Historical Documents* (London: Eyre & Spottiswoode, 1969) p. 407.
104. James Agate, *Red Letter Nights: a Survey of the Post-Elizabethan Drama in Actual Performance on the London Stage 1921–1943* (London: Jonathan Cape, 1944) p. 312.
105. *A True Relation of the Manner of the Deposing of King Edward II and also an exact account of the Proceedings and Articles against King Richard II: and the manner of his Deposition and Resignation According to the Parliament.* Roll itself, where they are recorded at large (London, 1689) p. 14. See also A. R. Myers (ed.), *English Historical Documents*, pp. 407–14.
106. Quoted in Vickers, *England in the Later Middle Ages*, p. 300.
107. *Early Stages*, p. 239.
108. *Richard II* (Cambridge University Press, 1941) pp. 2–8.
109. *The Royal Policy of Richard II: Absolutism in the Later Middle Ages*, pp. 25, 106, 111.
110. *Richard II and the English Nobility* (London: Edward Arnold, 1973) p. 133.
111. Foreword, in Gordon Daviot, *Plays*, p. xi.
112. Introduction, *Penguin Plays: Gallows Glorious, Lady Precious Stream, Richard of Bordeaux* (Middlesex, Harmondsworth: Penguin Books, 1958) p. 8.
113. *The Times*, 27/6/32.

CHAPTER 4: T. S. ELIOT: *MURDER IN THE CATHEDRAL*

1. 'Poetry and Poets,' in *On Poetry and Poets* (London: Faber & Faber, 1957) p. 81.
2. 'Rt. Hon. J. M. Robertson: Mr Shaw and "The Maid" ', *The Criterion*, 4, no. 2 (Apr. 1926) p. 390; 'A Commentary', *The Criterion*, 3, No. 9 (Oct. 1924) p. 4.
3. *Brecht on Theatre: the Development of an Aesthetic*, trans. by J. Willet (London: Methuen, 1964) p. 140.
4. Quoted in Brian Mitchell, 'W. H. Auden and Christopher Isherwood:

The "German Influence"', *Oxford German Studies*, 1 (1966) p. 166.

5. See John Willet, *The Theatre of Bertolt Brecht: A Study from Eight Aspects* (London: Eyre Methuen, 1959) pp. 220–1.

6. Quoted in J. Isaacs, *An Assessment of Twentieth-Century Literature* (London: Secker & Warburg, 1951) p. 155.

7. *W. H. Auden as a Social Poet* (Ithaca and London: Cornell University Press, 1973) p. 90.

8. Quoted in Joseph Warren Beach, *The Making of the Auden Canon* (Minneapolis: The University of Minnesota Press, [1957]) p. 148.

9. Stephen Spender (ed.), *W. H. Auden: a Tribute* (London: Weidenfeld & Nicolson, [1974]) p. 113.

10. 'So long as one was in Eliot's presence', Auden commented after Eliot's death in 1965, 'one felt it was impossible to say or do anything base'. See Humphrey Carpenter, *W. H. Auden: a Biography* (London: Allen & Unwin, 1981) p. 114.

11. Ibid., p. 333.

12. Ibid., p. 95.

13. Monroe K. Spears, *The Poetry of W. H. Auden: the Disenchanted Island* (New York: Oxford University Press, 1963) pp. 92–3.

14. See Edward Mendelson, *Early Auden* (London: Faber & Faber, 1981) pp. 271–4. Brian Finney, *Christopher Isherwood: a Critical Biography* (London: Faber & Faber, 1979) pp. 107–8.

15. See Edward Mendelson, *Early Auden*, p. 277.

16. Quoted in Humphrey Carpenter, *W. H. Auden: a Biography*, p. 194.

17. See Hubert Witt (ed.), *Brecht: as They Knew Him* (London: Lawrence & Wishart, 1974) p. 226.

18. 'Notes to *The Threepenny Opera*', *Plays*, vol. 1 (London: Methuen, 1960) p. 179.

19. *Brecht on Theatre: the Development of an Aesthetic*, p. 140.

20. 'A Commentary', *The Criterion*, 12, no. 46 (Oct. 1932) pp. 74–5.

21. Quoted in Keith A. Dickson, *Towards Utopia: a Study of Brecht* (Oxford: Clarendon Press, 1978) p. 63.

22. Ibid., p. 62.

23. All quotations from the text are cited from the following edition: *Murder in the Cathedral* (London: Faber & Faber, 1965).

24. 'Notes and Introduction', *Murder in the Cathedral*, pp. 116–7.

25. *The Irish Drama of Europe from Yeats to Beckett* (London: The Athlone Press, 1978) p. 204.

26. See T. S. Matthews, *Great Tom: Notes towards the Definition of T. S. Eliot* (London: Weidenfeld & Nicolson, 1974) pp. 67, 70.

27. *Eliot's Early Years* (Oxford University Press, 1977) pp. 98, 75.

28. Quoted in T. S. Matthews, *Great Tom*, p. 213.

29. Ibid., p. 75.

30. *Sweeney Agonistes* in *Collected Poems 1909–1962* (London: Faber & Faber, 1963) p. 131.

31. Part 1, Sc. 1, *The Family Reunion* (London: Faber & Faber, 1939) p. 27.

32. Op. cit., pp. 134–5.

33. Part 1, Sc. 1, *The Family Reunion*, pp. 28, 23.

34. 'Poetry and Drama' in *On Poetry and Poets*, pp. 80–1.

35. *Great Tom*, pp. 119, 116.

36. 'Archbishop Thomas Becket: A Character Study' in *The Historian and Character and other Essays* (Cambridge University Press, 1963) pp. 105–6.
37. Ibid., p. 112.
38. 'The Three Voices of Poetry,' in *On Poetry and Poets*, p. 91.
39. The Making of T. S. Eliot's Plays (Cambridge University Press, 1969) pp. 72–9.
40. *Murder in the Cathedral*, p. 20.
41. *English Historical Documents 1042–1189* (London: Eyre & Spottiswoode, 1953) p. 761.
42. Ibid., p. 764.
43. Ibid., p. 731.
44. Ibid., p. 747.
45. Ibid., p. 752.
46. Ibid., p. 751.
47. In Donald Adamson (ed.), *T. S. Eliot: a Memoir*, (London: Garnstone Press, [1971]) p. 138.
48. Douglas and Greenway, *English Historical Documents 1042–1189*, p. 758.
49. *The Making of T. S. Eliot's Plays*, p. 47.
50. This again links up with the fact that inner peace was a central issue for Eliot at the time because of the ordeal of his private life.
51. 'The Use of Original Sources for the Development of a Theme: Eliot in *Murder in the Cathedral*', *English*, 2, no. 61 (Spring 1956) pp. 2–8.
52. 'Mr Eliot's *Murder in the Cathedral*' in *The Cambridge Journal*, 4, no. 2 (Nov. 1950) pp. 83–95.
53. *The Making of T. S. Eliot's Plays*, p. 42.
54. 'Eliot and the Living Theatre' in Graham Martin (ed.), *Eliot in Perspective: a Symposium* (London: Macmillan, 1970) p. 156.
55. 'With Becket in *Murder in the Cathedral*' in Allan Tate (ed.), *T. S. Eliot: the Man and his Work* (London: Chatto & Windus, 1967) p. 189.
56. *The Art of T. S. Eliot*, (London: The Cresset Press, 1949) p. 134.
57. Op. cit., p. 185.
58. 'Tradition and the Individual Talent' in *Selected Essays* (London: Faber & Faber, 1932) pp. 17–21.
59. 'John Marston' in *Selected Essays*, p. 229.
60. 'Poetry and Drama' in *On Poetry and Poets*, pp. 86–7.
61. 'Dramatis Personae', *The Criterion*, 1, no. 3 (Apr. 1923) pp. 305–6.
62. 'Four Elizabethan Dramatists' in *Selected Essays*, p. 113.
63. 'Poetry and Drama,' in *On Poetry and Poets*, p. 80.
64. 'Religious Drama: Mediaeval and Modern', *University of Edinburgh Journal*, 9 (1937) p. 10.
65. Introduction, *Murder In the Cathedral*, p. 103.
66. *The Family Reunion*, Part 1, Sc. 1, p. 27.
67. Op. cit., pp. 106–7.
68. 'Dramatis Personae', *The Criterion*, 1, no. 3 (Apr. 1923) p. 304.
69. *The Times Literary Supplement* (3 Mar. 1927) p. 140.
70. 'Notes on the Blank Verse of Christopher Marlowe' in *Elizabethan Essays* (London: Faber & Faber, 1934) pp. 27–8.

71. Katharine Worth, *The Irish Drama of Europe from Yeats to Beckett*, p. 204.
72. *The Elder Statesman* (London: Faber & Faber, 1959) pp. 82–3.
73. E. H. Erikson, *Young Man Luther: a Study in Psychoanalysis and History* (London: Faber & Faber, 1959) p. 99.
74. 'With Becket in *Murder in the Cathedral*' in Allan Tate (ed.), *T. S. Eliot: the Man and his Work*, p. 191.
75. Katharine Worth. 'A New View of *Murder in the Cathedral*', *The London Review*, 9 (Winter 1976/77) p. 37.
76. 'Poetry and Drama' in *On Poetry and Poets*, p. 81.
77. *Drama: from Ibsen to Brecht* (London: Chatto & Windus, 1968) p. 182.
78. *The Plays of T. S. Eliot* (London: Routledge & Kegan Paul, 1960) p. 61.
79. '*Murder in the Cathedral*', *Plays and Players*, 20, no. 1 (Oct. 1972), p. 44.

CHAPTER 5: THREE PLAYS OF THE 1960s

1. All quotations from the text are cited from the edition in the following collection: *Three Plays* (London: Heinemann, 1963).
2. Frances Stephens, 'Plays at Chichester Reviewed', *Theatre World*, 60, no. 475 (Aug. 1964) p. 31.
3. All quotations from the text are cited from the following edition: *The Royal Hunt of the Sun: a Play Concerning the Conquest of Peru* (London: Hamish Hamilton, 1964).
4. All quotations from the text are cited from the following edition: *Luther: a Play* (London: Faber & Faber, 1961).
5. Preface, *A Man for All Seasons*, p. 94.
6. 'Dipsychus Among the Shadows' in J. R. Brown, ed., *Contemporary Theatre* (London: Edward Arnold, 1962) p. 140.
7. See R. Hayman, *Robert Bolt* (London: Heinemann, 1969) p. 74. Sally Emerson, 'Playing the Game', *Plays and Players*, 24 (June 1977) p. 12.
8. Introduction, *Vivat! Vivat Regina!*, p. xxi.
9. Ibid., pp. vii–viii.
10. See Frank Granville Barker, '*A Man for All Seasons*', *Plays and Players*, 8, no. 5 (Feb. 1961) p. 13; *The Times*, 2/7/60.
11. John McClain, 'New Hit Paced by British Star', *Journal American*, 24/11/61. Reprinted in *New York Theatre Critics' Reviews*, 22, no. 5 (1961) p. 164.
12. Richard Watts Jr., 'The Drama of a Man of Integrity', *New York Post*, 24/11/61. Reprinted in the *New York Theatre Critics' Reviews*, 22, no. 5 (1961) p. 167.
13. Robert Coleman, '*A Man for All Seasons* is Wonderful', *New York Mirror*, 23/11/61.
14. John McClain, 'New Hit Paced by British Star', *Journal American*, 24/11/61.
15. See R. Hayman, *Robert Bolt*, p. 81.
16. *Thomas More* (London: Jonathan Cape, 1935) p. 28.
17. Ibid., p. 32.
18. Ibid., p. 338.

19. Ibid., p. 177.
20. Ibid., p. 268.
21. Quoted in M. C. Fosbery, '*A Man for All Seasons*', *English Studies in Africa*, 6, no. 2 (Sept. 1963) p. 165.
22. *The Times*, 2/7/60.
23. Preface, *A Man for All Seasons*, p. 99.
24. '*A Man for All Seasons*' in C. Marowitz (ed.), *The Encore Reader: a Chronicle of the New Drama* (London: Methuen, 1965) p. 194.
25. *Tynan Right and Left*, pp. 28–30.
26. Preface, *A Man for All Seasons*, p. 94.
27. Ibid., p. 100.
28. Frank Granville Barker, '*A Man for All Seasons*', *Plays and Players*, 8, no. 5 (Feb. 1961) p. 13.
29. I have not been able to trace the source of this.
30. Preface, *A Man for All Seasons*, p. 96.
31. (a) E. F. Rogers (ed.), *The Correspondence of Sir Thomas More* (Princeton University Press, 1947) p. 516; (b) ibid., p. 516.
32. Quoted in Chambers, *Thomas More*, pp. 309–10.
33. Rogers, *The Correspondence*, pp. 516, 536–7.
34. *Robert Bolt*, p. 44.
35. See Chambers, *Thomas More*, p. 342.
36. Rogers, *The Correspondence*, p. 547.
37. Quoted in Chambers, *Thomas More*, p. 342.
38. Ibid., p. 338.
39. B. A. Young, '*A Man for All Seasons*', *The Times*, 20/10/76.
40. See Chambers, *Thomas More*, p. 324.
41. Ibid., p. 347; *Dictionary of National Biography*, p. 439.
42. Quoted in Chambers, *Thomas More*, p. 347. For another occasion when More voices a similar sentiment see Rogers, *The Correspondence*, p. 537.
43. *Tynan Right and Left* (London: Longmans, Green, 1967) p. 28.
44. See R. Hayman, *Robert Bolt*, p. 81.
45. Chambers, *Thomas More*, pp. 343, 307.
46. Richard Watts Jr, 'The Drama of a Man of Integrity', *New York Post*, 24/11/61.
47. See Chambers, *Thomas More*, p. 285.
48. J. Russell Taylor, *Anger and After: a Guide to the New British Drama* (London: Methuen, 1962) p. 367.
49. '1964 Chichester Festival', *Theatre World*, 60, no. 475 (Aug. 1964), p. 6; Frances Stephens, 'Plays at Chichester Reviewed', *Theatre World*, 60, no. 475 (Aug. 1964) p. 31.
50. *The Royal Hunt of the Sun*, *The Financial Times*, 29/8/73.
51. Charles Lewser, 'A Bantam puffed up as a Heavyweight: *The Royal Hunt of the Sun*', *The Times*, 29/8/73.
52. *Peter Shaffer*, (Essex: Longmans, 1974) p. 21.
53. 'To See the Soul of a Man . . .', *The New York Times*, 24/10/65.
54. 'In Search of a God: Peter Shaffer discusses his new play', *Plays and Players*, 12, no. 1 (Oct 1964) p. 22.

55. Preface, *The Conquest of the Incas* (London: Abacus, Sphere, 1970) pp. 18–19.
56. *The Ancient Civilization of Peru* (Harmondsworth, Middlesex: Penguin, 1957) p. 274.
57. Preface, *The Conquest of the Incas*, p. 18.
58. *The Vision of the Vanquished: the Spanish Conquest of Peru through Indian Eyes 1530–1570* (First published in France: Gallimard, [1971]; English translation by Ben and Sian Reynolds, Sussex: Harvester Press, 1977).
59. W. H. Prescott, *History of the Conquest of Peru* (London: Swan Sonnenschein, 1847) pp. 97–9.
60. *The Conquest of the Incas*, 548–9.
61. Op. cit., pp. 340–2.
62. Op. cit., p. 180.
63. J. Hemmings, *The Conquest of the Incas*, p. 155.
64. Introductory Note, *The Royal Hunt of the Sun* (New York, 1965) p. vi.
65. C. Marowitz, *Confessions of a Counterfeit Critic*, p. 89.
66. Op. cit., pp. 28–9.
67. Op. cit., pp. 80–2.
68. Introduction, *The Royal Hunt of the Sun* (New York, 1965) p. vii.
69. Walter Kerr, 'Review of *The Royal Hunt of the Sun*', *New York Herald Tribune*, 27/10/65. Reprinted in *New York Theatre Critics' Reviews* (1965) p. 295.
70. Op. cit., p. 226.
71. '*The Royal Hunt of the Sun*', *Financial Times*, 29/8/73.
72. 'Glittering Epic of Spanish Conquest', *The Times*, 8/7/64.
73. C. Marowitz, *Confessions of a Counterfeit Critic*, p. 89.
74. 'In Search of a God: Peter Shaffer discusses his new play', *Plays and Players*, 12, no. 1 (Oct. 1964) p. 22.
75. Op. cit., pp. 3–4, 15.
76. *The Conquest of the Incas*, pp. 79–80.
77. *The Vision of the Vanquished*, pp. 38–40, 56.
78. *The Times*, 8/7/64.
79. 'To See the Soul of a Man . . .', *The New York Times*, 24/10/65.
80. See K. Tynan, *Tynan Right and Left*, pp. 180–1. Richard Findlater, *Banned! a Review of Theatrical Censorship in Britain* (London: MacGibbon & Kee, 1967) pp. 186–7.
81. Caryl Brahms, 'Man Bites Dogma', *Plays and Players*, 8, no. 12 (Sept. 1961) p. 11.
82. 'Best Guarantee Yet of Mr Osborne's Stamina', *The Times*, 28/7/61.
83. *Tynan Right and Left*, p. 78.
84. John McClain, 'Brilliantly Acted Historical Drama', *Journal American*, 26/9/63. Reprinted in *New York Theatre Critics' Reviews*, 24, no. 22 (1963) p. 277.
86. Norman Nadel, 'Osborne's Overpowering *Luther*', *New York World-Telegram and The Sun*, 26/9/63. Reprinted in *New York Theatre Critics' Reviews*, 24, no. 22 (1963) p. 277.
87. Richard Watts Jr, 'Luther in a Memorable Portrayal', *New York Post*,

26/9/63. Reprinted in *New York Theatre Critics' Reviews*, 24, no. 22 (1963) p. 276.

88. 'Kerr on *Luther* at the St James', *New York Herald Tribune* 26/9/63. Reprinted in *New York Theatre Critics' Reviews*, 24, no. 22 (1963) p. 278.

89. 'That Awful Museum', *Twentieth Century*, 69 (Jan. – Mar. 1961) p. 216.

90. *Anger and After: a Guide to the New British Drama* (London: Methuen, 1962) p. 55.

91. *The Plays of John Osborne: an Assessment* (London: Victor Gollancz, 1969) p. 105. *John Osborne* (Essex: Longmans, Green, 1969) p. 18.

92. *Drama in the Sixties: Form and Interpretation* (London: Faber & Faber, 1966) p. 187.

93. *John Osborne* (Edinburgh: Oliver and Boyd, 1969) p. 87.

94. *Contemporary Playwrights: John Osborne* (London: Heinemann, 1968) p. 46.

95. 'They call it Cricket' in T. Maschler (ed.), *Declaration* (London: Mac-Gibbon and Kee, 1957) p. 105.

96. *Young Man Luther* (London: Faber & Faber, 1959) p. 7.

97. *The Journals of Søren Kierkegaard*, ed. and trans. by Alexander Dru (London: Oxford University Press, 1938) p. 508.

98. *A Better Class of Person: an Autobiography 1929–1956* (London: Oxford University Press, 1981) p. 508.

99. 'Osborne's Overpowering *Luther*', *New York World-Telegram and The Sun*, 26/9/63.

100. *Young Man Luther*, p. 115.

101. Ibid., pp. 247, 95, 16.

102. Ibid., p. 37.

103. *The Plays of John Osborne: an Assessment*, p. 105.

104. Contemporary Playwrights: John Osborne, p. 51.

105. It was subsequently published under the title, 'Luther and Mr Osborne' in *The Cambridge Quarterly*, vol. 1 (1965–66).

106. 'Luther and Mr Osborne' in *The Cambridge Quarterly*, 1 (Winter 1965–66) pp. 28–30.

107. Ibid., pp. 30, 42.

108. Ibid., pp. 32–3.

109. Ibid., pp. 34–7.

110. *Here I Stand: a Life of Martin Luther* (New York and Scarborough, Ontario: The New American Library, 1950) p. 281.

111. Erikson, *Young Man Luther*, p. 20.

112. *Here I Stand: a Life of Martin Luther*, p. 100.

113. Ibid., pp. 22–3.

114. Ibid., p. 56.

115. See for example, *Here I Stand*, pp. 160, 240–1.

116. Ibid., p. 44.

117. Ibid., pp. 281–3.

118. Harold Taubman, '*Luther* stars Albert Finney', *The New York Times*, 26/9/63. Reprinted in *New York Theatre Critics' Reviews*, 24, no. 22 (1963) p. 280.

119. Walter Kerr, 'Kerr on *Luther* at the St James,' *New York Herald Tribune*, 26/9/63. See also John McClain, 'Brilliantly Acted Historical Drama', *Journal American*, 26/9/63.

120. 'Shaw and John Osborne', *The Shavian*, 2 (Oct. 1964) p. 31.
121. Harold Taubman, '*Luther* stars Albert Finney', in *The New York Times*, 26/9/63.
122. *Here I Stand*, pp. 288–90.
123. Ibid., p. 198.
124. See John McClain, 'Brilliantly Acted Historical Drama', *Journal American*, 26/9/63. Norman Nadel, 'Osborne's *Luther*', *New York World-Telegram and The Sun*, 26/9/63.

CHAPTER 6: EDWARD BOND: *EARLY MORNING*

1. 'Us, Our Drama and the National Theatre', *Plays and Players*, 26, no. 1 (Oct. 1978) pp. 8–9.
2. *The Woman* (London: Eyre Methuen, 1979) pp. 126–7.
3. Bond expressed this view at a lecture he gave on 'Theatre as Education' at Riverside Studios, Hammersmith, on 17 Mar. 1982.
4. 'Us Our Drama and the National Theatre', *Plays and Players*, 26 no. 1 (Oct. 1978) pp. 8–9.
5. See Malcolm Hay and Philip Roberts, *Edward Bond: a Companion to the Plays* (London: TQ Publications, 1978) p. 14.
6. Ibid., p. 26.
7. See Tony Coult, 'Creating what is Normal: an Assessment and Interview', *Plays and Players*, 23, no. 3 (Dec. 1975) pp. 8–10.
8. Preface, *Lear* (London: Eyre Methuen, 1972) p. v.
9. Quoted in Lael Werternbaker, *The World of Picasso* (Nederland: Time-Life International [1967]) p. 42.
10. See Malcolm Hay and Philip Roberts, *Edward Bond: a Companion to the Plays*, p. 23.
11. 'Thoughts on Contemporary Theatre', *New Theatre Magazine*, 7, no. 2 (Spring 1967) p. 9.
12. *The New Cambridge Modern History vol. 12: The Era of Violence 1898–1945* (Cambridge University Press, 1960) p. 13.
13. Cited in Malcolm Hay and Philip Roberts, *Bond: A Study of His Plays* (London: Eyre Methuen, 1980) p. 22.
14. Hay and Roberts, *Edward Bond: a Companion*, p. 74.
15. *Revolutions in Modern English Drama* (London: G. Bell, 1973) pp. 171–2.
16. See 'Us, Our Drama and the National Theatre', *Plays and Players*, 26, no. 1 (Oct. 1978) p. 8.
17. Hay and Roberts, *Edward Bond: a Companion*, p. 26.
18. See Introduction, *Bingo* (London. Eyre Methuen, 1974) p. viii.
19. Cited in Tony Coult, *The Plays of Edward Bond* (London: Eyre Methuen, 1977) p. 19.
20. Introduction, *Bingo*, p. xiii.
21. See E. K. Chambers, *William Shakespeare: a Study of Facts and Problems*, vol. 2 (Oxford: Clarendon Press, 1930) pp. 141–52.
22. Hay and Roberts, *Edward Bond: a Companion*, p. 57.
23. See Michael Anderson, 'Exeter', *Plays and Players*, 21, no. 4 (Jan. 1974) p. 62.

24. *Bingo*, pp. vi–xv.
25. See Karl-Heinz Stoll, 'Interviews with Edward Bond and Arnold Wesker', *Twentieth-Century Literature*, 22 (4 Dec. 1976) p. 412.
26. Hay and Roberts, *Edward Bond: a Companion*, p. 75.
27. 'Has Mr Bond been saved?', *The Daily Telegraph*, 15/4/68.
28. Letter to Niloufer Harben, 26/10/82.
29. Letter to Niloufer Harben, 13/12/82.
30. *The Times*, 8/4/68. Wardle later recanted this view. See The 'Edward Bond View of Life', *The Times*, 15/3/69.
31. *The Observer*, 14/4/68.
32. Harold Hobson, *The Sunday Times*, reprinted in *The Critic*, 1, no. 8 (19 Apr. 1968) p. 9.
33. Oleg Kerensky, *The New British Drama: Fourteen Playwrights since Osborne and Pinter* (London: Hamish Hamilton, 1977) p. 20.
34. Ronald Bryden, *The Observer*, 14/4/68.
35. Katharine Worth, *Revolutions in Modern English Drama*, p. 175.
36. See Malcolm Hay and Philip Roberts, *Bond: a Study of His Plays*, pp. 84–8.
37. Irving Wardle, 'An Interview with William Gaskill', *Gambit*, 5, no. 7 (1970) p. 41.
38. Programme Note for *Narrow Road to the Deep North*, Belgrade Theatre, Coventry, June 1968. Cited in Hay and Roberts, *Bond: a Study of his Plays*, p. 88.
39. 'The Theatre of Edward Bond', *Times Educational Supplement*, 24/9/71.
40. *A Handbook of Contemporary Drama* (London: Pitman Publishing, 1972) p. 61.
41. 'The Edward Bond View of Life', *The Times*, 15/3/69.
42. 'The Bourgeois Bard', *New Statesman*, 86 (23 Nov. 1973) p. 783.
43. All quotations from the text are cited from *Early Morning* (London: Calder & Boyars, 1968).
44. Martin Esslin, 'A Bond Honoured', *Plays and Players*, 15, no. 19 (June 1968) p. 63.
45. See *The Critic*, 1, no. 8 (Apr. 1968) pp. 6–9.
46. B. A. Young, *Financial Times*, reprinted in *The Critic*, vol. 1, no. 8 (Apr. 1968) p. 8.
47. '*Early Morning*', *The Observer*' 14/4/68.
48. Cecil Woodham-Smith, *Queen Victoria: Her Life and Times*, vol. 1 (London: Hamish Hamilton, 1972) p. 200.
49. *The Political Influence of Queen Victoria 1861–1901* (London: Oxford University Press, 1935) pp. 138, 203, 120.
50. *Victoria R. I.* (London: Weidenfeld & Nicolson, 1964), p. 445.
51. *Op. cit.*, p. 236.
52. *Victoria R. I.*, pp. 305, 183, 222.
53. 'A Discussion with Edward Bond', *Gambit*, no. 17, p. 14.
54. George E. Buckle (ed.), *The Letters of Queen Victoria*, second series, vol. 2 (London: John Murray, 1926) p. 479. See also p. 363.
55. *Victoria R. I.*, pp. 323–4.
56. Ibid., p. 170.
57. Ibid., pp. 109, 137.

58. See George E. Buckle, *The Life of Benjamin Disraeli: Earl of Beaconsfield*, vol. 6 (London: John Murray, 1920) p. 245.
59. See Frederick Ponsonby, *Sidelights on Queen Victoria* (London: Macmillan, 1930) p. 145.
60. See Frank Hardie, *The Political Influence of Queen Victoria*, p. 34. Elizabeth Longford, *Victoria R. I.*, p. 401.
61. A. C. Benson (ed.), *The Letters of Queen Victoria* vol. 3 (London: John Murray, 1908) p. 170.
62. *The Plays of Edward Bond* (London: Eyre Methuen, 1977) p. 55.
63. *The Plays of Edward Bond* (Lewisburg: Bucknell University Press, 1976) pp. 111–2.
64. See Introduction, *The Fool* (London: Eyre Methuen, 1976) p. xi.
65. Quoted in Frank Hardie, *The Political Influence of Queen Victoria*, p. 162.
66. In G. E. Buckle (ed.), *The Letters of Queen Victoria*, second series, vol. 3, pp. 37–8.
67. Cited in Elizabeth Longford, *Victoria R. I.*, p. 279.
68. Cited in L. C. B. Seaman, *Victorian England: Aspects of English and Imperial History 1837–1901*, pp. 166–7.
69. *Days with Bernard Shaw* (New York: The Vanguard Press, [1949]) p. 231.
70. Op. cit., p. 47.
71. *Queen Victoria: Her Life and Times*, vol. 1, p. 431.
72. See Elizabeth Longford, *Victoria R. I.*, pp. 501, 436, 506.
73. Quoted in Frank Hardie, *The Political Influence of Queen Victoria*, p. 245.
74. Quoted in L. C. B. Seaman, *Victorian England: Aspects of English and Imperial History 1837–1901* (London: Methuen, 1973) p. 16.
75. A. R. Wallace, *The Wonderful Century* (London: Swann Sonnenschein, 1898) p. v.
76. See Zara S. Steiner, *Britain and the Origins of the First World War* (London and Basingstoke: Macmillan, 1977) p. 5.
77. Letter to Niloufer Harben, 10/6/82.
78. 'Creating what is Normal: an Assessment and Interview', *Plays and Players*, 26, no. 1 (Oct. 1978) p. 10.
79. Letter to Niloufer Harben, 3/6/82.
80. In his letter to me (3/6/82) Bond agrees that he knows this passage from Mill, but it was not in his mind when he wrote *Early Morning*, since he thinks he only came to know it after he had written the play.
81. *Principles of Political Economy: with some of Their Applications to Social Philosophy* (London: John W. Parker, 1848) p. 308.
82. See H. M. Lynd, *England in the Eighteen-Eighties: Towards a Social Basis for Freedom* (London: Frank Cass, 1945) p. 65.
83. *Signs of Change: Seven Lectures Delivered on Various Occasions* (London: Reeves & Turner, 1888) pp. 49–50.
84. *England in the Eighteen-Eighties: Towards a Social Basis for Freedom*, pp. 201, 223–4.
85. *Victorian England: Aspects of English and Imperial History 1837–1901* (London: Methuen, 1973) pp. 165, 168.

86. See Hay and Roberts, *A Companion*, p. 75.
87. Reproduced as an illustration in Asa Briggs, ed., *The Nineteenth Century: the Contradictions of Progress* (London: Thames & Hudson, [1970]) p. 31.
88. Letter to Niloufer Harben, 3/6/82.
89. I did therefore explore this area, but was unable to trace any unmistakable link between the drawings I came across and *Early Morning*.
90. Op. cit., p. 143.
91. Op. cit., p. 184.
92. In J. F. McCrindle (ed.), *Behind the Scenes: Theatre and Film Interviews from the 'Transatlantic Review'* (London: Pitman, 1971) p. 131.
93. 'Bond is out to make them laugh', *The Times*, 22/5/73.
94. *The Age of Capital 1848–1875* (London: Weidenfeld & Nicolson [1975]) p. 1.
95. Introduction, *The Fool*, pp. vi–xi.
96. John Rae, *Contemporary Socialism* (London: Wm Isbister, 1884) p. 61.
97. Quoted in H. M. Lynd, *England in the Eighteen-Eighties*, p. 5.
98. Introduction, *The Fool*, p. vii.
99. Ibid., p. viii.
100. *Industry and Empire: an Economic History of Britain since 1750* (London: Weidenfeld & Nicolson, 1968) p. 72.
101. *Victorian England: Aspects of English and Imperial History 1837–1901*, pp. 39–40.
102. See Jenifer Hart, 'Religion and Social Control in the Nineteenth Century' in A. P. Donajgrodski (ed.), *Social Control in Nineteenth-Century Britain* (London: Croom Helm, 1977) pp. 108–31.
103. L. C. B. Seaman, *Victorian England: Aspects of English and Imperial History 1837–1901*, p. 18.
104. Op. cit., p. 198.
105. 'Drama and the Dialectics of Violence', *Theatre Quarterly*, 2, no. 5 (Jan.–Mar. 1972) p. 13.
106. See Hay and Roberts, *Edward Bond: a Companion to the Plays*, p. 23.
107. 'Creating What Is Normal: Edward Bond: an Assessment and Interview', *Plays and Players*, 23, no. 3 (Dec. 1975) p. 13.

Index

277